did you know?

by Howie Schwab and Shelley Youngblut

did you know?

HYPERION
ESPN
BOOKS

ESPN's Did You Know?
© 1998 Hyperion/ESPN Books

ISBN 0-7868-8290-5

First Edition
10 9 8 7 6

Cover photographs:
Brett Favre: Scott Halleran/Allsport
Mark McGwire: Al Bello/Allsport
Michael Jordan: Brian Bahr/Allsport
Martina Hingis: Gary M. Prior/Allsport
Tiger Woods: David Cannon/Allsport
Dominik Hasek: Rick Stewart/Allsport

Title page photograph:
Chamique Holdsclaw: Otto Greule/Allsport

editorial director
Shelley Youngblut

writer/senior editor
Howie Schwab

design
Norman Hathaway

associate editor
Felicity Stone

assistant editor
Jim Minnich

stats class
Rob Neyer

hockey research
Vic Morren
Chuck Avellino
John Zoni

additional research
Shaun Assael
Russell Baxter
Jenny Ford
Paul Kinney
Jeff Rhode

contents

did you know?

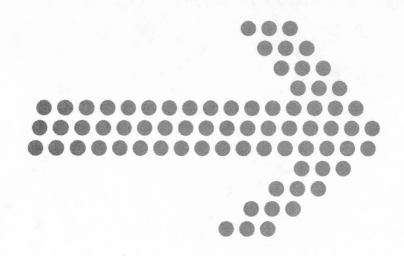

introduction

do not fold, bend
or mutilate

the genesis

chris myers

Bristol, Connecticut. 1991. The dead of winter. The dead of night. Inside ESPN headquarters, only a skeleton staff remained: the 2:30 a.m. SportsCenter producer Tim Kiley, coordinating producer Barry Sacks and a handful of production assistants fresh out of college, helping with the wire copy, highlights and scripts for the program. Monitors that had earlier blared out games in progress all around the country were now silent. My partner for the 2:30 a.m. broadcast, Mike Tirico, was tossing out facts about the games and information we were about to deliver to the audience. It wasn't enough. We reviewed the video, scanned the box scores and gathered the research—we always want to know more.

∴ At the end of the broadcast that night, we had time to fill. Mike Tirico came up with a gem of a fact, the kind of pertinent, resonant piece of information that totally satisfied that hunger for more. My delighted on-air response? "I did not know that." That is how one of my heroes outside the sports world, former king of late-night television Johnny Carson, used to respond to a great anecdote from a guest.

∴ As soon as we went off the air, we huddled in the conference room, knowing we were onto something. Let's face it, sports fans are as competitive as the athletes they admire. Even if you're just talking about sports, you want the edge. You want to know more than the other guy.

∴ Barry Sacks said we should throw out a great nugget every night on the 2:30 a.m. show. P.A. Edwin Van Duesen said we should make up a special graphic. Someone else suggested naming the segment I Did Not Know That. Rather than using Carson's exact phrase, I proposed Did You Know? And a little piece of SportsCenter history was made.

∴ The response was overwhelming. Whatever the top sports story was that day, we'd compete with each other to offer the best bonus piece of information. It wasn't that we were trying to outsmart the viewer.

We were the viewer: ready to be surprised, eager to be informed, generous with what we knew. Viewers would mail in or call to give us their own items for Did You Know? *—one of the first tangible links between the people who work at ESPN and our audience. Where else but* SportsCenter *could you learn that the only major league pitcher to match his age in strikeouts in a single game was Bob Feller, who, at 17, struck out 17 batters in 1936? Or that the NFL record for fewest rushing touchdowns in one season was set by the Brooklyn Dodgers—the football Dodgers—in 1934?*

∴ I finally met Johnny Carson a few years ago, at a celebrity tennis tournament at UCLA. When there was a break in Andre Agassi's match, I approached the Hollywood legend and told him about his role in the creation of one of America's most beloved sports slogans. Without missing a beat, he smiled and said, "I did not know that."

did you know?

In a Malibu real estate transaction with John McEnroe, Johnny Carson included personal tennis lessons from the four-time U.S. Open singles champion.

the process

**howie
schwab**

Being a true sports fan, I've always been intrigued by numbers and statistics, enjoying the way you can develop them to compare and contrast different teams and players. It has been a passion ever since I was a youngster.

·:· *I remember at age nine attending a Mets-Phillies game at Shea Stadium with my father. Nolan Ryan was on the mound for the Mets. Denny Doyle led off the game with a base hit. I turned to my dad, saying, "There goes his no-hitter!" Doyle's hit would be the only one allowed by Ryan that day. Two other base-runners reached on errors, while six others reached on walks. The date was April 18, 1970 (I checked).*

·:· *Did you know that Nolan Ryan finished his major league career with seven no-hitters and 12 one-hitters, including the one I witnessed? Imagine being so close to 19 no-nos. Did you know that the last time there were more than two official no-hitters in one season in the National League was 1976 (Larry Dierker, John Candelaria and John Montefusco did the honors).*

·:· *Sports demand comparisons. There are immediate ones: If you had to pick one pitcher to build a team around, would it be Roger Clemens or Greg Maddux? (I know some of you would choose Pedro Martinez, so hold those cards and letters! Me, I'm a Maddux man.) Then there are the historical arguments: Which team was better, the 1927 Yankees or the 1998 Yankees?*

·:· Did You Know? *is based on the premise that information is knowledge and knowledge is power. The goal is to come up with something that will (my apologies to Chris Myers for stealing his line) leave fans at the water cooler saying, I did not know that! We here in Bristol call it a Wow stat.*

·:· *Wow stats aren't easy to come by. Fortunately, ESPN has an extensive research staff and library to help unearth the nuggets good enough to go from a simple stat to on-air gold. Since I came on board in 1988, the research area has grown from a small room and one man—me—to 21 people* contributing to the department, complete with computers, on-line access, the support of outside statistical resources and floor-to-ceiling media guides.

∵ But no matter how sophisticated the process has become, the starting point remains the same: the news. For example, the four tennis Grand Slams in 1998 featured eight different men reaching the finals. The Australian Open had Petr Korda defeating Marcelo Rios; the French finals saw Carlos Moya over Alex Corretja. Then came Wimbledon, with Pete Sampras defeating Goran Ivanisevic. Finally, Patrick Rafter defended his '97 title at the U. S. Open, beating fellow Australian Mark Philippoussis.

∵ But why stop there? Take this information to the next level and add context—just how rare is this degree of wide-open competition on the men's side? The only way to know is to find the last time the four Grand Slams in one year all had different finalists.

∵ The answer: Never in the Open era. You have to go back to 1966, more than three decades, to get eight different men filling the slots of the four Grand Slam singles finals: Roy Emerson over Arthur Ashe in the Australian Open; Tony Roche over Hungarian Istvan Gulyas at the French Open; Manuel Santana over Dennis Ralston at Wimbledon; and ESPN's own Fred Stolle over John Newcombe at the U.S. Open. (Yes, I checked. And double-checked.)

∵ A Wow stat? You betcha. And it's just one of the thousands of Did You Knows? we've rounded up for your entertainment and enlightenment—and ours.

this is
sportscenter

- *SportsCenter* debuted on September 7, 1979, at 7 p.m. ET. Among the shows that aired that evening were *ABC Evening News with Frank Reynolds*, *The Dating Game*, *The Odd Couple*, *Over Easy with Hugh Downs* and the episode of *The Brady Bunch* that introduced Cousin Oliver. Rich Eisen was 10 years old.
- The first score reported was Chris Evert Lloyd defeating Billie Jean King 6-1, 6-0 at the U.S. Open.
- The first anchor was George Grande, now the TV voice of the Cincinnati Reds.
- The first live remote was from Boulder, Colo., and featured then-Patriots head coach Chuck Fairbanks. Unfortunately, there was video … but no audio.
- ESPN's signal of the debut telecast has traveled approximately 117,313,920,000,000 miles (19.66 light years) into outer space since September 7, 1979. The signal passed the star Ross 348 in November 1989 and recently reached the star ETA Cassiopeia A.
- Approximately 10,000 highlights are shown every year on *SportsCenter*.
- The current set is the fifth in 19 years, not including temporary sets built in the middle of the *SportsCenter* newsroom and in the ESPN lobby.
- The international version of *SportsCenter* is seen by more than 80 million viewers in 140 countries throughout Latin America and the Caribbean, Africa, Asia and the Middle East. The program is heard around the world in 15 languages, including English, Spanish, Portuguese, Mandarin, Cantonese and Japanese.
- Twenty-eight different mascots have appeared in the 'This is *SportsCenter*' promo campaign.
- *SportsCenter* celebrated its 10,000th telecast on December 2, 1988, and its 20,000th telecast on May 17, 1998.

total access

kenny mayne

"So it wasn't exactly like the Westminster Dog Show, which makes TV every year, but it was a big deal to me. In 1968, my dog (down to three legs because a panel station wagon had no brakes) made his dog show appearance at the Star Lake Elementary pet show. Ringo won Strangest Pet: while the other dogs were acting like show dogs are supposed to act, he peed in the vice-principal's parking spot."

personnel files

- ··· The first Chris Berman baseball nickname believed to have been uttered on *SportsCenter* (circa 1980) was John Mayberry "R.F.D."
- ··· On August 22, 1964, then-eight-year-old Dan Patrick threw a no-hitter for the Arizona Sun Shutters Little League team. He would repeat this feat on April 11, 1973, playing high school ball.
- ··· Dick Vitale pitched a no-hitter in Little League in Garfield, N.J., in 1951. In 1964, he coached an amateur baseball team (AAA) of 16-19-year-olds in Garfield to a state championship.
- ··· Nick "Tale of the Tape" Bakay is the voice of Salem, the cat on ABC's *Sabrina the Teenage Witch*, as well as Norbert on Nickelodeon's *Angry Beavers*.
- ··· When Karl Ravech was a junior in college, he served as an intern for Jack Edwards at WCVB-TV in Boston.
- ··· Writing for his high school student newspaper in Tarrytown, N.Y., Chris Berman used the byline Ilie Nastase for general features and Clifford Ray for basketball stories.
- ··· Then the program director of RKO Radio Network, Charley Steiner hired Keith Olbermann in 1981.
- ··· Chris Myers and high school classmate Dave Shula are both enshrined in the Chaminade Sports Hall of Fame in Hollywood, Fla.
- ··· Dan Patrick's first job after graduating from the University of Dayton was running religious tapes on a rock and roll radio station every Sunday from 2 a.m. until 9 a.m.
- ··· ESPNEWS anchor Trey Wingo's first job in television was as a page for *Late Night with David Letterman*. "More than once they would do a skit right in front of me, guarding the studio door," says Wingo. "This little voice inside my head kept saying, Do something! Make a television moment! But I never did—I wimped."
- ··· In 1997, Chris Berman was named one of *People's 40 Most Fascinating People*, the only sports figure to make the list. That same year, Rich Eisen and ESPNEWS anchor Andre Aldridge were featured bachelors in *Cosmopolitan All About Men*. Eisen described himself as turned on by "a baseball cap with a ponytail hanging out the back." Aldridge's ideal woman "looks good, has a sense of humor, is intelligent and isn't easily intimidated."

personnel files

··· Vice President Al Gore, Meat Loaf, Bob Weir and Bill Murray have all guest hosted on *Baseball Tonight's* Play of the Week segment. Hootie and the Blowfish introduced a *SportsCenter* Plays of the Week segment.

··· While working as ESPN pit reporter in 1988, Dr. Jerry Punch, a trauma specialist, helped save the lives of two drivers following crashes: Rusty Wallace and Don Marmor.

··· Rece is short for Rece Davis's middle name, Laurece (pronounced like Steve Miller's space cowboy—or the gangster of love—except with an L instead of an M). His first name is William.

··· While attending Yankee spring training in St. Petersburg in the '40s, *Sunday Countdown's* Hank Goldberg (then five) got his sportswriter father and his long-suffering mother evicted from the team hotel due to his rambunctious behavior. "I've been in kiddie rehab ever since," says Goldberg, who grew up to be the Miami Dolphins' play-by-play announcer for 15 years.

··· ESPNEWS anchor Jason Jackson and Dan Patrick both grew up north of Cincinnati, Ohio (Evendale and Mason respectively). "While I turned out to be a better snare drummer than a ballplayer, that Ohio passion for football never left me," says Jackson.

··· While she encourages everyone to sign up ESPN, ESPN2, ESPNEWS and Classic Sports, Chris McKendry did not have cable TV until 1991.

··· Bill Pidto and ESPNEWS's Dave Feldman played on the same Palo Alto high school basketball team as Jim Harbaugh. "He was a senior and a fierce competitor," says Pidto. "We were juniors and rode the pine."

··· Basketball analyst Quinn Buckner was a member of the last undefeated Division I men's basketball team (Indiana, 1976).

··· As a freshman at El Cajon Valley High School, *NFL 2Night* host Mark Malone set a world record for 14-year-olds for discus throw.

··· ESPNEWS anchor Dave Revsine played for the Trinity College "Runnin' Quatracentenarians" in 1992. "It was probably the worst college basketball team ever," says Revsine, who was in Ireland on a scholarship. "I'm convinced that every high school team in America could have beaten us."

··· College Basketball analyst Jay Bilas went to the same Rolling Hills High School in California that produced Tracy Austin, who in 1979 became the youngest woman to win the U.S. Open.

··· In his first job as an unpaid gofer at KFTW-AM in Fredericktown, Mo., then-17-year-old John Kernan (now the weekday host of *RPM 2 Night*) burned the antenna cable and put the station off the air for a week. "It was my responsibility to burn all the wire copy and trash. Surprisingly, I kept my job."

··· ESPNEWS anchor Betsy Ross's budding high school basketball career ended not in the gym but on the backyard court, when she bloodied her mother's nose in an especially tough game of one-on-one. "Hey, she was driving the lane, so what was I supposed to do?" says Ross.

··· *ESPN National Hockey Night's* Bill Clement and Guy Lafleur were both born in Thurso, Quebec, population 3,000. Only six months apart in age, the two future NHL rivals were teammates on several youth teams. Each now has a street named after him in Thurso.

··· ESPNEWS anchor Trey Wingo's full name is Hal Chapman Wingo III. His grandfather, Hal Chapman Wingo I, was a Baptist preacher, while his father, Hal Chapman Wingo II, was one of the founding editors at *People*. There's also a Hal Chapman Wingo IV who, Dad says, "can really smack a golf ball for a three-year-old."

··· Bob Stevens was at the largest crowd to ever watch an Oklahoma High School football game— in Leningrad. On July 4, 1989, more than 45,000 Russian fans watched two teams of traveling Oklahoma high school seniors, who had raised their own money to take football behind the Iron Curtain.

··· Dave Feldman, Bill Pidto and Karl Ravech shared the same bathroom. The trio of future ESPN anchors were roommates while working at the same station in Binghamton, N.Y.

··· Dan Patrick is a proud member of the Dick Trickle Fan Club.

··· Chris Berman has appeared in six movies: *Eddie*, *Celtic Pride*, *Little Big League*, *Necessary Roughness*, *Kingpin* and *The Program*. Oh yeah, and that Hootie video.

did you know?

Dan Patrick's trademark catch phrase "en fuego" was actually coined by someone else. Patrick was tired of using "on fire" to describe basketball highlights. A SportsCenter cameraman suggested he try saying it in Spanish.

Dan first tried "el fuego," which, as a Spanish teacher from Pennsylvania kindly pointed out, means "the fire."

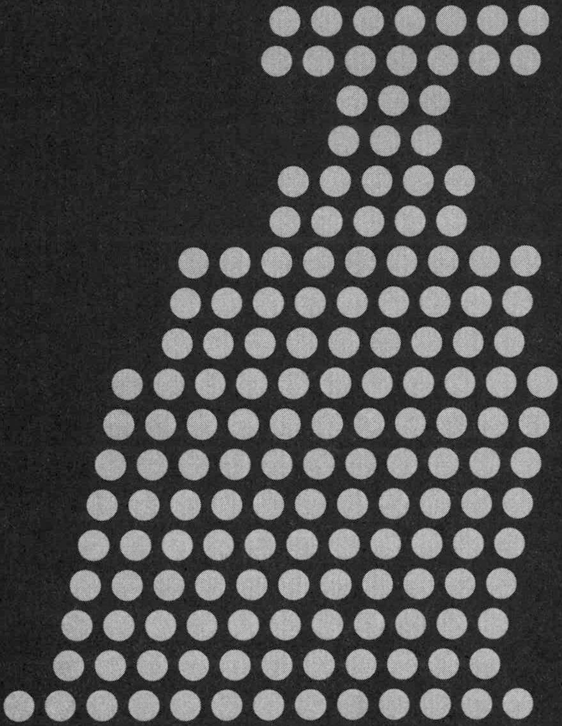

batteries not included

Stats are good up to the start of the 1998/99 NHL season.

did you know?

The National Hockey Night announcing team has four Stanley Cup rings to its credit: Brian Engblom won a pair with Montreal in 1978 and 1979, while Bill Clement earned two with Philadelphia in 1974 and 1975.

playoffs and championships

- In 1998, Detroit captured its ninth Stanley Cup, more than any other U.S.-based franchise but a long way from Montreal's 23 championships.
- Gordie Howe and Larry Robinson each competed in 20 postseasons. Mark Messier is the most experienced active playoff performer, with 236 playoff appearances in 17 postseasons.
- When the Devils, Penguins and Flyers were ousted in Round 1 of the 1998 Stanley Cup playoffs, it marked the first time in the NHL's current format that the top three seeds in a conference did not get past the first round.
- The Rangers have lost the first game in each of their last nine playoff series. However, they have gone on to win six of those nine series.
- The last non-NHL team to win the Stanley Cup was the Victoria Cougars of the Western Canada Hockey League. In 1925, the Cougars beat the Canadiens three games to one.
- The first Stanley Cup Finals series between two U.S.-based teams occurred in 1929. The Bruins swept the Rangers in a best-of-three series.
- In the post-expansion era, only two of 31 Stanley Cup Finals have included two Canadian teams. In 1986, Montreal defeated Calgary in five games. Three years later, the Flames took the Cup from the Canadiens in six.
- In their first 19 NHL seasons, the Oilers have won five Stanley Cups—that's as many as or more than three of the Original Six teams: Boston (5), Rangers (4) and Chicago (3).
- The Oilers were the first former WHA team to win a Stanley Cup. Ironically, of the four teams that joined the NHL in 1979, Edmonton was the only one *not* to win the WHA's Avco Cup title. Winnipeg (now Phoenix) won three Avco Cups, while New England/Hartford (now Carolina) and Quebec (now Colorado) each won one.
- Only two franchises have a winning percentage of .600 or better in postseason play: Edmonton at .637 and Montreal at .603.
- From 1951 through 1960, Montreal played in the Stanley Cup Finals a record 10 straight times, winning six championships.
- The only time every game in a Stanley Cup Finals series was decided in overtime was in 1951. Toronto emerged the winner, defeating Montreal in five games.
- Alexei Kovalev, Sergei Zubov, Alexander Karpovtsev and Sergei Nemchinov were the first Russian-born players to have their names inscribed on the Stanley Cup when they won the title with the Rangers in 1994.

- Being the best goalie in the regular season seldom translates into winning a championship. Since 1979/80, only two goaltenders have won the Vezina Trophy and a Stanley Cup title in the same campaign: Billy Smith with the Islanders in 1982 and Grant Fuhr with the Oilers in 1988.
- Only four players have won Stanley Cups with three different teams since the NHL took sole possession of the Cup in 1926: Gordon Pettinger (Rangers, Red Wings, Bruins), Al Arbour (Red Wings, Blackhawks, Maple Leafs), Larry Hillman (Red Wings, Maple Leafs, Canadiens) and Claude Lemieux (Canadiens, Devils, Avalanche).
- Ken Dryden holds the record for consecutive Cup Finals wins, with 10 between 1976 and 1978. Billy Smith and Turk Broda are second, tied at nine straight wins.
- In the 13 seasons that the President's Trophy has been awarded, only three teams with the best record over the regular season have gone on to win the Stanley Cup: Oilers (1986/87), Flames (1988/89) and Rangers (1993/94).
- Since the Finals went to a best-of-seven format in 1939, only two championship series have gone to overtime in the seventh and deciding game. Both times, the Red Wings came out on top: in 1950, Pete Babando scored in double OT to defeat the Rangers; four years later, Tony Leswick was the hero against the Canadiens.
- Calgary has not won a single playoff series since winning the Stanley Cup over Montreal in 1989. In addition, the Flames failed to win a playoff series during their eight seasons in Atlanta, dropping all six they appeared in.
- There have been 396 best-of-seven playoff series in NHL history. All seven games were won by the home team just six times.
- Since dropping the first 12 Finals games of his career while coaching St.Louis, Scotty Bowman has compiled a 32-9 record, winning eight Stanley Cup rings. Bowman has won 43 playoff series as a head coach, more than anyone in the NHL.
- Ralph "Scotty" Bowman won two Stanley Cups as a player for the Red Wings in 1936 and 1937. William "Scotty" Bowman has won two as a head coach with Detroit in 1997 and 1998.

inside the numbers

Of all players with over 300 combined goals (regular season and playoffs), only one player, Esa Tikkanen, has more than 20 percent of those goals coming in the playoffs, the true measure of a clutch performer:

player	total goals	regular season	playoffs	percentage
Esa Tikkanen	316	244	72	22.8
Claude Lemieux	371	298	73	19.7
Glenn Anderson	591	498	93	15.7
Mark Messier	706	597	109	15.4
Denis Potvin	366	310	56	15.3

for

the record

- The best recorded plus/minus in the NHL belongs to Bobby Orr, who went +124 in 1970/1971. Bobby Hull holds the mark in the WHA, going +65 for Winnipeg in 1975/76.
- Bobby Orr is also the only defenseman to lead the NHL in scoring. The Bruin won the Art Ross Trophy twice, notching 120 points in 1969/70 and 135 in 1974/75.
- The only defenseman to score five goals in a game isn't Bobby Orr, Denis Potvin or Paul Coffey. It is Toronto's Ian Turnbull, in a 9-1 rout of the Red Wings on February 2, 1977.
- The only player with at least 400 career goals (461) and 2,000 penalty minutes (2,532) is Pat Verbeek.
- The only player to record at least 400 penalty minutes twice in a season is Dave "The Hammer" Schultz. The Flyer enforcer spent an NHL record 472 minutes in the box in 1974/75 and logged 405 minutes in 1977/78.
- In 1997/98, the Capitals led the NHL in penalty killing at 89.2 percent efficiency, breaking the former record of 88.4 percent held by the 1973/74 Flyers.
- Only three players on a team in its first season in the NHL have led the league in goal scoring: Joe Malone had 39 goals for the Quebec Bulldogs in 1919/20, Bill Cook netted 33 for the Rangers in 1926/27 and Hartford's Blaine Stoughton's 56 goals in 1979-80 tied him with Los Angeles's Charlie Simmer and Buffalo's Danny Gare.
- Only three rookies have scored 50 or more goals in their freshman seasons: Teemu Selanne scored 76 for Winnipeg in 1992/93, Mike Bossy tallied 53 times for the Islanders in 1977/78 and Joe Nieuwendyk fired home 51 for Calgary in 1987/88.
- The record for most points in a game by a goaltender is three (all assists), credited to Jeff Reese in Calgary's 13-1 rout over San Jose on February 10, 1993.
- Tampa Bay G.M. Phil Esposito fired 550 shots on goal while with Boston in 1970/71. The mark is 124 shots more than the next highest total, Espo's 426 in 1971/72.
- Combining regular-season and playoff totals, only two players have amassed more than 4,000 penalty minutes: Dave "Tiger" Williams (4,421) and Dale Hunter (4,137). (Of course, Hunter had also contributed 575 more total points than Tiger entering the 1998/99 season.)
- 446 is the magic number for the most goals scored by one team in a season and the most goals allowed by one team in a season. Edmonton netted a record 446 goals in 1983/84. Washington allowed a record 446 goals in 1974/75.
- Only four players have scored 50 goals and recorded 200 penalty minutes in the same season: Kevin Stevens, Pittsburgh 1991/92 (54 goals/254 PIM); Gary Roberts, Calgary 1991/92 (53/207); Brendan Shanahan, St. Louis 1993/94 (52/211); and Keith Tkachuk, Phoenix 1996/97 (52/228).
- The most seasons one player has spent with the same club is 24, a record held by former Red Wing Alex Delvecchio. Stan Mikita was a 22-season Blackhawk, George Armstrong was a 21-season Maple Leaf, while Jean Beliveau wore the *bleu et rouge* for 20 seasons. 1998/99 will be Ray Bourque's 20th season in a Bruins uniform.
- The highest career point total by a goalie belongs to Grant Fuhr (46 points, all assists).

Q1

Only one NHL player has scored a goal five different ways in one game.

level 1   *Name the player.*

level 2   *List the five ways he scored.*

level 3   *When did he accomplish this feat and against which team?*

Q2

A six-team league until 1967, the NHL ballooned to 27 clubs for the 1998/99 season with the addition of the Nashville Predators. By the 2000/2001 campaign, the NHL will have 30 franchises.

level 1   *Name the three franchises that will enter the NHL by the 2000/2001 season.*

level 2   *Name the six franchises that entered the league in 1967.*

level 3   *Name the six franchises that entered the league in the '70s (excluding those from the WHA).*

---

question 1 answers

level 1   Mario Lemieux

level 2   *a* Even strength
           b Power play
           c Short-handed
           d Penalty shot
           e Empty net

level 3   December 31, 1988, against New Jersey

question 2 answers

level 1   The Atlanta Thrashers join the NHL for the 1999/2000 season, while the Columbus Blue Jackets and Minnesota Wild begin play the following season.

level 2   California Seals, Los Angeles Kings, Minnesota North Stars, Philadelphia Flyers, Pittsburgh Penguins and St. Louis Blues

level 3   Buffalo Sabres and Vancouver Canucks (1970/71), Atlanta Flames and New York Islanders (1972/73), Kansas City Scouts and Washington Capitals (1974/75)

wayne gretzky

- Wayne Gretzky was never selected in an NHL entry draft. The Great One signed with Indianapolis of the WHA in 1978 and was protected by Edmonton when the franchise joined the NHL in 1979. Although he was never eligible for the Calder Trophy, he did win the WHA's version of the award in 1978/79. The runner-up? Mike Gartner, who retired after the 1997/98 season.

- Mikko Leinonen shares one of Gretzky's 60-odd NHL records. The little-known former Ranger set a playoff record with six assists in a 7-3 win over Philadelphia on April 8, 1982, a mark No. 99 equaled against Los Angeles in a 13-3 trouncing on April 9, 1987.

- When Gretzky set up Ulf Samuelsson's goal on October 26, 1997, it gave The Great One 1,851 assists–more assists than any other player in NHL history has points.

- Gretzky has had seven streaks of 20 or more consecutive games with at least one point during his NHL career. That includes his record of 51 straight games in 1983/84.

- Through the 1997/98 season, only two active players had a career cumulative plus/minus rating above +500: Wayne Gretzky (+541) and Ray Bourque (+512).

❖ The Vancouver Canucks gave up three Gretzky goal-
scoring milestones: Glen Hanlon allowed Gretzky's
first goal on October 14, 1979, while Kirk McLean failed
to stop his record-setting 802nd on March 23, 1994.
The Great One also notched his 500th goal against
Vancouver, scoring into an empty net after the Canucks
pulled their goaltender on November 22, 1986.

❖ Gretzky is the all-time leader in regular-season hat
tricks, with 50. The Great One scored his 49th on
November 23, 1991, then proceeded to go the next 396
straight regular-season contests without one. His 50th
three-goal game finally came against, you guessed it,
Vancouver on October 11, 1997.

❖ Gretzky met his wife, Janet, while both were judges
on Dance Fever, the early '80s disco TV show hosted by
Deney Terrio. The prime minister of Canada and Hugh
Hefner were invited to their 1988 wedding.

❖ There is a 15-foot-tall bronze statue of The Great One
outside of Edmonton's Northlands Coliseum: chin up,
chest out, Oilers sweater tucked into his pants on one
side, Stanley Cup hoisted over his head.

the draft

-:- Of the 30 entry drafts since the current system was instituted in 1969, the first overall pick has been a center 15 times, more than any other position.

-:- Since 1969, only 10 goaltenders have been taken in the top 10. The first was current Carolina general manager Jim Rutherford, picked 10th by Detroit in 1969. The highest a goaltender has ever been taken is fourth (Roberto Luongo in 1997 by the Islanders).

-:- The first American-born player to be selected first overall was Brian Lawton, by Minnesota in 1983.

-:- Only one player from a U.S. college has been taken first overall. In 1986, Detroit picked Michigan State right wing Joe Murphy who, despite playing for MSU, was born in London, Ontario.

-:- The first European selected No. 1 overall was Mats Sundin, by Quebec in 1989. The Nordiques are the only team to have the first overall choice three years in a row: 1989 (Sundin), 1990 (Owen Nolan) and 1991 (Eric Lindros), none of whom still play for the franchise.

-:- The first Russian player selected in the first round was Alexei Kovalev, drafted 15th by the Rangers in 1991.

-:- The oldest player chosen first overall was Rob Ramage, who was 20 years, five months, when tabbed by the Colorado Rockies in 1979. The youngest chosen first overall was Pierre Turgeon, who was 17 years, 10 months when he was selected by Buffalo in 1987.

-:- Among players chosen first overall, only six have scored 30 or more goals in their first NHL season: Dale Hawerchuk (45), Mario Lemieux (43), Eric Lindros (41), Gilbert Perreault (38), Wendel Clark (34) and Dale McCourt (33).

-:- Montreal is the only team to have had the first two overall picks in the draft under the current system. The Canadiens were granted the selections in 1969 under a special rule allowing them to take the first two French-Canadian players (Réjean Houle and Marc Tardif).

-:- Before choosing Eric Chouinard 16th overall in 1998, Montreal had not selected a French-Canadian player in the first round since 1988, when they chose Eric Charron 20th overall.

-:- Six of the players selected first overall from 1969 to 1979 went on to win championships. Since then, only Mario Lemieux (Pittsburgh, 1991 and '92) and Joe Murphy (Edmonton, 1990) have gone on to hoist the Stanley Cup.

-:- Three former No. 1 overall picks went on to become NHL general managers: 1969's Réjean Houle (Montreal 1996-present), 1975's Mel Bridgman (Ottawa 1992/93) and 1978's Bobby Smith (Phoenix 1996-present).

did you know?

Linda Cohn played goal on her high school's men's hockey team. She had a butterfly style, was nasty with her stick in the crease ("I could start trouble and know I wouldn't have to finish it") and finished the season 3-3.

- Mike Gartner, selected fourth overall in 1979 by Washington, scored 708 goals in his career. The three players chosen before him that year—Rob Ramage, Perry Turnbull and Mike Foligno—combined to score 682.
- Paul Coffey was the fourth defenseman drafted in 1980, chosen sixth overall behind Dave Babych (Jets, second), Larry Murphy (Kings, fourth) and Darren Veitch (Capitals, fifth).
- Between 1969 and 1998, both Los Angeles and St. Louis have gone without a first round pick 16 times—more than any other franchise. (The Blues didn't participate in the 1983 entry draft due, in part, to a messy ownership transfer that nearly saw the team move to Saskatchewan.)
- The New York Rangers have selected players named York and Ranger in the entry draft. Michael York was chosen 136th in 1997, while Joe Ranger was taken 198th in 1986.
- Two of the top five active goalscorers were never drafted into the NHL. Wayne Gretzky was already Edmonton property before the Oilers' acceptance into the NHL for the 1979/80 season. Dino Ciccarelli was signed as a free agent out of the OHA by Minnesota in 1979.

inside the numbers

Atlanta Braves Cy Young-winner Tom Glavine was drafted in the fourth round of the 1984 entry draft by the Kings, 69th overall. Even more amazing is the starting lineup that can be built from players drafted after Glavine:

forwards	Brett Hull	Flames	117th overall
	Cliff Ronning	Blues	134th overall
	Luc Robitaille	Kings	171st overall
defensemen	Kjell Samuelsson	Rangers	119th overall
	Gary Suter	Flames	180th overall
goalie	Kirk McLean	Devils	107th overall

Since the current entry draft system was instituted in 1969, the top two selections in a given year have gone on to become teammates seven times:

year drafted	players (drafted by)	teammates	seasons
1969	No.1 Réjean Houle MTL, No. 2 Marc Tardif MTL	Canadiens	1969-73*
1971	No.1 Guy Lafleur MTL, No. 2 Marcel Dionne DET	Rangers	1988/89
1975	No.1 Mel Bridgman PHI, No. 2 Barry Dean KC	Flyers	1977-79
1978	No.1 Bobby Smith MIN, No. 2 Ryan Walter WSH	Canadiens	1983-90
1979	No.1 Rob Ramage COL, No. 2 Perry Turnbull STL	Blues	1982/83
1983	No.1 Brian Lawton MIN, No. 2 Sylvain Turgeon HFD	Whalers	1988/89
1991	No.1 Eric Lindros QUE, No.2 Pat Falloon SJ	Flyers	1995-98

*Houle and Tardif were also teammates with Quebec in the WHA from 1974 to '76.

closing the gap

You have to win the close ones. That's what separates the good teams from the bad ones.

⋰ But is it true? More precisely, do the good teams win more of the close ones than we would expect? After all, teams win because they're good, so doesn't it stand to reason that they'd win more squeakers than they'd lose?

⋰ To check this out, we made a list of the top six and bottom six teams at the close of the 1997/98 NHL season. The top six–New Jersey, Dallas, Detroit, Pittsburgh, St. Louis and Colorado–combined for a 265-147-80 record, or a .620 winning percentage. The bottom six–Anaheim, Vancouver, Tampa Bay, Florida, Calgary and the New York Rangers–combined for a 143-264-85 record, or a .377 winning percentage.

⋰ However, if we look just at the overtime records–and what's closer than OT?–the gap narrows considerably. The top six went 14-11-80, or a .514 winning percentage, while the bottom six went 12-19-85, or a .470 winning percentage.

⋰ Even if we subtract the ties–which, given their number, do influence the stats–and just look at overtime games that ended in a victory, the difference between the good and the bad still doesn't match the cliché (.560 versus .387).

June **9**

1948 Gary Thorne is born.
1993 The Montreal Canadiens defeat the Barry Melrose-led Kings 4-1 to win their 21st championship. "Take a good look at a Stanley Cup champion," exclaimed ESPN announcer Thorne, as Guy Carbonneau began the victory skate.

∴ Of course, one season is a small sample, so let's run the same test for the previous two campaigns, then add everything together. Now we've got 18 good teams, which combined for a .625 overall winning percentage. Our 18 bad teams combined for a pathetic .377 winning mark.

∴ But again, the difference isn't nearly so large in the overtime games. The good teams were a combined 51-40-216 (.518), the bad 32-46-204 (.475). The difference is more pronounced if we subtract the ties, but still not nearly as large as with the overall marks: .560 for the good teams in ties ending in a decision, .410 for the bad teams. That's a 150-point difference, substantially less than the difference between the overall marks.

∴ So do good teams win the close ones? Sure. But the key point is that overtime brings out the best in the worst, giving bad teams a fighting chance to win when the game is tight. *rob neyer*

total access
bill clement   national hockey night

"I am the only NHL player to have the dubious distinction of playing three games on three consecutive nights for three different teams. The first game was in Philadelphia, where I represented the Wales Conference in the 1976 All-Star Game. I drove back home to Washington, took the morning skate with the Capitals, then played the Islanders in Washington's 21st consecutive loss. After a hard practice the next morning, I heard I'd been traded to the Atlanta Flames, who wanted me to meet them in Philadelphia for a game that night. I drove back to Philly where, at 7:30 p.m., I took the ice for my third team in three nights."

streaks

- The Ottawa Senators lost the first 38 road games in their inaugural season, establishing the NHL record for the longest road losing streak. They finally posted a 5-3 win over the Islanders on April 10, 1993.
- From 1946 through 1987, the Canadiens won 18 straight playoff series against the Bruins. Boston finally ended the Habs' dominance with a four-games-to-one victory in the 1988 Adams Division Final.
- Patrick Roy has played in 40 or more games in each of the past 13 seasons, tying Tony Esposito for the most appearances by a goaltender in consecutive seasons.
- Hartford/Carolina has missed the playoffs six straight seasons. Among existing NHL teams, the Colorado/New Jersey franchise holds the record, with nine consecutive campaigns without a playoff berth (1979-87).
- The Blues have made it to the playoffs in 19 consecutive seasons, the longest active stretch in the NHL. The Boston Bruins hold the all-time mark of 29 seasons (1968-1996).
- New Flyers netminder John Vanbiesbrouck has the longest current streak of 10-plus win seasons. The Beezer has won at least 10 games in 14 straight campaigns entering 1998/99.
- Only two players have led their teams in scoring in each of the past five seasons: Wayne Gretzky (Kings and New York Rangers) and Doug Weight (Oilers).
- Jaromir Jagr is the only player to have scored at least 30 goals in each of the last seven seasons.
- Grant Fuhr started 76 consecutive games with the Blues in 1995/96, the longest streak of starts by a goalie in the post-expansion era.
- The Canadiens recorded the longest unbeaten streak on opening night, going 13-0-4 in 17 openers between 1963/64 and 1979/80.
- Between 1965 and 1975, the Maple Leafs lost the opening game in 10 straight playoff series, the longest such streak in NHL history. (Toronto won just three of those 10 series.)
- From 1979/80 to 1994/95, Mike Gartner scored at least 30 goals in 15 consecutive seasons (the NHL record).
- It has been 15 seasons since the team that gave up the fewest goals during the regular season went on to win the Stanley Cup. The Islanders were the last to accomplish this defensive feat, giving up 226 goals in the 1982/83 season.
- The Canadiens tallied 14 straight playoff overtime wins to set an NHL record. Vincent Damphousse began the streak on April 22, 1993, against Quebec; Buffalo's Geoff Sanderson ended it by beating the Habs on May 8, 1998.
- From 1980 to 1982, New York Islanders center Bryan Trottier put together a postseason record streak of 27 straight games in which he scored at least one point. Trottier had 16 goals and 26 assists during the streak.
- Mike Bossy and Wayne Gretzky share the record for most 50-goal seasons with nine. However, Bossy's nine 50-goal seasons for the Islanders were consecutive.
- Canadiens center Doug Jarvis is the NHL's Iron Man, playing in 964 consecutive games from 1975 to 1987.

inside the numbers

Only five teams have lost seven or more games to start a season:

team	season	straight start losses	final record
Rangers	1943/44	11	6-39-5
Blackhawks	1997/98	7	30-39-13
Capitals	1983/84	7	48-27-5
Blackhawks	1947/48	7	20-34-6
Canadiens	1938/39	7	15-24-9

Q3

Gordie Howe is second on the NHL's all-time goal-scoring list with 801 goals.

level 1 *For whom did he score his last goal?*

level 2 *One of Howe's teammates on that team was fellow goal-scoring legend Bobby Hull. Since Howe was already wearing No. 9 when Hull joined the team, what uniform number did the Golden Jet pick?*

level 3 *Howe and Hull were joined on that team by another future Hall of Famer. Name him.*

question 3 answers

level 1   Hartford Whalers

level 2   No. 16, the same number Hull originally wore when he came up with Chicago

level 3   Dave Keon

Q4

Eric Lindros was the first overall selection in the 1991 entry draft. While he has yet to win a Stanley Cup, six other players selected in the first round that year have.

level 1 *Name the six players.*

level 2 *In what year and for what team did they win the Stanley Cup?*

level 3 *Which teams drafted them and at what position overall?*

question 4 answers

level 1   a   Scott Niedermayer
          b   Aaron Ward
          c   Peter Forsberg
          d   Martin Lapointe
          e   Brian Rolston
          f   Alexei Kovalev

level 2   a   New Jersey 1995
          b   Detroit 1997 and 1998
          c   Colorado 1996
          d   Detroit 1997 and 1998
          e   New Jersey 1995
          f   Rangers 1994

level 3   a   New Jersey (3rd)
          b   Winnipeg (5th)
          c   Philadelphia (6th)
          d   Detroit (10th)
          e   New Jersey (11th)
          f   Rangers (15th)

dubious distinctions

- The most one-goal losses suffered by a team in a season is 21, shared by the 1992/93 Sharks, the 1993/94 Mighty Ducks and the 1997/98 Blackhawks.

- Only two teams in NHL history have lost 70 or more games in a season, and they did it the same year: San Jose (71) and Ottawa (70) both reached the mark during the 1992/93 season.

- The Blues have participated in more playoff games (246) without winning the Stanley Cup than any other team.

- The worst recorded plus/minus in the NHL belongs to Bill Mikkelson of the expansion 1974/75 Capitals. In only 59 games, Mikkelson, a defenseman, posted a dubious rating of -82. His teammates weren't much better, as the Caps allowed the most goals that season (446), with four players finishing with a plus/minus rating of -65 or worse: Mikkelson, Tommy Williams (-69), Greg Joly (-68) and Mike Marson (-65).

- Mike Gartner played in 1,554 regular season and playoff contests without having won the Stanley Cup, more than any other NHL player.

- Billy Reay coached and won more games than any head coach not to win a Stanley Cup. Reay guided Toronto and Chicago to victory in 542 games in 1,102 regular-season contests over 16 seasons but never won the big one.

- Brad Park was a six-time runner-up for the Norris Trophy, finishing second to Bobby Orr four times and to Denis Potvin twice.

- Patrick Roy is the only goaltender to allow a player's 500th career goal twice. Roy succumbed to Steve Yzerman on January 17, 1996, and surrendered Joe Mullen's milestone goal on March 14, 1997.

- John Vanbiesbrouck was the opposing goalie for 30 of Mario Lemieux's 613 regular-season goals, more than any other NHL netminder.

- Blackhawks goalie Sam LoPresti set an NHL record in futility in 1941, stopping 80 shots in a 3-2 loss to the Bruins.

- Tampa Bay averaged just 1.84 goals per game in 1997/98, becoming the first team in the post-expansion era to average fewer than two goals per game for an entire season.

- Including their earlier incarnations as the Kansas City Scouts and the Colorado Rockies, the Devils have played 24 straight seasons without a 50-goal or 100-point scorer. In 1987/88, Pat Verbeek scored 46 goals and Kirk Muller notched 94 points, the franchise marks.

did you know?

While with the Cincinnati Stingers in 1978/79, Barry Melrose was fourth in the WHA in penalty minutes, with 222. Just 10 PIMs behind was Birmingham's Dave Hanson, who portrayed one of the infamous Hanson brothers in the 1977 movie Slap Shot (real-life brothers, Steve and Jeff Carlson, played the other Hansons).

- In their 11 years of existence from 1967 to 1978, the Oakland Seals/California Seals/Cleveland Barons franchise never had a winning season.
- Dallas defenseman Craig Muni has played in 113 career playoff games without scoring a goal, the worst playoff scoring performance of any player, excluding goalies.
- The Blackhawks hold the records for fewest goals scored in a season of 70 games or more (133 in 1953/54) and the fewest goals scored in any season (33 in 1928/29).
- The post-expansion record for fewest shots on goal in a playoff win is 10, shared by the Devils (April 9, 1990, against Washington) and the Blackhawks (April 13, 1974, against Los Angeles).
- Detroit's Sid Abel is the only coach in NHL history to have made at least four trips to the Stanley Cup Finals and not gone home with a Cup ring.
- Of all netminders, Gilles Meloche played in more regular-season games (788) without winning a Stanley Cup than any other goaltender. Among active goalies, John Vanbiesbrouck entered 1998/99 with the most games played without a Cup ring (717).
- Michel Petit has suited up for a record 10 franchises. Drafted 11th overall by Vancouver in 1982, the defenseman then moved around to the Rangers, Quebec, Toronto, Calgary, Los Angeles, Tampa Bay, Edmonton, Philadelphia and Phoenix.
- King defenseman Randy Holt is the most penalized player in a single period, tallying 67 minutes (three majors, one minor and five misconducts) on March 11, 1979, in the most penalized period in NHL history. The Kings were assessed a total of 184 minutes, while the Flyers (who won 6-3) peaked with 199 minutes.
- The only forfeited game in modern NHL history occurred in the Boston Garden on March 14, 1933. Bruin Eddie Shore scored a disputed goal at 19:58 of the third period to give Boston a 3-2 lead over Chicago. When Blackhawk coach Tommy Gorman was ejected for arguing with referee Bill Stewart, he pulled his team off the ice with two seconds left and the game was declared forfeit.

inside the numbers

Since the NHL went to a multi-divisional format in 1967/68, only six teams have been able to finish at the top of their division in four or more consecutive seasons:

team	consecutive seasons in first place
Canadiens	8 (1974/75 to 1981/82)
Oilers	6 (1981/82 to 1986/87)
Nordiques/Avalanche	4 (1994/95 to 1997/98)
Bruins	4 (1975/76 to 1978/79)
Flyers	4 (1973/74 to 1976/77)
Blackhawks	4 (1969/70 to 1972/73)

The last time five or more clubs racked up more than 100 points in a season was back in 1992/93 (Montreal won the Stanley Cup):

teams	points
Penguins	119
Bruins	109
Blackhawks	106
Nordiques	104
Red Wings	103
Canadiens	102
Canucks	101

teammates

-:- Only two members of the 1980 gold-medal-winning U.S. Olympic team went on to win Stanley Cups: Ken Morrow won four with the New York Islanders from 1980 to 1983 while Neal Broten won with New Jersey in 1995. Morrow is the only player to win Olympic gold and Stanley Cup silver in the same season.

-:- The only teammates to each score at least 70 goals in the same season are Edmonton's Wayne Gretzky (73) and Jari Kurri (71) in 1984/85 .

-:- Mighty Ducks left winger Paul Kariya, Predators goalie Mike Dunham and Canucks goalie Garth Snow were all members of the University of Maine's 1992/93 NCAA championship team.

-:- Washington centers Adam Oates and Joe Juneau both played college hockey for RPI. Oates starred from 1982 to 1985, while Juneau wore the school colors from 1987 to 1991.

-:- San Jose left winger Stephane Matteau and St. Louis center Pierre Turgeon were both members of the team representing Canada in the 1982 Little League World Series. They did not win.

-:- Current Carolina Hurricanes Gary Roberts and Steve Chiasson were also teammates on a Memorial Cup-winning team in 1986. The pair celebrated Canada's junior hockey championship as members of the Guelph squad.

-:- Toronto's Curtis Joseph and Tie Domi co-own a racehorse named Ice Tie.

-:- In 1997/98, Washington's Adam Oates, Phil Housley and Dale Hunter all registered their 1,000th career point, the first time three players from the same team reached the mark during the same season.

-:- Brothers Maurice and Henri Richard were teammates on Montreal's five straight Stanley Cup winners from 1956 through 1960. The Rocket earned a total of eight Cup rings while the Pocket Rocket amassed a record 11.

-:- Two members of the great dynasties of the 1980s—Islander Bryan Trottier and Oiler Paul Coffey—helped Pittsburgh win its first Stanley Cup in 1991.

-:- The Bruins are the only team to have the top four players in the league scoring race—and they've done it twice. In 1970/71, Phil Esposito 152 pts., Bobby Orr 139, Johnny Bucyk 116 and Ken Hodge 105 finished 1-2-3-4. In 1973/74, the top four were Esposito 145 pts., Orr 122, Hodge 105 and Wayne Cashman 89.

-:- Three Oilers scored 50 or more goals in the same season twice in the '80s. In 1983/84, Wayne Gretzky scored 87 goals, Glenn Anderson notched 54 and Jari Kurri tallied 52. The same three turned the trick again two seasons later, as Kurri scored 68, followed by Anderson's 54 and Gretzky's 52.

-:- Jacques Plante (second all-time in career wins with 434) and Glenn Hall (fourth with 407) were teammates with the St. Louis Blues during the 1968/69 and 1969/70 seasons.

-:- All three players with at least 10 shorthanded goals in their playoff careers are former Edmonton Oilers: Mark Messier 14, Wayne Gretzky 11 and Jari Kurri 10.

inside the numbers

Since the institution of the red line in 1943/44, a player has scored at least one quarter of his team's goals on just five occasions:

player	team	season	goals	team goals	percentage
Brett Hull	STL	1990/91	86	310	27.7
Teemu Selanne	ANA	1997/98	52	205	25.4
Brett Hull	STL	1991/92	70	279	25.1
Maurice Richard	MTL	1949/50	43	172	25.0
Peter Bondra	WSH	1994/95*	34	136	25.0

*Lockout shortened season

Q5

One of the most powerful hockey figures from the '70s and '80s took a big fall in the '90s.

level 1   *Name the former executive director of the NHL Players Association who served time in prison for fraud and theft involving players' insurance premiums.*

level 2   *What international hockey tournament did this individual help create?*

level 3   *Which prestigious group was he forced to resign from? How many other members have been expelled?*

question 5 answers

level 1   Alan Eagleson

level 2   Canada Cup

level 3   The Hockey Hall of Fame. Inducted in the Builders category in 1989, the Eagle is the only member to have been expelled.

Q6

The New York Islanders are the only U.S.-based team to win four consecutive Stanley Cup championships.

level 1   *Name the teams the Islanders defeated in 1980, 1981, 1982 and 1983.*

level 2   *Name the four Islanders who won the Conn Smythe Trophy as playoff MVP in 1980, 1981, 1982 and 1983.*

level 3   *The Islanders' run was finally halted by the Oilers in 1984, but not before they set a record for consecutive playoff series wins. How many consecutive wins did they notch?*

question 6 answers

level 1	
1980	Philadelphia
1981	Minnesota
1982	Vancouver
1983	Edmonton

level 2	
1980	Bryan Trottier
1981	Butch Goring
1982	Mike Bossy
1983	Billy Smith

level 3   19 consecutive wins

behind the bench

-:- Toe Blake is the only person to have won the Hart Trophy as MVP (1939) and won the Stanley Cup as a head coach.

-:- Blake won Stanley Cups in his first five seasons as Montreal head coach (1955/56 to 1959/60). Blake won eight championships in all behind the bench, a record he shares with his protégé, Detroit's Scotty Bowman.

-:- Only three coaches have won Stanley Cups with more than one team since 1926: Tommy Gorman with Chicago and the Montreal Maroons, Dick Irvin with Toronto and Montreal and Scotty Bowman with Montreal, Pittsburgh and Detroit.

-:- Scotty Bowman is the only coach to record at least 200 wins with three different teams: 419 with Montreal, 210 with Buffalo and 223 going into the 1998/99 season with Detroit. Dick Irvin won 431 games with Montreal and 216 with Toronto, the only coach to record 200 wins with two different teams.

-:- Scotty Bowman leads all head coaches in regular-season wins, with 1,057. Of active coaches, the next closest is Vancouver's Mike Keenan, with 491.

-:- Al Arbour is second all-time for the most regular-season coaching losses (577) and second on the all-time victory list (781).

-:- In 1998/99, new Chicago coach Dirk Graham will become the fourth former Selke Trophy winner (awarded to the top defensive forward) to lead a team behind the bench. The others are Bob Gainey (Stars 1990-96), Steve Kasper (Bruins 1995-97) and Craig Ramsay (interim coach for Buffalo in 1986/87).

-:- Former Bruins coach Tom Johnson owns the highest regular-season winning percentage among those who have coached at least 200 games. Johnson compiled a .738 winning percentage with Boston (1970-1973).

-:- The entire 1998/99 Rangers coaching staff has Edmonton connections. Head coach John Muckler led the Oilers in 1990 to their last championship, while assistants Keith Acton, Charlie Huddy and Craig MacTavish won Cups while playing for Edmonton (one, five and three respectively).

-:- Pat Burns is the only head coach to win the Jack Adams Award three times: Montreal (1989), Toronto (1993) and Boston (1998).

-:- Jacques Demers is the only coach to win the Jack Adams Award in back-to-back seasons (Detroit, 1986/87, 1987/88).

-:- Roger Neilson is the most traveled head coach in the NHL, having led seven different clubs: Philadelphia, Toronto, Buffalo, Vancouver, Los Angeles, New York Rangers and Florida.

total access
al morganti   national hockey night

"I grew up in Needham, Massachusetts, and found out very early that hockey was the biggest game in town. The Needham high school team won two state championships, led by Robbie Ftorek, now the coach of the Devils, and backstopped by Cap Raeder, a former assistant coach for Barry Melrose with the Kings. The all-time attendance record at the old Boston Garden was not for the Bruins or Celtics, but to see those Ftorek-led teams play in the state hockey tournaments."

Q

Wayne Gretzky finally broke Gordie Howe's goal-scoring mark of 801 goals in 1994.

level 1 *Whose goal-scoring record did Howe break and what was the mark?*

level 2 *How many 50-goal seasons did Howe have in his 26-year NHL career?*

level 3 *Who held the record before the player whose record Howe broke?*

Q

The National Hockey League shut down its schedule for 17 days during the 1997/98 season to allow its players to participate in the Winter Olympics in Nagano.

level 1 *Which team was accused of causing property damage to the Olympic village?*

level 2 *How much money was paid out to cover the damage?*

level 3 *Who paid for the damage?*

family secrets

-:- Philadelphia goaltender Ron Hextall is a third-generation NHLer: his grandfather, Bryan Hextall Sr., and his father, Bryan Jr., combined to play 19 seasons, while his uncle Dennis played for six teams over 13 seasons.

-:- Manon and Pascal Rheaume are the first brother-sister combination to have played in any major professional team sport.

-:- Nikos Tselios, Carolina's first-round draft pick in 1997, is a cousin of Chicago's Chris Chelios.

-:- New Jersey goalie Martin Brodeur's father, Denis, is the official photographer for both the Montreal Canadiens and Montreal Expos. The elder Brodeur was also a goaltender for Canada's 1956 Olympic hockey team, which won a bronze medal.

-:- Phoenix defenseman Gerald Diduck's sister, Judy, was a member of Canada's first women's Olympic hockey team. Of course, San Jose forward Tony Granato's sister, Cammi, captained the U.S. squad to the gold medal in Nagano in 1998.

-:- Chicago center Chad Kilger's father, Bob, was an NHL referee from 1970 until 1980.

-:- Phoenix center Jeremy Roenick's brother, Trevor, was a fourth-round draft choice by the Hartford Whalers in 1993.

-:- Ken and Dave Dryden were the first brothers to play goal opposite each other in the NHL. Playing in only his second NHL game, Ken led the Canadiens to a 5-2 victory over Dave's Sabres on March 20, 1971.

-:- Phoenix's Keith Tkachuk and Nashville's Tom Fitzgerald are first cousins, as are Dallas's Joe Nieuwendyk and the Rangers' Jeff Beukeboom.

-:- Oiler Mike Grier's father, Bob, is director of player personnel for the NFL's New England Patriots.

-:- Hurricane Kevin Dineen's father, Bill, was head coach of the Flyers from 1991 to 1993. Bill also won two Avco Cups as head coach of the WHA's Houston Aeros in 1974 and 1975.

-:- Mighty Duck Ted Drury's brother, Chris, was a pitcher on the Trumbull, Connecticut, 1989 Little League World Championship team. Chris also won the 1998 Hobey Baker Award while at Boston University.

-:- Pittsburgh G.M. Craig Patrick and Washington president Dick Patrick are cousins, members of hockey's most illustrious family. Four members of the Patrick family have been head coach of the Rangers, including Craig, who guided the Blueshirts on two occasions in the 1980s. Craig's uncle, Muzz, was Ranger coach from 1953 to 1955. Craig's father, Lynn, guided New York from 1948 to '50, while Craig's grandfather, Lester, was the Rangers' first coach from 1926 to '39. And Craig's grandfather, Joseph, the Patrick patriarch, helped build the first artificial ice rinks in Canada.

inside the numbers

No set of brothers has combined for more NHL goals than the Sutters. Of course, it helped that there were six of them:

brothers	goals through 1997/98
Sutters	1,311 (Brent 363, Brian 303, Ron 196, Darryl 161, Rich 149, Duane 139
Hulls	913 (Bobby 610, Dennis 303)
Richards	902 (Maurice 544, Henri 358)
Gretzkys	886 (Wayne 885, Brent 1)
Stastnys	823 (Peter 450, Anton 252, Marian 121)

Q

The Pittsburgh Penguins selected Mario Lemieux first overall in the 1984 entry draft.

level 1   *Name the junior team from which Lemieux was drafted.*

level 2   *Although Lemieux has retired, the four players selected after him are still active. Name them in descending order.*

level 3   *The Penguins had two other first-round picks in 1984. Name them.*

Q

The last arena from the Original Six era will close during the 1998/99 season.

level 1   *Name the arena and the city.*

level 2   *Which Hall of Famer was the driving force behind the construction of the original building?*

level 3   *After this building closes, which NHL rink will briefly become the league's oldest?*

question 9 answers

level 1   Laval

level 2   2   Kirk Muller
3   Ed Olczyk
4   Al Iafrate
5   Petr Svoboda

level 3   No. 9 Doug Bodger and No. 16 Roger Belanger

question 10 answers

level 1   Maple Leaf Gardens, Toronto

level 2   Conn Smythe

level 3   The temporary home of the Carolina Hurricanes, Greensboro Coliseum, which opened in 1959. When the Hurricanes move into their permanent home in Raleigh, Pittsburgh's Civic Arena will become the league's oldest structure. The Igloo opened in 1961.

franchise history

- Since 1944, the Montreal Canadiens have not gone more than seven seasons without winning the Stanley Cup. The Habs won their last Cup in 1993.
- After joining the NHL in 1970, the Vancouver Canucks spent their first three seasons in the East Division.
- The team with the shortest tenure in NHL history was the Montreal Wanderers. A member of the league in its inaugural season of 1917/18, the Wanderers played just six games (1-5-0) before fire claimed their home rink, the Westmount Arena, and forced them to withdraw from the league.
- The Washington Capitals failed to make the playoffs in each of their first eight seasons. Of the 20 teams that joined the NHL in the post-expansion era, it took the Caps more seasons than any other newcomer to reach the postseason for the first time.
- The Rangers have had only two 50-goal scorers in their 72 NHL seasons. Vic Hadfield scored 50 in 1971/72 and Adam Graves scored 52 in 1993/94.
- The Winnipeg Jets/Phoenix Coyotes franchise is 0-3 in seventh games in their NHL playoff history. The only Game 7 win in franchise history occurred when the Jets were in the WHA and defeated San Diego 7-3 in the 1977 Western semifinals.
- The Oilers made the playoffs in each of their first 13 NHL seasons (1979/80 to 1991/92).
- During 1993/94, the Panthers posted an 18-16-8 mark, the only expansion team to have a winning record away from home in their first season.

- Of the top 10 goalscorers of all time through 1997/98, six spent at least part of their career with the Rangers. They are Wayne Gretzky, Marcel Dionne, Phil Esposito, Mike Gartner, Jari Kurri and Mark Messier.
- The Penguins own two of the top five power play goal totals for a single season: a record 119 in 1988/89 and 110 in 1987/88 (good for a tie for fourth spot).
- The Devils have dressed six Hobey Baker Award winners (top collegiate hockey player): Neal Broten, George McPhee, Tom Kurvers, David Emma, Scott Pellerin and Brendan Morrison.
- Since the NHL first instituted All-Rookie selections in 1982/83, Chicago has had the most goaltenders named to the squad: ESPN analyst Darren Pang (1987/88), Ed Belfour (1990/91) and Dominik Hasek (1991/92).
- Of the six players and two draft picks obtained by Quebec from Philadelphia in the deal for Eric Lindros on June 30, 1992, only one player remains with the franchise (now based in Colorado): Peter Forsberg.
- Minnesota and Ohio have a unique link in hockey history. After the Cleveland Crusaders of the WHA ceased operations in 1975/76, the franchise re-emerged the following season as a short-lived second version of the Minnesota Fighting Saints. Following the 1977/78 season, the Cleveland Barons merged with the Minnesota North Stars. Now in the 1999/2000 season, the states are linked again as the Minnesota Wild and Columbus Blue Jackets will become the 29th and 30th teams in the NHL.

inside the numbers

Of the 27 teams that skated into the 1998/99 season, six have changed cities:

team	previous homes
Carolina Hurricanes	Hartford 1979-97
Calgary Flames	Atlanta 1972-80
Colorado Avalanche	Quebec 1979-95
Dallas Stars	Minnesota 1967-93
New Jersey Devils	Kansas City 1974-76, Colorado 1976-82
Phoenix Coyotes	Winnipeg 1979-96

Q11

Five of the NHL's top 10 all-time goalscorers also played in the World Hockey Association (WHA).

level 1 *Name the five players in descending order of ranking in the NHL top 10.*

level 2 *Name all the WHA clubs that the five played for.*

level 3 *Which of the five scored the most regular-season WHA goals and which player scored the fewest?*
Bonus: What were their respective WHA regular-season goal totals?

question 11 answers

level 1	a	Wayne Gretzky 1st
	b	Gordie Howe 2nd
	c	Mike Gartner 5th
	d	Bobby Hull 7th
	e	Mark Messier 10th

level 2	a	Indianapolis, Edmonton
	b	Houston, New England
	c	Cincinnati
	d	Winnipeg
	e	Indianapolis, Cincinnati

level 3 Hull scored 303 goals. Messier scored 1 goal.

Q12

Five NHL players have tallied seasons of 150 points or better.

level 1 *Name the five players.*

level 2 *Name the franchises they accomplished this feat with.*

level 3 *How many times has each player hit that 150-point mark?*

question 12 answers

level 1	a	Phil Esposito
	b	Wayne Gretzky
	c	Mario Lemieux
	d	Bernie Nicholls
	e	Steve Yzerman

level 2	a	Boston
	b	Edmonton, Los Angeles
	c	Pittsburgh
	d	Los Angeles
	e	Detroit

level 3	a	1
	b	9
	c	4
	d	1
	e	1

personal files

- Esa Tikkanen was a national junior figure skating champion in Finland.
- Philadelphia's three-time 50-goal scorer John LeClair was cut from his high school hockey team in Vermont when he was a freshman.
- Edmonton's Bill Guerin was an honorable mention All-American in lacrosse while in high school in Massachusetts.
- Devils head coach Robbie Ftorek was the first American player to be named MVP of a major pro hockey league. He was the WHA's MVP in 1977 while with the Phoenix Roadrunners.
- Vancouver's Peter Zezel once played professional soccer for the NASL's Toronto Blizzard. Zezel also made a cameo appearance in the 1986 Rob Lowe movie *Youngblood*.
- San Jose's Bernie Nicholls is part owner of the New Mexico Scorpions of the Western Professional Hockey League. Other part owners of the Scorpions include St. Louis right wing Joe Murphy and Texas Rangers relief pitcher John Wetteland.
- San Jose left wing Shawn Burr and Florida right wing Dino Ciccarelli are owners of the Sarnia Sting of the Ontario Hockey League.
- San Jose's Todd Ewen wrote and illustrated *A Frog Called Hop*, a children's book.
- San Jose's Marty McSorley appeared in *Con Air* and *Forget Paris*, while Luc Robitaille played himself in *Sudden Death*.
- Islanders coach and G.M. Mike Milbury was recruited to play both hockey and football at Colgate University.
- Islanders center Sergei Nemchinov roomed with legendary Soviet goaltender Vladislav Tretiak while the two were with Russia's Central Red Army team.
- Devils owner John McMullen owned baseball's Houston Astros from 1979 to '92. Devils G.M. Lou Lamoriello was a player, coach and manager in the Cape Cod Baseball League.
- Sharks owner George Gund III, who also owns the NBA's Cleveland Cavaliers, was the owner of the Cleveland Barons during their two NHL seasons from 1976 to '78.
- Kelvington, Saskatchewan (pop. 900), has produced five NHL players: Lloyd Gronsdahl (Boston, 1941/42); Barry Melrose; his cousin, Wendel Clark; and the Kocur brothers, Joey and Kory (who played one game for Detroit).
- Rangers G.M. Neil Smith was an All-American defenseman during his freshman season at Western Michigan University. One of Smith's teammates during his time at WMU was *ESPN National Hockey Night's* John Saunders.

did you know?

While millions refer to Milton Berle as Uncle Miltie,
Steve Levy is one of the few who can say it and mean it:
Levy's father's first cousin married Berle's brother, making
him a distant uncle, but a relative nonetheless.

Q13

Hockey is known for its colorfully named forward trios, including the Triple Crown Line, the Punch Line, the Kraut Line, the GAG Line, the Production Line, the Kid Line (also known as the Kitchener Kids), the French Connection and, most recently, the Legion of Doom and the Crash Line.

level 1   *Name the members of the KLM Line and the team they played for in the '80s.*

level 2   *Name the members of Chicago's 1961 Million Dollar Line. How did they get their nickname?*

level 3   *The 1961 Stanley Cup champion Blackhawks had a second line with a nickname. Who played on it and what was it called?*

question 13 answers

level 1   Vladimir Krutov, Igor Larionov and Sergei Makarov (Red Army)

level 2   Murray Balfour, Bill Hay and Bobby Hull. The line got its name after head coach Rudy Pilous commented he wouldn't trade the trio for a million dollars.

level 3   Ab McDonald, Stan Mikita and Ken Wharram were known as the Scooter Line.

Q14

During the 1998 off-season, coaches were coming and going almost as much as players.

level 1   *Including the 1998/99 season, name the only NHL team that started each of the last three seasons with a new head coach.*

level 2   *Name the three head coaches.*

level 3   *This club also named a new team president and general manager. Who is he, and what position did he leave to take his new job?*

question 14 answers

level 1   Mighty Ducks of Anaheim

level 2   Ron Wilson 1996/97
Pierre Page 1997/98
Craig Hartsburg 1998/99

level 3   Pierre Gauthier, who left his job as general manager of the Ottawa Senators to go to Anaheim

awards

:: In 1997/98, Dominik Hasek became the first goaltender to win the Hart Trophy as league MVP in consecutive seasons. Three other goalies won it once: Roy Worters (1928/29), Charlie Rayner (1949/50), Al Rollins (1953/54) and Jacques Plante (1961/62).

:: Since expansion in 1967/68, Bobby Orr (1970 and 1972), Bobby Clarke (1975), Guy Lafleur (1977 and 1978), Wayne Gretzky (1984, 1985 and 1987) and Mark Messier (1990) are the only players to win the Hart Trophy and the Stanley Cup in the same season.

:: The Selke Trophy has gone to a Montreal Canadien on seven occasions. However, only two Habs have actually won the award: Bob Gainey took the honor four times (1978-81), while Guy Carbonneau won it three times (1988, 1989, 1992).

:: No U.S.-born player has ever won the Hart Trophy. In fact, only two non-Canadians have ever claimed the award: Russian Sergei Fedorov (1994) and Czech Dominik Hasek (1997, 1998).

:: Only two European goaltenders have ever won the Vezina Trophy: Sweden's Pelle Lindbergh (1985) and Dominik Hasek (1994, 1995, 1997, 1998).

:: Only three defensemen have won the Norris Trophy with two different teams. Doug Harvey won six with Montreal and one with the Rangers; Chris Chelios won his first with Montreal and two more with Chicago; Paul Coffey won twice with Edmonton and once with Detroit.

:: Patrick Roy was the youngest player to ever win the Conn Smythe Trophy (just 20 when he was named playoff MVP in 1986 with Montreal).

bill clement   total access
national hockey night

"My first year out of Junior A, I was playing for the Flyers farm team, the Quebec Aces, to improve my scoring. In one memorable weekend series, we played two games against the Canadiens farm team, the Montreal Voyageurs. I scored my first professional hat trick in the first game, then scored two more in the second–five goals in six periods against the same goalie, a tall, awkward string bean that I thought didn't have a chance in the NHL. Later that season, that goalie got called up to the Canadiens and helped them win the Stanley Cup, earning both the Conn Smythe and the Calder Trophy. He's also enshrined in the Hockey Hall of Fame. And that's the last time I underestimated Ken Dryden."

Q 15

A fluke goal put a dramatic stop to Edmonton's quest for a third straight Stanley Cup in 1986, when an Oiler defenseman inadvertently banked an outlet pass off the skate of goaltender Grant Fuhr in Game 7 of the Smythe Division final.

level 1   *Who were the Oilers playing?*

level 2   *Name the Oiler defenseman who scored on his own goalie.*

level 3   *Who was credited with the winning goal?*

Q 16

Brett Hull will be loading up his gun in the Lone Star State after signing with the Dallas Stars as an unrestricted free agent on July 3, 1998.

level 1   *Which NHL team originally drafted Hull?*

level 2   *How many 50-goal seasons has Hull amassed during his career?*

level 3   *What was his highest goal total and in what season did his reach that number?*

awards

- Players from New York-based teams have won the Lady Byng Trophy on 18 occasions: 13 Rangers, four Islanders and Billy Burch of the Americans in 1927.
- Since the inception of the Conn Smythe Trophy in 1965, the award has gone to a player on the losing team in the Finals just four times: Detroit's Roger Crozier in 1966, St. Louis's Glenn Hall in 1968, Philadelphia's Reg Leach in 1976 and Philadelphia's Ron Hextall in 1987.
- From 1943 to 1945, Toronto had a record three straight Calder Trophy winners: Gaye Stewart, Gus Bodnar and Frank McCool.
- Only four goaltenders have won the Calder and Vezina Trophies in the same season: Frank Brimsek 1938/39, Tony Esposito 1969/70, Tom Barrasso 1983/84 and Ed Belfour 1990/91.
- Boston's Sergei Samsonov won rookie of the year awards in two leagues in consecutive seasons. He was the International Hockey League's top freshman in 1996/97 and the NHL's Calder Trophy winner in 1997/98.
- Only two players have won the Conn Smythe Trophy in consecutive seasons: Bernie Parent (Philadelphia, 1974-75) and Mario Lemieux (Pittsburgh, 1991-92).
- Only three players on a last-place team have won the Hart Trophy: Tom Anderson of the 1941/42 Brooklyn Americans, Al Rollins of the 1953/54 Chicago Blackhawks and Mario Lemieux of the 1987/88 Pittsburgh Penguins.
- Of the four top-scoring defensemen of all time (Paul Coffey, Ray Bourque, Larry Murphy and Denis Potvin), only Murphy has failed to win the Norris Trophy. The other three have 11 Norrises among them.

inside the numbers

Only four times in NHL history has a postseason award been won by the same player five or more consecutive seasons:

player	award		consecutive seasons
Bobby Orr	Norris	8	1968-75
Wayne Gretzky	Hart	8	1980-87
Wayne Gretzky*	Ross	7	1981-87
Jacques Plante	Vezina	5	1956-60

*During the 1979/80 season, Gretzky tied Marcel Dionne in points with 137. However, Dionne was awarded the Art Ross Trophy based on his 53 goals to Gretzky's 51.

Q17

In the early '80s, it looked certain that Wayne Gretzky would wear one NHL jersey his entire career. Instead, The Great One has donned No. 99 for several teams.

level 1   *Name the NHL teams.*

level 2   *What was the only team with which Gretzky did not play a full season?*

level 3   *When Gretzky joined his current team in 1996, a former teammate was the head coach. Name him and the team, position and season he played with Gretzky.*

Q18

The 1998 off-season saw front office changes to several NHL teams, some of which extended to the league's hierarchy.

level 1   *Name the former head coach who is the new senior vice-president, director of hockey operations for the NHL.*

level 2   *Name the person he replaced and the position that person left the league's New York office to take.*

level 3   *What was that person's job before his stint with the NHL?*

question 17 answers

level 1   *a*   Edmonton
          b   Los Angeles
          c   St. Louis
          d   New York Rangers

level 2   St. Louis (18 regular-season games and 13 playoff games in 1995/96)

level 3   Colin Campbell, defenseman Edmonton (1979/80)

question 18 answers

level 1   Colin Campbell

level 2   Brian Burke left the NHL to become president/general manager of the Vancouver Canucks, where he'd been the vice-president and director of hockey operations from 1987 to '92.

level 3   General manager of the Hartford Whalers (1992-94)

the
last time

∴ The last time a player other than Wayne Gretzky, Mario Lemieux or Jaromir Jagr led the NHL in scoring was 1979/80. Los Angeles center Marcel Dionne notched 137 points along with Gretzky, but was awarded the title based on having scored 53 goals to Gretzky's 51.

∴ The last Montreal Canadien to lead the NHL in goal scoring was Guy Lafleur in 1978, with 60 goals.

∴ The last player to win the Lady Byng Trophy and play for the Stanley Cup champion in the same season was Calgary's Joe Mullen in 1988/89.

∴ The last Ranger to lead the NHL in scoring was Bryan Hextall in 1942, with 56 points.

∴ The last defenseman to register 100 points in a season was Brian Leetch of the Rangers, who notched 102 points on 22 goals and 80 assists in 1991/92.

∴ Excluding the lockout-shortened 1994/95 season, the last time a player led the NHL in scoring with less than 100 points was during the 1967/68 season. That year, Chicago's Stan Mikita topped the circuit with 87.

∴ The last and, thus far, only time a Penguin won the Norris Trophy as top defenseman was in 1981, when Randy Carlyle took the hardware.

∴ The last player to average more than one goal per game for a season was Boston's Cam Neely. In 1993/94, Neely tallied 50 goals in just 49 games played.

∴ The last player born outside of North America to be picked first overall in the entry draft was Roman Hamrlik (Tampa Bay, 1992).

∴ The last time a goalie was named team captain was in 1946-48, when Bill Durnan wore the C for two seasons with the Montreal Canadiens.

∴ The last time Stephane Matteau scored a playoff goal was his Game 7, double-overtime winner against New Jersey that propelled the Rangers into the 1994 Stanley Cup Finals. Since that May 27th tally, Matteau has gone 36 consecutive playoff contests without scoring.

∴ The last time a netminder won 40-plus games in back-to-back seasons was in 1975/76 and 1976/77, when Ken Dryden turned the trick for the Canadiens.

∴ The last time the Kings won a playoff game was June 1, 1993, when Barry Melrose guided the team to a 4-1 win over Montreal in Game 1 of the Finals. The Kings lost the next four games, missed the playoffs the next four seasons and were swept in the opening round by St. Louis in 1998.

total access
nick bakay   espn: the magazine

"While growing up in Buffalo, I attended the Bobby Orr-Mike Walton hockey camp for four summers, where I took elbows to the head from former Broadstreet Bully Bill Barber, watched former Canadien Doug Jarvis call all the kids with long hair 'Alice,' and was frequently shown preferential treatment by future broadcaster John Davidson, who liked to try to stump me on music trivia. I have since gone on to score against Kelly Hrudey and the Beezer, proudly wearing the Cooper hockey gloves in which Rick Martin became the first Buffalo Sabre to score 50 goals in a season."

Q19

Of the many top goalies who were free agents in 1998, Mike Richter and Curtis Joseph were considered the prizes. Richter eventually re-signed with the New York Rangers, while Cujo left the Oilers for the Maple Leafs.

level 1   *In what season did both Richter and Joseph make their regular-season NHL debuts?*

level 2   *What U.S. college did both goaltenders attend?*

level 3   *Of the two, which goalie has collected more regular-season wins?*

question 19 answers

level 1   1989/90

level 2   The University of Wisconsin

level 3   Entering the 1998/99 season, Joseph had 213 regular-season wins to Richter's 203. Richter has one Stanley Cup ring, as well as the edge in playoff wins, 41-26.

Q20

The Stanley Cup has been awarded since 1893 in all but one season.

level 1   *Which year had no Stanley Cup winner?*

level 2   *What was the reason the Finals series was never completed?*

level 3   *Name the Montreal Canadien who died in a Seattle hospital as a result.*

question 20 answers

level 1   1919

level 2   Influenza epidemic

level 3   Joe Hall

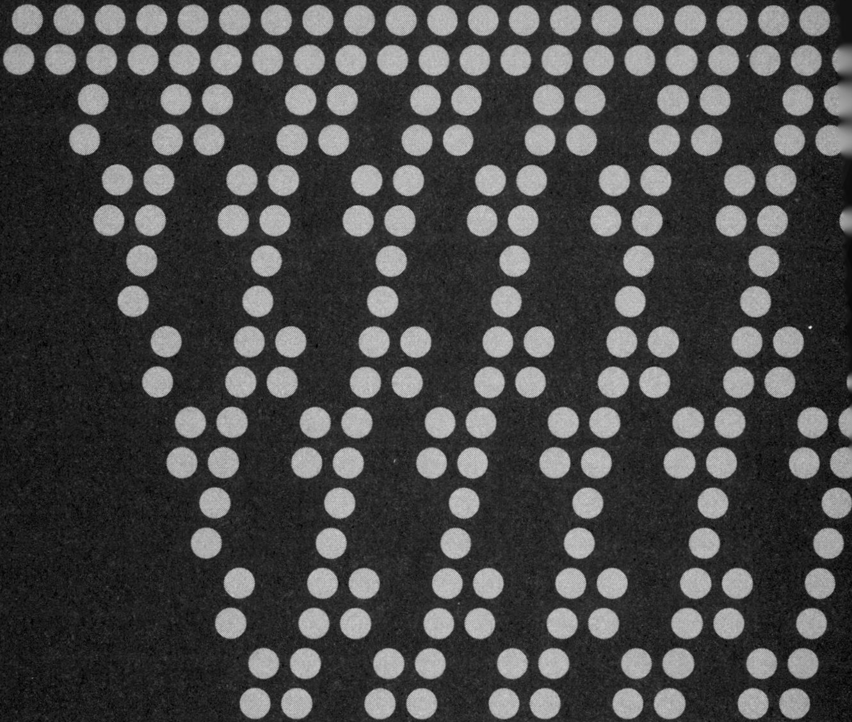

college basketball

no preservatives

Stats are good up to the start of the 1998/99 NCAA season.

did you know?

Dick Vitale's first ESPN telecast was Wisconsin versus
De Paul at Alumni Hall on December 16, 1979. The Blue
Demons beat the Badgers, 84-78.

championships

-:- The NBA and NCAA basketball champions have come from the same state three times: 1989 (Pistons, Michigan), 1975 (Warriors, UCLA) and 1972 (Lakers, UCLA). Utah claimed both runners-up in 1998.

-:- The only team to win consecutive postseason NIT titles is St. John's (1943/44). Six different schools have won back-to-back NCAA championships: Duke, UCLA, Cincinnati, San Francisco, Kentucky, Oklahoma State. St. John's has the most men's college basketball victories: 1,554 wins in 91 years without ever winning an NCAA title, although they have won a record five NIT titles. The closest the Red Storm (née Redmen) came to winning the Big Dance was in 1952, when they lost 80-63 to Kansas in the championship game.

-:- The ACC is the only Division I conference in which each member institution has a winning record in NCAA tournament competition.

-:- The 1985 and '86 Louisville Cardinals are the last teams to make the NIT Final Four and the NCAA Final Four in consecutive seasons.

-:- The largest margin of victory in a women's NCAA championship game is 23 points, by Tennessee over Louisiana Tech in 1987 when the Lady Vols won their first of five titles. Tennessee also holds the record for the largest margin of victory in a women's Final Four, beating Arkansas by 28 points in 1998.

-:- The largest margin of victory in a men's NCAA championship is held by UNLV, beating Duke by 30 points in 1990.

-:- Since 1980, 15 of the 19 national men's championship games were decided by single figures.

-:- No team has ever won the NIT and NCAA titles in consecutive years.

-:- The 1979 McDonald's All-American Class has the most combined NCAA and NBA championships, with 18 (five NCAA and 13 NBA). The class included James Worthy, Isiah Thomas, Byron Scott, Greg Kite, Sidney Lowe, Derek Whittenberg and Jim Braddock.

-:- Chamique Holdsclaw is the only NCAA basketball player, male or female, to play on teams that won four consecutive high school state championships and the NCAA championship in each of the first three years in college.

-:- Bob Bender is the only player to appear in the NCAA title game for two different schools (Indiana in 1976 and Duke in 1978). Bender has made two NCAA appearances as a head coach (Illinois State in 1990 and Washington in 1998).

- The only time the same two teams met in the NCAA title game in consecutive years was in 1961 and '62. Cincinnati defeated Ohio State to win the NCAA championship both years.
- Louisville is the only team since 1985 to win the NCAA tournament after missing it the year before.
- Denny Crum, Jerry Tarkanian, Lute Olson and Nolan Richardson all coached at the junior college level and also won national championships in Division I.
- The 1957 NCAA championship game is the only multiple OT game in finals history (North Carolina beat Kansas, 3 OT).
- UCLA's Sidney Wicks is the only male player to win three national championships after spending his first season at a junior college.
- LSU (1985/86) and Kansas (1992/93) are the only schools whose teams went to the Final Four, a bowl game and the College World Series in the same academic year.
- For winning the NCAA men's championship in 1942, Stanford received $93.75. That wouldn't cover the cost of two good tickets at the 1998 Final Four, where the SEC shared a payoff of $5,618,279 after Kentucky won the title.

inside the numbers

Kentucky's 1998 NCAA men's championship team moved into a select circle of schools with three or more consecutive trips to the NCAA title game:

school	consecutive finals	years
UCLA	7	1967-73
Ohio State	3	1960-62
Cincinnati	3	1961-63
Duke	3	1990-92
Kentucky	3	1996-98

Only three women's schools have entered the NCAA tournament unbeaten and still won the national championship:

title	school	regular season	postseason
1986	Texas	29-0	5-0
1995	Connecticut	29-0	6-0
1998	Tennessee	33-0	6-0

the no.1s

✕ Six of the nine NCAA champions in the '90s have been No. 1 seeds. The exceptions were Kentucky (No. 2) in 1998, Arizona (No. 4) in 1997 and Duke (No. 2) in 1991.

✕ Since seeding began in 1979, No. 1 seeds have met in the NCAA title game only twice: 1993 (North Carolina, Michigan) and 1982 (North Carolina, Georgetown), with the Tar Heels winning both times. Four top seeds have never advanced to the Final Four in the same year.

✕ Michigan (1985), Michigan State (1990) and Connecticut (1990) are the only teams who became top seeds after not making the NCAA tournament the year before.

✕ Harvard is the only 16th seed to upset a No. 1 seed in the first round of the NCAA women's tournament, beating Stanford 71-67 in 1998.

✕ The 1985 St. John's team that made the Final Four (losing to Georgetown in the national semifinal) included three current NBA players: Chris Mullin, Mark Jackson and Bill Wennington.

✕ The 1998 men's championship game did not have a No. 1 regional seed participating. Before '98, the last time that happened was 1991, when Duke beat Kansas.

inside the numbers

Since 1979, only four conferences have boasted two No.1 men's seeds in the same year:

year	conference	no. 1 seeds
1980	SEC	Kentucky, LSU
1982	ACC	North Carolina, Virginia
1985	Big East	Georgetown, St. John's
1993	Big Ten	Michigan, Indiana
1998	ACC	Duke, North Carolina

Since 1985, only seven No.1 regional men's seeds have lost in the second round:

year	no.1 seed	lost to
1985	Michigan	Villanova
1986	St. John's	Auburn
1990	Oklahoma	North Carolina
1992	Kansas	UTEP
1994	North Carolina	Boston College
1996	Purdue	Georgia
1998	Kansas	Rhode Island

total access
mimi griffin   women's college basketball analyst

"Contrary to what people might think, Chamique Holdsclaw does not wear No. 23 as a tribute to Michael Jordan. The religious Tennessee star chose the number because it represents her favorite psalm, which includes the famous opening line: 'The Lord is my Shepherd, I shall not want.'"

Q1

In 1998, three men joined the select group of 15 coaches who have taken three different schools to the Big Dance.

level 1 *Name the three coaches.*

level 2 *Name the three schools and the years.*

level 3 *Name the only coach who has led four different schools to the NCAA tournament, along with the schools and the years.*

question 1 answers

level 1   *a*   Jim Harrick
        b   Tubby Smith
        c   Billy Tubbs

level 2   *a*   Pepperdine 1982-83, 1985-86,
            UCLA 1989-96,
            Rhode Island 1998

        b   Tulsa 1994-95,
            Georgia 1996-97,
            Kentucky 1998

        c   Lamar (1979-80),
            Oklahoma (1983-90, 1992),
            TCU (1998)

level 3 Eddie Sutton: Creighton 1974,
           Arkansas 1977-85,
           Kentucky 1986-88,
           Oklahoma State 1991-95, 1998

Q2

Kentucky has had a great tradition on the hardwood.

level 1   *How many Kentucky men's basketball coaches have taken the Wildcats to the Final Four?*

level 2 *Name them.*

level 3 *How many Final Four appearances did each make while at Kentucky?*

question 2 answers

level 1   Four

level 2   *a*   Adolph Rupp
        b   Joe B. Hall
        c   Rick Pitino
        d   Tubby Smith

level 3   *a*   Six
        b   Three
        c   Three
        d   One

john wooden

- John Wooden almost became an English professor but instead went into coaching.
- Wooden coached two seasons at Indiana State (1946/47 and 1947/48) before going to UCLA.
- In his first season as head coach at Indiana State, he turned down an invitation to the NAIA postseason tournament because he had an African-American player on his team. Back then, black players were not permitted to play in that event.
- He was inducted into the Basketball Hall of Fame as both a player (1960) and coach (1972).
- The closest he came to a losing season at UCLA was 14-12 in 1959/60.
- His Bruins won 13 conference championships in his last 14 seasons at the helm. Only the 1965/66 team fell short of the league crown.
- While most remember Wooden's glory days, UCLA was actually 3-9 under the Wizard of Westwood in NCAA tournament games from 1950 to '63.

- Wooden is one of only two coaches to beat his alma mater in the NCAA men's basketball championship game: in 1969, UCLA beat Purdue 92-72. The other coach to accomplish that feat was Denny Crum: in 1980, Louisville beat UCLA 59-54.
- Wooden coached against Jerry Tarkanian in the 1971 NCAA tournament. His Bruins edged Tark's Long Beach State squad 57-55.
- Wooden coached against Bobby Knight in the 1973 NCAA tournament. His Bruins beat Knight's Hoosiers 70-59.
- During his first 17 years as head coach at UCLA, Wooden and the team managers used to sweep and mop the floor every day before practice.
- Wooden's final game as UCLA coach was the 1975 NCAA championship game. His Bruins beat Kentucky 92-85.

the final four

-:+ In 1983, Georgia became the only school to have both its men's and women's basketball teams make the NCAA Final Four in the same year.

-:+ Tennessee's 86-58 win over Arkansas in the 1998 women's Final Four was the largest margin of victory in an NCAA women's national semifinal.

-:+ Tennessee's 1996/97 national championship team is the only champ in NCAA women's history to finish with 10 or more losses (29-10).

-:+ The only team to make the men's Final Four in its only appearance in the NCAA tournament is Indiana State. The 1979 Sycamores, led by Larry Bird, lost the title game 75-64 to the Michigan State Spartans, led by Magic Johnson.

-:+ In 1998, only one of the top four women's seeds made the Final Four, the fewest to advance that far since 1985.

-:+ North Carolina has made it to the men's Final Four in each odd year in the '90s.

-:+ Kansas has been a top four regional seed in the men's NCAA tournament every year in the '90s.

-:+ Only four of the past 21 men's national semifinal games have been decided by double figures.

-:+ Since 1988, only three men's teams seeded below No. 4 have made it to the Final Four: Mississippi State (No. 5) in 1996, Michigan (No. 6) in 1992 and Kansas (No. 6) in 1988 (the Jayhawks walked away with the big prize).

-:+ No men's team seeded below No. 6 has made the Final Four since Dale Brown led LSU as an 11th seed in 1986 (the lowest seed to make the Final Four since seeding began in 1979).

-:+ UNLV's 1977 men's Final Four representative had six players average in double figures. Future NBA star Reggie Theus was the No. 4 scorer that season, averaging 14.5 points per game.

inside the numbers

The SEC has put at least one team in the women's Final Four every year in the '90s except 1992 (the six-year current streak is the longest active streak of any conference):

year	teams
1990	Auburn
1991	Tennessee
1992	(none)
1993	Vanderbilt
1994	Alabama
1995	Tennessee, Georgia
1996	Tennessee, Georgia
1997	Tennessee
1998	Tennessee, Arkansas

Since 1988, at least one men's ACC team has made it to the Final Four every year except 1996:

year	teams
1988	Duke
1989	Duke
1990	Duke, Georgia Tech
1991	Duke, North Carolina
1992	Duke
1993	North Carolina
1994	Duke
1995	North Carolina
1996	(none)
1997	North Carolina
1998	North Carolina

Q3

John Wooden took UCLA to the NCAA tournament 12 times, winning 10 national championships.

level 1   *Since Wooden retired in 1975, how many coaches have led the Bruins to the Big Dance?*

level 2   *Name them.*

level 3   *Of this group, how many have won a national championship as a head coach?*

question 3 answers

level 1   Seven

level 2   a   Gene Bartow
b   Gary Cunningham
c   Larry Brown
d   Larry Farmer
e   Walt Hazzard
f   Jim Harrick
g   Steve Lavin

level 3   Two. Jim Harrick won at UCLA and Larry Brown won at Kansas.

Q4

Pat Summitt won her first and sixth NCAA women's championships on March 29.

level 1   *What years did Summitt win them?*

level 2   *Which school lost to the Lady Vols both times?*

level 3   *How many coaches have won more NCAA Division I championships?*

question 4 answers

level 1   1987, 1998

level 2   Louisiana Tech

level 3   Summitt's six NCAA titles rank No. 1 among women's coaches. Only John Wooden has won more Division I championships.

the bad seed

Impossibly awful. That's the best that can be said about Purdue coach Gene Keady's NCAA tournament record. Every year, you expect him to turn things around. But Keady—or if you prefer, his team—never does.

∴ Any number of well-known coaches have struggled in March but eventually tasted success: Dean Smith, Jim Harrick and Lute Olson all won championships after years of disappointments. But Keady's been struggling for nearly two decades, and the disappointments never seem to stop.

∴ His first tournament was in 1980, when he coached Western Kentucky. Since then, he's taken the Purdue Boilermakers to a dozen tourneys. And here's the key stat: Keady-coached teams have never beaten a team seeded higher than themselves. Not once. Not ever. By way of contrast, in 1998 another Indiana school, tiny Valparaiso, beat not one, but two higher-seeded teams.

∴ If you assume that a team should win a certain number of games based on its seed—that is, a No. 2 seed should win three games, a No. 15 shouldn't win any—consistently higher-seeded Purdue should have won 26 games under Keady. His tally? Twelve. That's right, fewer than half as many as expected.

did you know?

The school with the most wins over a top-ranked men's college basketball team is Notre Dame, with nine. ESPN's Digger Phelps coached Notre Dame to seven of those wins, the last one over North Carolina in 1987. Runner-up Maryland has upset the national No. 1 team five times.

∴ In 1996, Keady's Boilermakers won the Big Ten championship, which in turn earned them a No. 1 seed in the NCAA tournament. The results? In the first round, Purdue very nearly became the first No. 1 to lose to a No. 16 seed in the first round, as they barely escaped Western Carolina, 73-71. Bullet dodged? Hardly. Purdue tanked in the second round to No. 8 Georgia, 76-69.

∴ Purdue fared somewhat better in 1998 as a No. 2 seed, trouncing No. 15 Delaware and No. 10 Detroit before bowing to No. 3 Stanford, an eventual Final Four team. But yet again, Keady's charges lost to a team seeded lower than themselves.

∴ One of these years, Keady may get lucky and (a) beat the teams he should beat, then (b) beat a team he shouldn't. But I wouldn't bet on it.

rob neyer

inside the numbers

Don't bet on a men's No. 16 seed shocking a No. 1.
It hasn't happened in 56 chances, although there have
been close calls since the field went to 64 teams in 1985:

year	no. 1 sneaks by no. 16
1985	Michigan 59, Fairleigh Dickinson 55
1989	Oklahoma 72, East Tennessee State 71
1989	Georgetown 50, Princeton 49
1990	Michigan State 75, Murray State 71 (OT)
1996	Purdue 73, Western Carolina 71

Don't bet on a men's No. 2 seed being stunned by a
No. 15 seed. Since 1985, it's happened just three times:

year	no. 15 seed over no. 2 seed
1991	Richmond over Syracuse
1993	Santa Clara over Arizona
1997	Coppin State over South Carolina

dubious distinctions

- Oregon has gone the longest since its last appearance in the men's Final Four. The Ducks won the first-ever NCAA tournament in 1939 and have only appeared in the Big Dance four times since, reaching the regionals in 1945 and 1960.

- The University of Houston, with five, has the most Final Four appearances without ever winning the men's national championship. Coach Guy Lewis's best chance came in 1983. Despite Clyde Drexler, Hakeem Olajuwon and Larry Micheaux leading "Phi Slamma Jamma," the Cougars lost to N.C. State, 54-52.

- Jim Boeheim has the most all-time NCAA tournament wins (29) among men's coaches who have never won a championship. His Orangemen have reached the Final Four twice, losing to Indiana in 1987 and Kentucky in 1996.

- The men's schools that have played in their conference tournament the most without winning a championship are The Citadel (45 Southern appearances) and Clemson (45 ACC appearances).

- In 1976, Davidson's Kevin Doheny set an NCAA record when he fouled out in five minutes and six seconds after entering it. His first foul, for charging, came two seconds after he first touched the ball, with three more following in the next 36 seconds.

- The school that had gone the longest since its last NCAA men's tournament appearance is Harvard. The Crimson went 19-1 during the 1945/46 regular season before losing to Ohio State in the first round and NYU in a consolation game in their first and only postseason berth in 1946. Harvard has also never won the Ivy League title.

- Bradley and USC hold the record for most losses by a Final Four team, with 12 each in 1954.

inside the numbers

Only four men's schools seeded below 12th have made it to the Sweet Sixteen. All lost their regional semifinal:

year	school	seed	winner
1986	Cleveland State	14	Navy
1988	Richmond	13	Temple
1997	Tennessee-Chat.	14	Providence
1998	Valparaiso	13	Rhode Island

did you know?

When men's college basketball analyst Jay Bilas was in his teens, he appeared on The White Shadow as a member of the opposing team: "I assumed Coolidge, Salami and the rest of the Carver High cagers were also in high school but was disappointed to find out all of them were around 30."

.×: The schools with the most losses while ranked No. 1 in a season are North Carolina (1993/94) and Michigan (1964/65), with four each. Both were signs of bad things to come: the Tar Heels would bow out of the 1994 men's tournament in the second round, while the Wolverines lost to UCLA in the 1965 title game.

.×: Since 1938, the fewest points scored in a Division I college basketball game is 17, on December 15, 1973 (Tennessee 11, Temple 6). The half-time score was 7-5 in favor of Tennessee, so the teams combined for just five points in the second half. In a preshot clock snoozer, the Vols went 3-for-10 from the field, while the Owls sank 2-for-11.

.×: The record for fewest points scored by one team in a Division I game is six, shared by Arkansas State (1945) and Temple (1973).

.×: The record for most consecutive losses to a single opponent is held by Brown, who has been defeated at Ivy League rival Princeton 48 consecutive times dating back to 1929. Runner-up Clemson has lost 45 straight times to North Carolina at Chapel Hill.

.×: The NCAA Division I men's college basketball record for most consecutive home defeats is 32, by New Hampshire. The Wildcats didn't win a home game from February 9, 1988, to February 2, 1991, finally snapping the losing streak by defeating Holy Cross 72-56.

.×: Since the NCAA tournament expanded to 64 teams in 1985, Howard (1987), Southern Illinois (1990) and UNLV (1992) have won the most games (26) in the regular season without gaining a tournament berth.

.×: The widest margin of victory in a college basketball game is 118 points. On December 9, 1971, Mississippi College beat Dallas Bible 168-50. Long Island University fell just short of that mark, beating Medgar Evers 179-62 on November 26, 1997.

.×: Although the Carrier Dome in Syracuse bears the name of one of the world's top air-conditioning manufacturers, the arena is not air-conditioned.

inside the numbers

Beginning in 1989, a men's No. 12 seed has defeated a No.5 seed 13 times:

year	conference	no. 12 seed over no. 5 seed
1989	West	DePaul over Memphis
1990	West	Ball State over Oregon State
1990	Midwest	Dayton over Illinois
1991	East	Eastern Michigan over Mississippi State
1992	West	New Mexico State over DePaul
1993	West	George Washington over New Mexico
1994	West	Wisconsin-Green Bay over California
1994	Midwest	Tulsa over UCLA
1995	Midwest	Miami-Ohio over Arizona
1996	West	Drexel over Memphis
1996	East	Arkansas over Penn State
1997	Southeast	College of Charleston over Maryland
1998	Midwest	Florida State over TCU

teammates

-:- Before 1998, the only time two schools each had two consensus All-Americans in the same season was 1930. John Thompson and Frank Ward were named All-Americans with Montana State, while the legendary John Wooden and Charles Murphy were nominated from Purdue. Rounding out the 1930 team was Pittsburgh's Charles Hyatt and Indiana's Branch McCracken. The consensus All-American teammates in 1998 were Raef LaFrentz and Paul Pierce of Kansas, and Arizona's Mike Bibby and Miles Simon.

-:- UCLA is the only NCAA champion to return the following season with its starting lineup intact and successfully defend its title. The starters on the 1967/68 Bruins were Lew Alcindor (C), Mike Warren (G), Lynn Shackelford (F), Lucius Allen (G) and Kenny Heitz (F).

-:- Current Division I women's coaches Theresa Grentz (Illinois), Rene Portland (Penn State) and Marianne Stanley (California) were college teammates at Immaculata in 1972/73 and 1973/74.

-:- Nick Anderson and Kendall Gill teamed up to take Illinois to the Final Four in 1989. Gill is the school's 10th all-time leading scorer, while Anderson, despite playing just two seasons, is 21st all-time.

-:- Five of Mark Jackson's St. John's teammates went on to play in the NBA: Chris Mullin, Bill Wennington, Shelton Jones, Walter Berry and Ron Rowan (who dressed for seven games with the Trail Blazers in 1986/87).

inside the numbers

Indiana's 1976 national championship team was the last men's team to go undefeated. There were a number of close calls that season. Look at the margins and win-loss records:

margin	win-loss record
0-9	11-0
10-19	9-0
20-29	8-0
30+	4-0

Meanwhile, six of Indiana's games were decided by five points or less:

opponent	margin of victory	final score
At Ohio State	2 points	66-64
Notre Dame	3 points	63-60
At Purdue	3 points	74-71
Purdue	4 points	71-67
Alabama (NCAA)	5 points	74-69
Michigan	5 points	72-67 (OT)

Q5

While he never won a national title, Shaquille O'Neal had a fine collegiate career at LSU.

level 1   *In five NCAA tournament games, what was LSU's record with Shaq?*

level 2   *What was his top single-season scoring average at LSU?*

level 3   *What was his career free-throw shooting percentage in college?*

question 5 answers

level 1   Two wins, three losses

level 2   27.6 ppg. as a sophomore

level 3   57.5 percent

Q6

The 1989 Michigan squad is the last Big Ten team to win the national championship.

level 1   *Who took over as head coach just before the start of the 1989 tournament?*

level 2   *Which four future NBA first-round picks were members of that team?*

level 3   *Which fellow Big Ten member did the Wolverines beat in the national semifinals? What was the score?*

question 6 answers

level 1   Steve Fisher

level 2   *a*   Glen Rice
       b   Terry Mills
       c   Rumeal Robinson
       d   Loy Vaught

level 3   Illinois, 83-81

- The record for most consecutive conference tournaments won is seven, by Kentucky in the SEC (1944-50) and North Carolina A&T in the Mideastern Conference (1982-88).
- The record for most consecutive NCAA tournament appearances is 24, by North Carolina (active).
- The Division I record for free throws attempted in a game by one team is 79, by Northern Arizona on January 26, 1953. The Lumberjacks made 46 but still lost to Arizona 90-70.
- The most overtime periods ever in an NCAA tournament game is four: Canisius beat N.C. State (1956-first round) and St. Joseph's beat Utah (1961-national third place).
- The Lady Vols finished the 1997/98 season with a 39-0 record, the most wins by a Division I women's team in one season.
- The largest deficit to start a college game occurred in 1990, when Connecticut jumped out to a 32-0 lead en route to destroying New Hampshire 85-32. But starting with a big lead doesn't always mean finishing with one. On January 27, 1977, New Mexico State trailed Bradley 28-0 after the first 6:11 but rallied to win 117-109.
- Providence's Eric Murdock holds the NCAA career steals record with 376, set over 117 games (3.2 steals per game) from 1988-91.
- Bevo Francis of Division II Rio Grande College (Ohio) scored a record 113 points against Hillsdale on February 2, 1954. Francis's teammates combined to score 21 in the 134-95 victory.
- Ginny Doyle of Richmond holds the NCAA women's record for best free-throw shooting percentage in one season, an impressive 95 percent in 1992.
- Villanova's women's basketball team set an NCAA record with 18 three-pointers made against Penn on December 20, 1997.
- Cindy Brown of Long Beach State holds the women's record for most points in a single game, tallying 60 (20 field goals, 20 free throws) against San Jose State on February 16, 1987. That season, she scored a record 974 points.

did you know?

Robin Roberts is among the all-time women's basketball leading scorers at Southeastern Louisiana. She scored 1,446 points and grabbed 1,034 rebounds during her collegiate career.

Q7

The 1982 NCAA men's championship game featured two future NBA superstars, Michael Jordan and Patrick Ewing.

level 1   *Name the future Lakers teammates who were stars on that North Carolina team.*

level 2   *Name the teams Georgetown and North Carolina defeated in the national semifinals to set up this championship clash.*

level 3   *Who scored more in the championship game, Jordan or Ewing?*

question 7 answers

level 1   James Worthy and Sam Perkins

level 2   Georgetown defeated Louisville; North Carolina beat Houston.

level 3   Ewing outscored Jordan 23-16, but North Carolina won the war 63-62.

Q8

One of the most notable championship games featured Larry Bird and Indiana State against Magic Johnson and Michigan State in the 1979 final.

level 1   *Where was the championship game held?*

level 2   *Entering the title game, how many losses had Indiana State suffered?*

level 3   *Where did Larry Bird transfer from before attending Indiana State?*

question 8 answers

level 1   Salt Lake City, Utah

level 2   None

level 3   Indiana

head of the class

-:+ Only two women have won back-to-back NCAA women's Division I scoring titles: Mercer's Andrea Congreaves in 1992 and '93, and Maine's Cindy Blodgett of Maine in 1996 and '97.

-:+ Texas Tech's Sheryl Swoopes averaged 35.4 points per game in the NCAA tournament as she led the Red Raiders to the national championship in 1993.

-:+ Lynette Woodard scored 3,649 points while at Kansas, more than any player, male or female, in school history.

-:+ The first college player to score 50 points in one game was Stanford's Hank Luisetti against Duquesne in 1938. (Luisetti is also noteworthy for sinking the first one-handed shot).

-:+ Cheryl Miller was the first athlete, male or female, to have a basketball jersey retired at USC.

-:+ Xavier McDaniel, Kurt Thomas and Hank Gathers are the only players to lead the NCAA in both scoring and rebounding in the same season.

-:+ Speaking of Hank Gathers, he scored 41 points and grabbed 29 rebounds in Loyola Marymount's 181-150 win over now-defunct U.S. International on January 31, 1989. The 331 points were the most scored by two Division I teams.

inside the numbers

In the '90s, four teams from the same conference have made the men's Sweet Sixteen seven times:

year	conference	teams
1990	ACC	Duke, North Carolina, Clemson, Georgia Tech
1992	ACC	Duke, North Carolina, Georgia Tech, Florida State
1993	ACC	Florida State, North Carolina, Wake Forest, Virginia
1995	ACC	North Carolina, Maryland, Wake Forest, Virginia
1996	SEC	Arkansas, Kentucky, Georgia, Mississippi State
1997	Pac-10	UCLA, Arizona, California, Stanford
1998	Pac-10	UCLA, Arizona, Stanford, Washington

total access
jay bilas   men's college basketball analyst

"Along with Johnny Dawkins (2,556 career points), Mark Alarie (2,136) and David Henderson (1,570), I was part of the highest-scoring class in ACC history (and, I believe, NCAA history). I contributed 1,062 points in my career at Duke, which was even more remarkable considering how few shots were left over from that trio. In 1986, we went 37-3, including a winning streak of 21 games. In the '86 title game, I guarded Pervis Ellison, holding him to a meager 25 points (although Louisville won 72-69). Ellison was so hot in that game that he would have exploded against a less skilled defender."

Q 9

In the 1988 men's championship game, two teams from the same conference met.

level 1   *Name the conference and the schools.*

level 2   *What was the final score?*

level 3   *Name the MVP of the 1988 Final Four.*

Q 10

Tennessee does not hold the record for most points per game in a season in NCAA Division I women's basketball. That honor goes to Providence, which turned the trick in 1991.

level 1   *What did Providence average per game that season?*

level 2   *What was the team's record in its 32 games that season?*

level 3   *How many times did Providence score 100 or more points in a game in 1991?*

question 9 answers

level 1   Big 8, Kansas and Oklahoma

level 2   Kansas won 83-79.

level 3   Kansas's Danny Manning

question 10 answers

level 1   96.7 points per game

level 2   26-6

level 3   Providence went to the century mark or beyond 13 times.

streaks

---- The only two players to lead the Missouri Valley Conference in scoring for three straight seasons were Larry Bird and Oscar Robertson.

---- Pete Maravich scored 60 or more points on four occasions during his three years at LSU.

---- The only time the same two teams have played twice in the regular season as No. 1 versus No. 2 was in 1974. In the first meeting, No. 2 Notre Dame snapped No. 1 UCLA's 88-game win streak in South Bend. When the teams met one week later in Los Angeles, No. 2 UCLA returned the favor by dethroning No.1 Notre Dame.

---- The ACC has put at least two teams in the Sweet Sixteen every year since 1979 (that year, in the second round, Penn stunned North Carolina and St. John's upset Duke, a day referred to as Black Sunday on Tobacco Road).

---- North Carolina has made the longest active streak for consecutive trips to the Big Dance (24), followed by Arizona (14), Indiana (13), UCLA (10) and Kansas and Temple (nine each).

---- The only coach to go undefeated in NCAA tournament play is Stanford's Everett Dean, who went 3-0 in 1942, leading the Cardinals to victory in an eight-team field. Dean knew to quit when he was ahead; Stanford would not return to the Big Dance until 1989.

---- Since 1938, the only time two college basketball teams went unbeaten in the same season was 1973, with N.C. State (27-0) and UCLA (30-0). The Wolfpack was on probation and therefore ineligible for the NCAA tournament. The following season, Norm Sloan's squad would dump UCLA in the Final Four and then beat Marquette for the NCAA title.

---- The best start by a first-year Division I college basketball coach is 33-0 by Indiana State's Bill Hodges in 1978/79. Hodges' first loss came in the 1979 title game versus Michigan State.

---- UConn and Louisiana Tech women's programs are the only two in men's or women's Division I history to reach 30 wins four years in a row.

---- The last 12 teams to make it to the NCAA tournament with records below .500 all lost in the first round. The most recent was Prairie View in 1998.

did you know?

In 1980, Mimi Griffin (a four-year member of the University of Pittsburgh's women's team), became the first woman to do color commentary for an NCAA men's tournament game, a first-round match-up between Notre Dame and Virginia on ESPN.

Q11

Jerry West was a great college player long before starring with the Lakers.

level 1 *For what college did he play?*

level 2 *What year was he NCAA Tournament MVP?*

level 3 *What was his college's record during his three seasons there?*

Q12

The 1984 men's final featured future No.1 NBA draft picks Hakeem Olajuwon and Patrick Ewing.

level 1 *For which teams did each play? What was the final score of the championship game?*

level 2 *Who scored more in the title tilt, Ewing or Olajuwon?*

level 3 *List the years each was drafted No. 1.*

question 11 answers

level 1   West Virginia
level 2   1959
level 3   81 wins, 12 losses

question 12 answers

level 1   Ewing's Georgetown beat Olajuwon's Houston 84-75.
level 2   Olajuwon, 15-10.
level 3   Olajuwon 1984, Ewing 1985

personal files

-:- Pat Riley played for Kentucky in the 1966 NCAA championship game loss to Texas Western. Riley shot eight of 22 from the floor and finished with 19 points.

-:- Tony Gwynn, the all-time assists leader at San Diego State, was named to the All-WAC first team in 1981. His backcourt mate on the All-WAC squad was BYU's Danny Ainge.

-:- The MVP of the 1963 NIT, Ray Flynn of Providence, went on to become mayor of Boston.

-:- Many know Bill Bradley for his days as a New Jersey senator. Remembered on the collegiate hardwood for his scoring, Bradley was also the top rebounder in the 1965 NCAA tournament, averaging 11.4 boards per game, and was named Most Outstanding Player.

-:- Dave Winfield, known more for his baseball exploits, participated for the University of Minnesota basketball team in the 1972 NCAA tournament. Winfield scored eight points in a 70-56 loss to Florida State.

-:- Tim Stoddard was a member of the 1974 NCAA championship team at N.C. State and the winner of Game 4 of the 1979 World Series for the Orioles.

-:- Illinois's Dike Eddleman was the top scorer on the school's Final Four team in 1949 (13.1 ppg.). He also played both offense and defense on the football team and competed in the 1947 Rose Bowl.

-:- Wilt Chamberlain scored 23 of Kansas's 53 points in the 1957 NCAA championship game against North Carolina. The Tar Heels won, 54-53 in their second triple overtime in two nights.

-:- Arkansas athletic director and former football coach Frank Broyles played college basketball at Georgia Tech.

-:- NFL commissioner Paul Tagliabue played college basketball at Georgetown.

-:- Stanford women's basketball coach Tara VanDerveer played collegiately at Indiana. She graduated in 1976, the same year the Hoosiers' men's team went unbeaten.

-:- The Atlanta Hawks tabbed current Illinois coach Lon Kruger in the ninth round in 1974.

-:- The Bulls drafted current University of Minnesota coach Clem Haskins in the first round in 1967, third overall.

-:- While most know that former USC women's star Cheryl Miller and ex-UCLA standout Reggie Miller are sister and brother, it was Cheryl who averaged 20 or more points per game in all four collegiate seasons (20.4, 22.0, 26.8, 25.4).

-:- Ed Diddle Sr. of Western Kentucky faced his son, Ed Diddle Jr. of Middle Tennessee State, 12 times, a record for father-versus-son coaching match-ups. Father knew best: Ed Sr. won 11 of those 12 meetings.

-:- Ray Meyer of DePaul never coached against his son Joey but he did coach against son Tom (Illinois-Chicago). The elder Meyer came out on top, as Ray's Blue Demons scored a 78-53 rout on December 1, 1981.

-:- Tubby Smith had the pleasure of coaching two different sons on two different Division I teams: G.G. at Georgia and Saul at Kentucky.

-:- Moses Malone Jr. and Gee Gervin, sons of Moses Malone and George Gervin, are slated to play together at the University of Houston for the 1998/99 season, where their head coach is Clyde Drexler.

-:- Lucy Harris of Delta State was the first women's college player inducted into the Basketball Hall of Fame (1992).

Q13

The late *Monday Night Football* director Chet Forte was a former first-team All-America basketball player.

level 1 *For what school did he play?*

level 2 *What year was he All-America?*

level 3 *What was his highest-scoring season? In what year?*

question 13 answers

level 1 Columbia

level 2 1957

level 3 28.9 ppg. in 1957

Q14

Dr. J came into his own in the pros, but the signs of greatness were there in college.

level 1 *Where did Julius Erving attend college and how many years did he play?*

level 2 *How many times did his teams play in the NCAA tournament?*

level 3 *What was his points-per-game average in college?*

question 14 answers

level 1 The University of Massachusetts, two seasons (1970 and '71)

level 2 His Minutemen never made the NCAA tournament.

level 3 26.3 ppg.

the coaches

-:- Kentucky is the only school to reach consecutive men's NCAA title games with different head coaches. UCLA came close when Gene Bartow reached the Final Four in 1976, the year after John Wooden ended his incredible run of 10 titles in 12 years.

-:- Five men's coaches have led Kansas to the Final Four: Phog Allen, Dick Harp, Ted Owens, Larry Brown and Roy Williams. In 1998, Bill Guthridge became the fourth coach to take North Carolina to the Final Four, along with Dean Smith, Frank McGuire and Ben Carnevale.

-:- Hall of Fame coaches Adolph Rupp and Dean Smith both played on national men's championship teams at the University of Kansas. Rupp was on the 1922 and '23 champions, while Smith was a member of the 1952 champion.

-:- Jim Phelan, who took over the Mount St. Mary's men's program in 1955, leads all active Division I coaches in longevity with a single school. UTEP's Don Haskins, who started in 1962, is next.

-:- Lillian Haas holds the women's record for coaching the most consecutive seasons at the same school. Haas spent 29 seasons at Drexel from 1964 to '92.

-:- Connecticut men's coach Jim Calhoun has completed the Boston Marathon four times.

-:- Missouri men's coach Norm Stewart was the school's leading scorer during the 1955/56 season.

-:- Houston Rockets coach Rudy Tomjanovich averaged 25.1 ppg. during his collegiate career at Michigan (1968-70).

-:- Bob Cousy served as a men's head coach at Boston College from 1963 to '69, where his record was 117-38.

total access
mimi griffin   women's college basketball analyst

"People marvel not only at Pat Summitt's success as a coach but also at her ability to juggle so many other responsibilities, such as doing color commentary on network television, writing books, appearing in instructional videos, delivering commencement speeches and running clinics. But when Pat first came to Tennessee 24 years ago, she had to do it all. She not only coached the women's team but attended classes toward a master's degree, taught physical education and trained to earn herself a place on the first U.S. women's Olympic basketball team in 1976."

Q15

Duke has had a great hoops tradition.

level 1 *How many national championships has Duke won in men's basketball? Name the years.*

level 2 *Mike Krzyzewski has taken the Blue Devils to the tournament the most times (14). Which Duke coach ranks second?*

level 3 *How many times did the No. 2 coach take them to the NCAAs?*

Q16

The late Jimmy Valvano was a special member of the ESPN family.

level 1 *What year did he lead N.C. State to the NCAA championship?*

level 2 *Name the team his Wolfpack beat in the championship game. What was the final score?*

level 3 *Name the college that gave Jimmy V. his first head coaching job.*

the coaches

-:- Only three coaches have led teams to the NCAA Final Four and the NBA Finals: Fred Schaus, Butch van Breda Kolff and Jack Ramsay. None of them has ever won a national championship.

-:- North Carolina men's coach Bill Guthridge was once the golf coach at Kansas State, where he taught Jim Colbert, now a standout on the Senior Tour.

-:- Al McGuire and Adolph Rupp coached against each other in the 1969 NCAA tournament. McGuire's Warriors beat Rupp's Wildcats 81-74.

-:- North Carolina's 1982 men's national championship team had three assistant coaches who went on to become head coaches competing in the 1998 tournament: Bill Guthridge, Roy Williams and Eddie Fogler.

-:- Bobby Knight and Dean Smith are the only two coaches to coach and play for NCAA championship teams. Knight has three titles as Indiana coach (1976, 1981, 1987), while he won as a player with Ohio State in 1960. Smith won as a player with Kansas in 1952 and led the Tar Heels to victory in 1982 and 1993.

-:- A Kansas chemistry professor coined the phrase "Rock, Chalk, Jayhawk" almost 100 years ago.

-:- Jody Conradt, currently at the University of Texas, holds the Division I women's record for most 20-win seasons (23).

-:- Clem Haskins is the only man to be a consensus All-American (at Western Kentucky), a first-round NBA draft pick (Bulls in 1967) and head coach in the Final Four (Minnesota 1997).

inside the numbers

If you want to root for a men's team from a certain conference, you'll do well with the ACC.
Look at the national champions by conference over the past 17 seasons:

conference	titles
ACC	5
SEC	3
Big East	2
Big Ten	2
Pac-10	2
Others	3

If you're looking for offense, UNLV and Loyola-Marymount are good places to go. They dominate the top five highest-scoring teams in Division I men's history:

school	season	ppg.
Loyola-Marymount	1989/90	122.4
Loyola-Marymount	1988/89	112.5
UNLV	1975/76	110.5
Loyola-Marymount	1987/88	110.3
UNLV	1976/77	107.1

Q17

Jerry Tarkanian has had a long, solid coaching career.

level 1   *How many different schools has he taken to the NCAA tournament?*

level 2   *Name the schools.*

level 3   *What NBA team did he serve as head coach?*

Q18

At the start of the 1997/98 NBA season, six head coaches had also been head coaches in the NCAA tournament.

level 1   *Name the coaches.*

level 2   *Name the schools.*

level 3   *What was the farthest they took their team(s) and in what year?*

question 17 answers

level 1   Two

level 2   Long Beach State and UNLV

level 3   San Antonio Spurs

question 18 answers

level 1   a   Larry Brown
         b   John Calipari
         c   P.J. Carlesimo
         d   Chuck Daly
         e   Bill Fitch
         f   Rick Pitino

level 2   a   Kansas/UCLA
         b   Massachusetts
         c   Seton Hall
         d   Penn
         e   Bowling Green
         f   Boston U/Providence/Kentucky

level 3   a   1988/championship
                 1981/quarterfinals
             b   1996/semifinals
             c   1989/finals lost in OT to Michigan
             d   1972/quarterfinals
             e   1968/first round
             f   1983/first round
                 1987/semifinals
                 1996/championship

**the
last time**

∴ Before University of the Pacific's Michael Olowokandi in 1998, the last No. 1 overall NBA draft pick to not play in the previous NCAA tournament was Minnesota's Mychal Thompson in 1978. The Golden Gophers went 17-10 overall and 12-6 in the Big Ten (second place), but were not invited to the NCAA tournament. Future Celtic star Kevin McHale (then a sophomore) was one of Thompson's teammates.

∴ The last non-ACC men's team from the state of North Carolina to beat the Tar Heels is Davidson (76-71) in 1952.

∴ Before Kentucky's Tubby Smith in 1998, Cincinnati's Ed Jucker was the last men's coach to win the NCAA title in his first full season at a school. Jucker led the Bearcats to the NCAA final in his first three years, winning in 1961 and '62. (Michigan's Steve Fisher "interimed" his way to the title in 1989.)

∴ For the 1997/98 season, Kentucky (Tubby Smith) and North Carolina (Bill Guthridge) had new men's head coaches. Before 1997/98, the last time North Carolina and Kentucky men's basketball programs started the same season with new head coaches was in 1927 (James Ashmore, UNC; Basil Hayden, UK). Ashmore went 80-37 in five seasons with the Tar Heels, while Hayden lasted just one season at Kentucky, going 3-13.

inside the numbers

In the 1992 NCAA women's tournament, there were plenty of close calls. Six games were decided by one point:

round	teams and scores
East 1st round	George Washington over Vermont 70-69
East 2nd round	West Virginia over Clemson 73-72
Midwest 2nd round	SW Missouri State over Iowa 61-60
Midwest 2nd round	UCLA over Texas 82-81
West 2nd round	Stephen F. Austin over Creighton 75-74
National semifinals	Stanford over Virginia 66-65

total access
larry beil

"I was broadcasting the Rainbow Classic in Hawaii when I was recruited by Gene Keady of Purdue. All of the TV guys were playing in a pickup game when I was en fuego, hitting several outside shots. When I sat down later to interview Keady, he asked me if I had any eligibility left. He was half-serious and half-kidding, I think!"

Q 19

The NCAA basketball tournament has become a television viewing staple.

level 1   *When was the first men's basketball championship game televised?*

level 2   *Who broadcast the game?*

level 3   *Name the teams. What was the final score?*

question 19 answers

level 1   1946
level 2   WCBS-TV
level 3   Oklahoma State 43, North Carolina 40

Q20

Talk about a crossover. One Heisman Trophy winner actually played in an NCAA Final Four.

level 1   *Name the player.*

level 2   *For what school did he play?*

level 3   *Give the year.*

question 20 answers

level 1   Terry Baker
level 2   Oregon State
level 3   1963

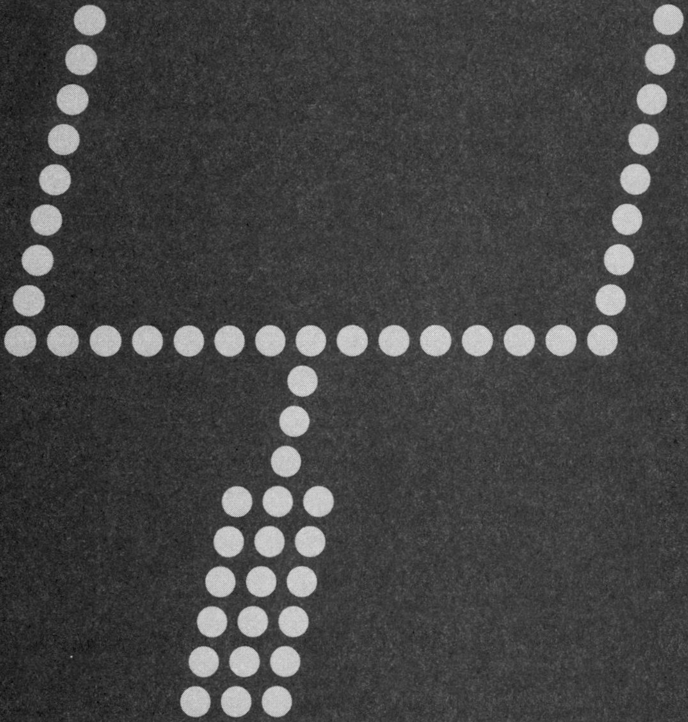

college football

some assembly required

Stats are good up to the start of the 1998 season.

did you know?

Analyst Todd Blackledge was the second quarterback chosen in that famous class of 1983 (seventh overall), with only John Elway (first overall) going earlier. Among those chosen later in the first round were Jim Kelly (14th), Tony Eason (15th), Ken O'Brien (24th) and Dan Marino (27th).

bowls

-:- In the first bowl game, Michigan whipped Stanford 49-0 in the Rose Bowl on January 1, 1902. The second Rose Bowl did not take place until 1916.

-:- The only two schools to have won each of the five major bowl games—the Cotton, Fiesta, Orange, Rose and Sugar Bowls—are Notre Dame and Penn State. Nebraska won its eighth Orange Bowl in 1998, the Cornhuskers' 13th overall major bowl triumph. Yet they never managed a Rose Bowl win before it became an annual Big Ten/Pac-10 affair, losing in their only shot 21-13 to Stanford.

-:- Paul "Bear" Bryant still holds the record for most bowl games as a coach: 29, going 15-12-2. Heading into the 1998 season, Joe Paterno is just one win away from tying Bryant. Tom Osborne retired with 25 bowl appearances, while Bobby Bowden has 21.

-:- The major bowl game that has gone the longest without having a No. 1 versus No. 2 match-up is the Cotton Bowl. In 1964, top-ranked Texas won the national championship 28-6 over No. 2 Navy.

-:- The most combined points in a bowl game is 91: BYU beat SMU 46-45 in the 1980 Holiday Bowl and Richmond defeated Ohio 49-42 in the 1968 Tangerine Bowl.

-:- Former Georgia football coach Vince Dooley was the co-MVP of the 1954 Gator Bowl as a member of Auburn.

-:- Bo Jackson (1984 Sugar, 1984 Liberty and 1986 Cotton) and Ty Detmer (1988 Freedom, 1989 Holiday and 1991 Holiday) are the only two Heisman Trophy winners to also earn three MVP awards in bowl games.

-:- In back-to-back seasons, Penn State beat the Heisman-winning running back in a bowl game. First came USC's Marcus Allen in the 1982 Fiesta (26-10), then Georgia's Herschel Walker in the 1983 Sugar (27-23).

-:- In 1990, the final season it was known as the All-American Bowl (it later became the Hall of Fame Classic), the MVP was future Packers quarterback Brett Favre.

-:- As Nebraska's head coach, Tom Osborne was 8-13 in bowl games before winning his final four pre-retirement bowls.

-:- Troy Aikman (UCLA) and Emmitt Smith (Florida) played against each other at the Aloha Bowl in 1987. Aikman's Bruins beat Smith's Gators 20-16.

inside the numbers

Between 1986-92, Joe Paterno had a six-game bowl streak where he went up against coaches who had won or would win national championships:

year	bowl	opponent	opposing coach	penn state result
1986	Orange	Oklahoma	Barry Switzer	lost 10-25
1987	Fiesta	Miami-Fla.	Jimmy Johnson	won 14-10
1988	Fla. Citrus	Clemson	Danny Ford	lost 10-35
1989	Holiday	BYU	LaVell Edwards	won 50-39
1990	Blockbuster	Florida St	Bobby Bowden	lost 17-24
1992	Fiesta	Tennessee	Johnny Majors	won 42-17

total access
chris fowler

"In the wake of Tom Osborne's retirement, it's not widely known that the only program he considered leaving Nebraska for was Colorado's (now NU's biggest rival). In the '70s, with the pressure to fill Bob Devaney's legacy weighing on him, Osborne was open to rebuilding at CU and, the story goes, would probably have moved over if Colorado officials had shown more interest. How might that have affected the balance of power in college football?"

**the
first time**

-:- Paul "Bear" Bryant's first bowl appearance was the 1947 Great Lakes Bowl. Kentucky beat Villanova 24-14.

-:- Woody Hayes's first bowl appearance was the 1951 Salad Bowl. His Miami-Ohio squad beat Arizona State 34-21.

-:- Knute Rockne's first bowl game was also his only bowl appearance. In the 1925 Rose Bowl, Notre Dame beat Stanford, coached by Pop Warner, 27-10.

-:- Lou Holtz's first bowl appearance as a head coach was in 1970. He coached William and Mary in a 40-12 loss to Toledo in the Tangerine Bowl.

-:- Lou Holtz also has interesting ties with Bobby Bowden. Back in the 1972 Peach Bowl, Bowden coached West Virginia against the Holtz-led N.C. State Wolfpack (N.C. State won 49-13). Three years later, Bowden's Mountaineers edged Holtz's Wolfpack in the Peach in a rematch 13-10.

-:- Bo Schembechler's first bowl game as a head coach came against USC and veteran coach John McKay in the 1970 Rose Bowl. The Trojans beat the Wolverines, 10-3.

-:- Joe Paterno had to settle for a tie in his first bowl game as a head coach, 17-17 against Florida State in the 1967 Gator Bowl. Twenty-three years later, Paterno's Nittany Lions lost to Bobby Bowden's Seminoles in the Blockbuster Bowl 24-17.

-:- Texas's Darrell Royal was 0-2-1 as a head coach before leading the Longhorns to a bowl victory. Royal's postseason debut was a 39-7 drubbing by Mississippi in the 1958 Sugar Bowl.

inside the numbers

In 1997, Iowa senior Tavian Banks became the fastest player to reach 1,000 yards in Division I-A history:

season	player	school	no. of carries to reach 1,000 yards
1997	Tavian Banks	Iowa	125
1996	Byron Hanspard	Texas Tech	129
1988	Barry Sanders	Oklahoma State	130
1983	Mike Rozier	Nebraska	133
1981	Marcus Allen	USC	140

Q1

Only one man has won the Heisman while playing on a losing team.

level 1   *Name the player.*

level 2   *Name the school.*

level 3   *What was the year and the school's record?*

question 1 answers

level 1   Paul Hornung

level 2   Notre Dame

level 3   Two wins, eight losses in 1956

Q2

Bobby Bowden has certainly enjoyed his share of success as a head coach.

level 1   *Entering 1998, what was his record in 21 bowl games?*

level 2   *When was the last time his Seminoles missed a bowl berth?*

level 3   *At which school did Bowden begin his head coaching career?*

question 2 answers

level 1   16-4-1

level 2   1981

level 3   Samford

paul bryant

- "Bear" Bryant got his nickname from wrestling a bear.
- At 13, he was 6 foot 1 and 180 pounds (6 foot 3 and 210 pounds in his prime).
- He earned a scholarship to the University of Alabama without graduating from high school (he had failed a foreign language class).
- He was secretly married for five months because Crimson Tide coach Frank Thomas didn't allow scholarship players to get hitched.
- As a player at Alabama (1933-35), his teams went 23-3-2.
- During the 1935 season, Bryant broke his leg playing Mississippi State. The next week against archrival Tennessee, No. 34 dressed for moral support, but no one expected him to play. Instead, Bryant had the game of his career, scoring two TDs in a 25-0 rout.
- As an assistant coach, he went to the Rose Bowl with Alabama in 1938. While he was there, he was offered a Hollywood screen test and an agent offered him double his salary to try an acting career. He declined.
- While serving as a lieutenant-commander on the USS Uruguay, Bryant and the rest of the crew were ordered to abandon ship in the spring of 1942. By the time the

captain realized the ship wasn't going to sink, more than 200 of Bryant's fellow crewmembers had already jumped overboard and drowned.

- After spring practice in 1982, the 67-year-old Alabama head coach told everyone he was on vacation in North Africa. Instead, Bryant had plastic surgery–a neck job–to make himself look as young as he still felt.

- During the pregame festivities of Super Bowl I, which took place inside the Louisiana Superdome, Joe Paterno asked Bryant why he wasn't wearing his trademark houndstooth hat. "My mama always told me to take my hat off inside," Bear replied.

- He met Lyndon Johnson at a presidential luncheon in the '60s. LBJ said to Bryant, "Well, now, you're a big 'un, ain't you?" Bryant replied, "You're a pretty big sonofab____ yourself."

- He started a scholarship program at the University of Alabama for the children of his former players. Over the past 16 years, hundreds of students have benefited.

- He is credited with coining the phrase "A tie is like kissing your sister."

- He was honored with a commemorative postage stamp.

the draft

-:- Since 1993, only three defensive backs have been chosen with a top five pick in the NFL Draft: Shawn Springs, Bryant Westbrook and Charles Woodson.

-:- There were no players picked from Ohio State in the 1998 draft, the first time not a single Buckeye was selected.

-:- When Peyton Manning was chosen No. 1 overall by the Colts in 1998, it marked the first time an SEC player was picked first overall since Aundray Bruce of Auburn in 1988.

-:- The SEC had at least one player picked from all 12 schools in 1998. No other conference had each school represented.

-:- When the Chargers chose Ryan Leaf with their first pick in the 1998 NFL draft, it marked the first time San Diego had used its first-round choice on a quarterback since Marty Domres in 1969.

-:- Chicago halfback Jay Berwanger was the first player to win the Heisman (1935) and the first player selected in the NFL draft (by the Eagles in 1936).

-:- In 1953, the Redskins drafted two-time Olympic decathlon champion Bob Mathias as a running back out of Stanford.

-:- The most first-round selections from one college in one year is five, from USC in 1968 (OT Ron Yary, OT Mike Taylor, DE Tim Rossovich, RB Mike Hull and WR Earl McCullough).

-:- The Trojans are the only school since the common draft (NFL-AFL) to have players chosen No. 1 overall in consecutive years (Ron Yary in 1968, O.J. Simpson in 1969).

-:- Notre Dame has had the most No. 1 overall draft choices–five: QB Angelo Bertelli (1944-Boston), QB Frank Dancewicz (1946-Boston), E Leon Hart (1950-Detroit), HB Paul Hornung (1957-Green Bay) and DE Walt Patulski (1972-Buffalo).

-:- The Fighting Irish also had the most players chosen in a single NFL draft–18 in 1946.

-:- Only twice since 1967 have players from the same school been chosen first and second overall. In 1967, Michigan State's DT Bubba Smith went first to Baltimore while RB Clint Jones went second to Minnesota. In 1984, Nebraska's Irving Fryar went first to New England while G Dean Steinkuhler was the second choice, by Houston.

lee corso

total access
college gameday

"When I was playing at Florida State, our No. 46 was the toughest, most aggressive, best-looking running back I'd ever seen. In one game, I watched that same No. 46, who you'd know as Burt Reynolds, run for 50 yards before being hauled down from behind by a future governor of Alabama, Fob James."

Q3

Tennessee boasts the dubious distinction of producing the most Heisman runners-up without actually winning the award.

level 1   *How many runners-up has Tennessee had?*

level 2   *Name the school that's produced the second most runners-up without winning a Heisman.*

level 3   *List the Volunteer runners-up, the year and who won.*

question 3 answers

level 1   Four

level 2   Purdue (three)

level 3   *a*   Hank Lauricella, 1951, Dick Kazmaier
       b   Johnny Majors, 1956, Paul Hornung
       c   Heath Shuler, 1993, Charlie Ward
       d   Peyton Manning, 1997, Charles Woodson

Q4

Northwestern holds the Division I-A record for consecutive losses.

level 1   *How many games did the streak last?*

level 2   *What years did the streak run through?*

level 3   *Name the school the Wildcats beat to break their losing streak.*

question 4 answers

level 1   34

level 2   1979-82

level 3   Northern Illinois

take my state, please

Florida-Florida State, Michigan-Michigan State.

∴ And it's not just Florida and Michigan. When the two biggest football teams in any state get together on Saturday afternoon for an internecine battle, you get the feeling bragging rights are at stake from one corner of the region to the other.

∴ We looked at 11 Division I University-versus-State series having at least 40 games each and discovered an interesting pattern to the results. In every one, the U. leads the all-time series, generally by a healthy margin.

winner	wins	losses	ties	win %	loser
Oklahoma	72	12	7	.830	Okla. St.
Colorado	53	15	2	.771	Colorado St.
Iowa	33	12	0	.733	Iowa St.
North Carolina	57	4	6	.690	N.C. St.
Michigan	59	26	5	.683	Mich. St.
Kansas	61	29	5	.668	Kansas St.
Washington	57	27	6	.667	Wash. St.
Florida	26	14	2	.643	Florida St.
Mississippi	54	34	6	.606	Miss. St.
Arizona	41	29	1	.585	Arizona St.
Oregon	51	40	10	.554	Oregon St.
totals	**564**	**262**	**50**	**.672**	

∴ In many cases, the school with State in its name was established after its University sister, thus starting at a disadvantage. Can this state of affairs be changed? Kansas State boasts a much stronger program than Kansas these days, and in 1997 the Ryan Leaf-led Washington State Cougars topped Washington for the Pac-10's Rose Bowl berth. Oklahoma State also beat Oklahoma, but the U.'s were 8-3 against States in 1997, and even if the States do turn things around, they'll still have a long way to go to even the all-time numbers. *rob neyer*

did you know?

Mark Malone was Arizona State's top rusher in 1978 (705 yards, 4.9 yards per carry), finishing his collegiate career with 1,390 rushing yards, the most of any Sun Devil quarterback. "I had a 98-yard touchdown run against Utah, one yard short of the team record," says Malone. "But the highlight was handing eventual national champion USC—featuring my future ESPN colleague Anthony Muñoz—its lone defeat of the '78 season."

inside the numbers

Fourteen players have rushed for 100 or more yards in 11 regular-season games in one year:

year	player	school	total yards
1997	Ahman Green	Nebraska	1,877
1996	Troy Davis	Iowa State	2,185
1995	Wasean Tait	Toledo	1,905
1995	Darnell Autry	Northwestern	1,675
1993	Brent Moss	Wisconsin	1,637
1988	Barry Sanders	Oklahoma State	2,628
1987	Craig Heyward	Pittsburgh	1,655
1983	Mike Rozier	Nebraska	2,148
1981	Herschel Walker	Georgia	1,891
1981	Marcus Allen	USC	2,342
1980	George Rogers	South Carolina	1,781
1977	Terry Miller	Oklahoma State	1,680
1976	Tony Dorsett	Pittsburgh	1,948
1974	Archie Griffin	Ohio State	1,695

dubious distinctions

- The Division I-A college football program that has gone the longest without winning a conference title is Iowa State, which last won in 1912 as a member of the Missouri Valley Intercollegiate Athletic Association.
- The Division I-A college football program that has gone the longest without ever playing in a bowl game is Southwestern Louisiana (1908-97). The Ragin' Cajuns, who have been an independent since the 1982 season, finished 1-10 in 1997.
- The longest drought between Rose Bowl victories belongs to Michigan State, which won it in 1954 and did not win it again until 1988.
- On September 13, 1980, East Carolina fumbled the ball five times on five straight possessions, losing 27-21 to Southwestern Louisiana.
- The most lopsided score in sports history was Georgia Tech's whupping of Cumberland College 222-0 on October 7, 1916. Tech never threw a single pass and rushed for 528 yards.
- As a freshman, future Heisman Trophy winner Andre Ware actually threw more interceptions (5) than touchdown passes (4).
- Paul Hornung never had a 500-yard rushing season or a 1,000-yard passing season at Notre Dame.
- In 1997, Alabama's Mike DuBose became the first Tide coach to lose seven games on the field since the team went 2-7-1 in 1957 (Alabama's official 1993 record was 1-12 after the school was penalized for using an ineligible player).

inside the numbers

Jim Brown was one of the greatest running backs in NFL history, yet he never had a 1,000-yard rushing season in three years at Syracuse. That said, his yard-per-carry average was pretty good, helping the Orangemen to a .667 winning percentage:

year	yards	yards per carry	team win-loss record
1954	439	5.9	4-4
1955	666	5.2	5-3
1956	986	6.2	7-1
total	2,091	5.8	16-8

did you know?

Kirk Herbstreit was Ohio State's starting quarterback in 1992. The starters in 1991 (Kent Graham) and 1993 (Bobby Hoying) both now play in the NFL.

Q5

Oklahoma holds the Division I-A record for the longest win streak.

level 1   *How many games did the streak last?*

level 2   *What years did the streak run through?*

level 3   *Which school beat the Sooners to end the streak?*

question 5 answers
level 1   47
level 2   1953-57
level 3   Notre Dame upended Oklahoma, 7-0.

Q6

Retired Nebraska coach Tom Osborne was more than just a solid college head coach.

level 1   *What rank did he have in the Army National Guard?*

level 2   *How many years did he play in the NFL? At what position?*

level 3   *Which team did he have his longest stint with?*

question 6 answers
level 1   Sergeant
level 2   Three, wide receiver
level 3   Two seasons with the Washington Redskins

awards

- The only player to win both the Heisman Trophy and Pro Bowl MVP Award is O.J. Simpson. Simpson won the Heisman with USC in 1968 and the Pro Bowl MVP while with the Bills in 1973, after running for 112 yards and a TD.
- There have been 10 Heisman winners who also won the national championship in the same season. Between 1950 and 1995, only Pittsburgh's Tony Dorsett in 1976 and Florida State's Charlie Ward in 1993 accomplished both, followed in 1996 and 1997 respectively by Florida's Danny Wuerffel and Michigan's Charles Woodson. No player has ever repeated this double the following season.
- Since 1970, only two Heisman winners have played on a team that finished out of the AP Top 20-25 rankings: South Carolina's George Rogers in 1980 and Auburn's Bo Jackson in 1985.
- The first non-senior to win the Heisman was Army's Doc Blanchard in 1945.
- Notre Dame's Frank Leahy is the only man to coach four different Heisman winners (Angelo Bertelli, Johnny Lujack, Leon Hart and John Lattner). Woody Hayes coached four winners at Ohio State, but Archie Griffin won it twice.
- Archie Manning finished in the top five in the Heisman voting twice: fourth in 1969 and third in 1970.
- Dick Butkus finished third in the Heisman voting in 1964, following John Huarte and Jerry Rhome.
- Don Meredith finished third in Heisman voting in 1959, following Billy Cannon and Richie Lucas (Cannon had come in second the previous year).
- Troy Aikman finished third in Heisman voting in 1988, following Barry Sanders and Rodney Peete.
- Defensive back Jack Tatum, known more for his days as The Assassin with the Oakland Raiders, was 10th in the 1969 voting and seventh in the 1970 balloting for the Heisman.
- 1941 Heisman Trophy-winner Bruce Smith from the University of Minnesota was nominated for sainthood in the Roman Catholic Church for his work with cancer patients.

total access
chris fowler

"Charles Woodson's first experience as a defensive back was a disaster. The future Heisman winner had been a high school running back but wanted to play defense at Michigan. In his first practice at cornerback, Woodson looked so lost that defensive backfield coach Vance Bedford shook his head and laughed that there was no way the kid would ever be a DB. A few months later, Woodson was blanketing Biletnikoff Award-winner Terry Glenn and making a key interception against the Buckeyes. So much for first impressions!"

Q

Only one Division I-A football program has had three consecutive coaches win 100 games.

level 1   *Name the school and the coaches.*

level 2   *Name the schools that have had two consecutive coaches win 100 games.*

level 3   *Name the coaches.*

Q

In 1998, two Heisman finalists played each other in a bowl game.

level 1   *Name the players and the bowl.*

level 2   *When was the last time two Heisman finalists met in a bowl game?*

level 3   *Name the players and the bowl. **Bonus**: Which team won and what was the score?*

question 7 answers

level 1   *a*   Georgia Tech
        b   John Heisman, William Alexander and Bobby Dodd

level 2   *a*   Penn State
        b   Nebraska

level 3   *a*   Rip Engle, Joe Paterno
        b   Bob Devaney, Tom Osborne

question 8 answers

level 1   Washington State's Ryan Leaf and Michigan's Charles Woodson in the Rose Bowl

level 2   1980

level 3   South Carolina's George Rogers and Pittsburgh's Hugh Green in the Gator Bowl. The Panthers won 37-9.

the heisman definition of second best

∴ Alex Karras was runner-up to John David Crow in the Heisman voting in 1957.

∴ Joe Theismann was runner-up to Jim Plunkett in 1970.

∴ Billy Sims, who won the 1978 Heisman Trophy, was runner-up to Charles White the next season.

∴ John Elway was runner-up to Herschel Walker in 1982.

∴ Herschel Walker was runner-up to Marcus Allen in 1981 (Jim McMahon was third and Dan Marino came in fourth).

∴ Steve Young was runner-up to Mike Rozier in 1983 (Doug Flutie came in third).

∴ Peyton Manning was runner-up to Charles Woodson in 1997.

inside the numbers

In the season before winning the Heisman, Bo Jackson, Barry Sanders and Rashaan Salaam were each held below 1,000 yards rushing:

year	player	team	rushing	touchdowns
1985	Bo Jackson	Auburn	475 yards	5
1988	Barry Sanders	Oklahoma State	603 yards	8
1994	Rashaan Salaam	Colorado	844 yards	8

1987 Heisman Trophy winner Tim Brown actually had some better numbers the year before he won the Heisman:

year	receptions	receiving yards	all-purpose yards
1986	45	910	1,937
1987	39	846	1,847

total access
dave revsine   espnews

"My single life-long sports passion is Northwestern football, and I've been through all the highs and lows. I was at the 1981 game against Michigan State when NU broke the all-time Division I-A losing streak record with its 29th straight loss. Fortunately I was also there the next year when NU beat Northern Illinois 31-6 to finally to snap the streak at 34 games. And, if that isn't sweet enough, I was at the Rose Bowl rooting the Cinderella 'Cats in 1996."

Q9

It is rare in Division I-A college football for there not to be an unbeaten, untied team at the end of the regular season.

level 1   *How many times has this happened?*

level 2   *In which years did this happen?*

level 3   *Who won the national title in those years?*

question 9 answers

level 1   Three

level 2   *a*   1927
          b   1936
          c   1990

level 3   *a*   Illinois
          b   Minnesota
          c   Colorado and Georgia Tech

Q10

The Four Horsemen are well known in college football lore.

level 1   *For what school did they play?*

level 2   *Name the Four Horsemen.*

level 3   *Which one was the quarterback?*

question 10 answers

level 1   Notre Dame

level 2   Jim Crowley, Elmer Layden, Don Miller, Harry Stuhldreher

level 3   Stuhldreher

streaks

---- The last time before 1997 that both Michigan and Nebraska finished the regular season unbeaten was 1971. Nebraska finished the 1971 regular season 12-0, while Michigan went 11-0. The No. 1 Cornhuskers beat Alabama in the Orange Bowl, winning the national title, while the Wolverines lost to Stanford in the Rose Bowl.

---- The Division I-A record for longest winning streak belongs to the University of Oklahoma, which won 47 straight games from 1953 to '57. (The Sooners' streak was snapped in 7-0 squeaker by Notre Dame.) Washington holds the second-longest streak, 39 straight wins from 1908 to '14.

---- The longest uninterrupted series in the history of college football is 95 games between Kansas and Oklahoma (1903-97). The next-longest streak is Kansas and Nebraska at 92 straight games (1906-97).

---- The last time five teams finished the regular season unbeaten was in 1979, when Alabama, BYU, Florida State, Ohio State and McNeese State all went 11-0. However, the Crimson Tide was the only one of the five to win its bowl game.

---- After winning the 1996 Division I-AA Championship, Marshall joined the 1989 Georgia Southern squad as the only two teams to finish a season with a 15-0 record.

---- The most-played rivalry in college football is 133 games between Lehigh and Lafayette. At the end of the 1997 season, Lafayette leads 71-57-5.

---- The Division I-A record for consecutive 100-yard rushing games is 31, set by Ohio State's Archie Griffin between 1973 and '75.

---- Marshall's Randy Moss concluded his collegiate career with at least one touchdown catch in each of his last 28 games. Moss was drafted in the first round by the Minnesota Vikings in the 1998 NFL draft.

---- Entering the 1998 season, Notre Dame had won 34 straight meetings versus Navy. The last Midshipmen win came in 1963, when Roger Staubach was the school's quarterback.

---- Entering the 1998 season, Nebraska had gone 29 straight meetings against Kansas State without a loss. The last time the Wildcats beat the Cornhuskers was 1968.

---- Speaking of Nebraska, the members of the 1997 senior class went 49-2 in its four years. The Cornhuskers also sport the longest current streak of years with a bowl appearance: 29.

inside the numbers

Tony Dorsett was never held below 100 yards in three bowl appearances for Pittsburgh. And he got better each season:

year	bowl	opponent	rushes	yards
1973	Fiesta	Arizona State	30	100
1975	Sun	Kansas	27	142
1977	Sugar	Georgia	32	202

Q

Teammates have finished 1-2 in the Heisman voting only once.

level 1   *Name the players and the year.*

level 2   *Name the school.*

level 3   *Who finished third?*

question 11 answers

level 1   Doc Blanchard and Glenn Davis in 1945

level 2   Army

level 3   HB Bob Fenimore from Oklahoma State

Q

In 1997, Oklahoma State alumni Barry Sanders and Thurman Thomas gained enough pro yardage to become the all-time NFL rushing combo to graduate from the same college.

level 1   *Name the No. 2 rushing combo and their alma mater.*

level 2   *Name the No. 3 rushing combo and their alma mater.*

level 3   *How many pro yards had Sanders and Thomas gained entering the 1998 season?*

question 12 answers

level 1   Marcus Allen and O.J. Simpson, USC

level 2   Jim Brown and Larry Csonka, Syracuse

level 3   25,183 yards

-:- The NCAA Division I-A record for most consecutive conference championships is 14, by Oklahoma from 1946 to '59.

-:- The Division I-A record for yards in a single game by two teams is 1,563, set by Houston and TCU in 1990. Houston won 56-35.

-:- The highest scoring total ever in a Division I-A or I-AA game is 124 points. In 1980 Oklahoma rocked the scoreboard with an 82-42 win over Colorado. The most lopsided college game ever was in 1916, when Georgia Tech beat Cumberland College 222-0.

-:- The Division I-A record for passing touchdowns in a game is 11, set by David Klingler of Houston against Eastern Washington in 1990.

-:- The Division I-A record for pass attempts in a single game is held by TCU's Matt Vogler, who threw 79 passes on November 3, 1990, against Houston, connecting on 44. Vogler followed up with 72 attempts against Texas Tech that same season.

-:- The NCAA Division I record for the highest points per game average in a season is 56.0, set by Army in 1944. Army posted four shutouts and outscored its opponents 504-35 en route to a 9-0 national championship season.

-:- Brigham Young's Jay Miller caught a record 22 passes for 263 yards in a 56-21 victory over New Mexico on November 3, 1973.

-:- In 1977, Tennessee-Chattanooga had a pair of freshmen each rush for over 1,000 yards: Mike Smith (1,062) and Gwain Durden (1,049).

inside the numbers

Four coaches have led four different schools to a bowl game:

coach	schools
Larry Smith	Tulane, Arizona, USC, Missouri
Earle Bruce	Tampa, Iowa State, Ohio State, Colorado State
Lou Holtz	Wm. & Mary, N.C. State, Arkansas, Notre Dame
Bill Mallory	Miami-O, Colorado, Indiana, N. Illinois

total access
dan davis   espn radio

"Many people associate my broadcasting career with a particular moment. I was lucky enough to be in the broadcast booth at the Orange Bowl, calling the Boston College-Miami football game, on November 23, 1984. Doug Flutie heaved one to Gerard Phelan with time expiring, and the rest, as they say, is history. Boston College took possession on its own 20-yard line with 28 seconds left, down four points. The Eagles had two timeouts available to them, but in their 80-yard drive, culminated by Flutie to Phelan, they never used either of them. That offense was so much on the same page, they didn't need a timeout. I still believe it was the best college offense ever."

Q13

Future Packers star Brett Favre threw a game-winning 79-yard touchdown pass on the final play of a game in 1989.

level 1   *For what college did Favre play?*

level 2   *Who was that opponent?*

level 3   *What was the final score?*

question 13 answers

level 1   Southern Mississippi
level 2   Louisville
level 3   Southern Miss. won 16-10.

Q14

Rivalries are a big part of college football. The winners also receive special trophies. Name the schools that are involved in these trophy showcase games.

level 1   *Little Brown Jug*

level 2   *Old Oaken Bucket*

level 3   *Bourbon Barrel*

question 14 answers

level 1   Michigan-Minnesota
level 2   Purdue-Indiana
level 3   Indiana-Kentucky

the coaches

- Only three Oklahoma coaches have made a bowl appearance in their first season: Jim Tatum in the 1947 Gator Bowl (beat N.C. State 34-13), Gomer Jones in the 1965 Gator (lost to Florida State 36-19) and Chuck Fairbanks in the 1968 Orange (beat Tennessee 26-24).

- Raiders owner Al Davis was an assistant coach at USC from 1957 to '59. The Trojans posted a record of 13-16-1 during his tenure.

- Bear Bryant was 43-6 coaching against former staff and players, including Charley McClendon (14-2), Steve Sloan (5-0) and Howard Schnellenberger (1-0). The only ex-player or assistant to have a winning record versus Bryant was Gene Stallings.

- The youngest head coach in a bowl game is South Carolina's Johnny McMillan, who was 26 when his Gamecocks lost to Wake Forest in the 1946 Gator Bowl.

- Steve Spurrier's first head coaching job was with the USFL's Tampa Bay Bandits in 1983. Spurrier spent three seasons with Tampa Bay, compiling a 35-19 record.

- Colorado head coach Rick Neuheisel set the NCAA record for highest percentage of passes completed in a single game, going 25 for 27 (.926) as UCLA defeated Washington on October 29, 1983.

- Eddie Robinson, college football's all-time winningest coach with 408 victories, sent more than 200 players on to the pros in his 55 seasons as Grambling head coach. Four of his former Tigers are in the Pro Football Hall of Fame: Willie Brown, "Buck" Buchanan, Willie Davis and Charlie Joiner.

- Virginia football coach George Welsh was third in the Heisman voting in 1955 as a quarterback at Navy. Howard "Hopalong" Cassady took home the trophy.

- Jimmy Johnson was 3-4 in bowl games while coaching at Oklahoma State and Miami. He did win his last two, with victories over Barry Switzer and Tom Osborne.

- Future NFC Central coaches Dennis Green and Bobby Ross went against each other in the 1991 Aloha Bowl. Ross's Georgia Tech team edged Green's Stanford squad 18-17.

inside the numbers

Lloyd Carr's three-year rise to the top is tied for the third-quickest among coaches winning their first national title since polling began in 1936. The only coach to win the championship in his first season is Bennie Oosterbaan, who coincidentally led the Wolverines to their last national title in 1948. Barry Switzer won titles in his second and third seasons with Oklahoma:

coach	school	first season	first title	years to the top
Bennie Oosterbaan	Michigan	1948	1948	1
Paul Brown	Ohio State	1941	1942	2
Barry Switzer	Oklahoma	1972	1974	3
Lloyd Carr	Michigan	1995	1997	3
John Robinson	USC	1976	1978	3
John McKay	USC	1960	1962	3

Q 15

Overtime came into play in Division I-A in 1996.

level 1   *What was the first game to go into OT between two Division I-A schools?*

level 2   *What was the score?*

level 3   *How many overtime games were there in the first year?*

question 15 answers

level 1   Oregon versus Fresno State
(SW Missouri State of Division I-AA played Division I-A Oklahoma State that same weekend and the game went into overtime.)

level 2   Oregon 30, Fresno State 27

level 3   26

Q 16

Barry Sanders won the Heisman in 1988.

level 1   *How many rushing yards did he accumulate?*

level 2   *How many total all-purpose yards did he gain?*

level 3   *How many total rushing yards did he have in the two years before winning the Heisman?*

question 16 answers

level 1   2,628

level 2   3,250

level 3   928

college files

- Jerry Rice had 301 receptions in four seasons at Mississippi Valley State (1981-84).
- Deion Sanders, then of Florida State, led the nation in punt returning in 1988, averaging 15.2 yards per runback.
- The only players to lead the NCAA in rushing and then lead the NFL in rushing the following season are George Rogers (1981), Earl Campbell (1978) and Byron White (1938).
- The last Heisman Trophy winner to play in the Super Bowl was Desmond Howard in Super Bowl XXXI.
- Jim McMahon set or tied 70 NCAA records in three seasons at Brigham Young (1977-78 and 80/81).
- Ahmad Rashad caught three touchdown passes in his first collegiate game at Oregon. The three scoring strikes were thrown by Hall of Famer Dan Fouts (Rashad's name back then was Bobby Moore).
- Frank Thomas of White Sox fame also played football at Auburn.
- Davey O'Brien was the first Heisman winner to sign a pro contract, but after two years he left to join the FBI.
- 1955 Heisman winner Howard "Hopalong" Cassady served as a baseball scout for the New York Yankees.
- Heisman winner Doc Blanchard never played pro football, instead going to active duty for the army. He also served as a jet pilot in Korea and Vietnam, retiring with the rank of colonel. Blanchard was also a member of the honor guard at FDR's funeral in 1945.
- Former Supreme Court judge Byron "Whizzer" White was officially the first 1,000-yard rusher in NCAA history, with 1,121 yards in 1937 (official because the NCAA did not always keep statistics in the '20s).
- Florida QB John Reaves threw nine interceptions versus Auburn on November 1, 1969.
- More than just a gridiron star, Jim Brown won 10 athletic letters at Syracuse: three in football, three in lacrosse, two in track and field and two in basketball.
- Current Baltimore Ravens head coach Ted Marchibroda led the nation in passing for the University of Detroit in 1952.
- Bo Jackson turned down a $250,000 offer to join the New York Yankees before deciding to attend Auburn on a football scholarship.

Q17

Before his stints as an actor on *Hill Street Blues* and *Sisters*, Ed Marinaro was a pretty good football player.

level 1   *What position did he play?*

level 2   *What college did he attend?*

level 3   *In 1971, he led the nation in three categories. Name them and his stats.*

question 17 answers

level 1   RB

level 2   Cornell

level 3   Rushing yards (1,881), all-purpose yardage (214.7 ypg.) and scoring (16.4 ppg.)

Q18

Four players named White are in the College Football Hall of Fame.

level 1   *Name them.*

level 2   *Name their schools.*

level 3   *Which White was the first to be inducted?*

question 18 answers

level 1   *a*   Byron
          b   Charles
          c   Danny
          d   Randy

level 2   *a*   Colorado
          b   USC
          c   Arizona State
          d   Maryland

level 3   Byron White in 1938

family secrets

⁘ Former Nebraska QB Scott Frost's mother, Carol, won the gold medal in the discus at the 1967 Pan-American Games. She also competed in the 1968 Olympics.

⁘ Former Heisman Trophy winner O.J. Simpson is a cousin of Baseball Hall of Famer Ernie Banks.

⁘ Michigan running back Justin Fargas is the son of actor Antonio Fargas, better known as Huggy Bear on *Starsky and Hutch*.

⁘ Former Texas free safety Chris Carter is the cousin of major league baseball player and former World Series hero Joe Carter.

⁘ Former Michigan State offensive lineman Flozell Adams is a cousin of NBA guard Hersey Hawkins.

⁘ Sons of two famous coaches have played for Duke: Steve Spurrier's son, Steve Jr., and Kyle Shanahan, son of Super Bowl champion Mike Shanahan.

inside the numbers

The Pac-10 had a different school lead the league in total offense in five straight years from 1993 to '97:

year	school	total ypg.
1993	California	403.2
1994	Stanford	444.5
1995	USC	414.3
1996	Arizona State	492.5
1997	Washington State	502.2

total access
kenny mayne

"I didn't play often and I didn't play well, but I did play once in awhile ... and I got to go to school for free. It was the summer of 1981, the UNLV practice field, and the quarterbacks were warming down before the finale in which we'd launch the ball toward the athletic building to prove our manhood or something. Steve White and I bounced up short but we were still proud of our arms. Then the skinny freshman, this kid from Santa Barbara, the guy whose brother scored a bunch of TDs for USC (Sam the Bam), this kid Randall Cunningham threw the ball and hit the wall with it. We figured he'd probably stay in the game a few years."

Q 19

Florida and Florida State have had a heated rivalry over the years.

level 1   *Entering 1998, how many meetings have the teams had?*

level 2   *Who leads the series?*

level 3   *What is their head-to-head bowl record?*

Q 20

College football fans know the phrase "Win one for the Gipper."

level 1   *For whom was the phrase named?*

level 2   *At what school did he play?*

level 3   *What year was that player first named All-America?*

question 19 answers

level 1   42

level 2   Florida, 26-14-2

level 3   Tied 1-1. Florida won the 1997 Sugar Bowl. Florida State won the 1995 Sugar Bowl.

question 20 answers

level 1   George Gipp

level 2   Notre Dame

level 3   1920

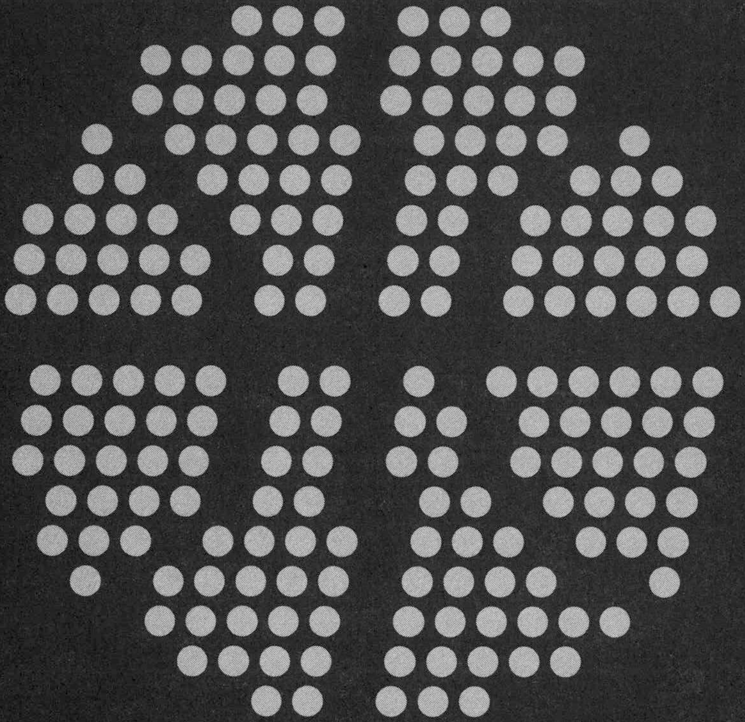

caution: avoid extreme heat

Stats are good up to the start of the 1998/99 season.

did you know?

Nick Bakay and Christian Laettner attended the same
Buffalo, New York, high school, where Bakay claims he was
the first guy to wear a headband.

playoffs and championships

-:- The only time both the East and West finals ended in a series sweep was in 1957. The Celtics
swept the Syracuse Nationals three games to none in the Eastern Division finals. The St. Louis
Hawks swept the Minneapolis Lakers three games to none in the Western Division finals.
The Celtics went on to defeat the Hawks four games to three, including a 125-123 double
overtime win in Game 7. This was the first of 16 Boston NBA titles.

-:- The only two NBA postseasons since 1955 to go without a 40-point scorer were in 1971 and
1982, both of which featured the game's greatest scorer, Kareem Abdul-Jabbar.

-:- The only teams to win the NBA title despite having the league's worst regular-season free-
throw percentage are the 1982 Lakers, the 1978 Bullets and the 1967 76ers.

-:- Wilt Chamberlain and Rick Barry share the record for the most field goal attempts in a playoff
game. Both were playing for the Warriors when they threw up 48 shots from the field, with
each hitting 22 (Chamberlain scored his 56 points in 1962, while Barry tallied 55 in 1967).

-:- The only Bull other than Michael Jordan to score 40 or more points in a playoff game is Flynn
Robinson, who had 41 points versus the Lakers on March 27, 1968 (Chicago won 104-98).

-:- Game 1 of the 1998 NBA Finals between the Bulls and the Jazz, which Utah won 88-85,
was the lowest-scoring overtime game in the NBA playoffs since 1954/55. The 173 total
points also broke the record for lowest-scoring playoff game, period. The record was
previously held by Detroit and New York, who put up 177 points in the Eastern Conference first
round in 1992 (Knicks won 90-87).

-:- The 1958 St. Louis Hawks are the only team to win four games by three points or less in one
playoff series. They needed all four of those close wins—2, 3, 3 and 1 point respectively—
to hand the Celtics their only finals loss in the Bill Russell era.

-:- The 1977/78 champion Bullets didn't have a player average at least 20 points per game
during the regular season. Elvin Hayes was their top scorer at 19.7 points per game.

-:- Back in 1985/86, six teams with losing records made the playoffs: Washington (39-43),
New Jersey (39-43) and Chicago (30-52) from the Eastern Conference, and Portland (40-42),
Sacramento (37-45) and San Antonio (35-47) from the Western Conference.

-:- Dennis Rodman and Bill Russell are the only two players in NBA history to lead the league in
rebounding and win the NBA championship in the same season three times.

-:- Since 1954/55, the only NBA team to win a title without one of the NBA's "50 Greatest
Players" is the 1979 Sonics. Led by Gus Williams, Dennis Johnson, Jack Sikma and Dick
Snyder, the Sonics did have a top 50 player on their bench: coach Lenny Wilkens.

inside the numbers

This just in: the Bulls are good! Here's how Chicago's record in the '90s stacks up against the best teams in each previous decade:

decade	team	winning pct.	titles
'90s	Bulls	.747	6
'80s	Lakers	.724	5
'70s	Celtics	.615	2
'60s	Celtics	.677	9
'50s	Celtics	.624	2

These NBA champions won titles despite having a leading scorer who averaged fewer than 20 ppg. during the regular season (minimum 40 games played):

year	team	high scorer	ppg.
1990	Detroit Pistons	Isiah Thomas	18.4
1989	Detroit Pistons	Adrian Dantley	18.4
1979	Seattle Sonics	Gus Williams	19.2
1978	Washington Bullets	Elvin Hayes	19.7
1976	Boston Celtics	Dave Cowens	19.0
1964	Boston Celtics	John Havlicek	19.9
1963	Boston Celtics	Sam Jones	19.7
1955	Syracuse Nationals	Dolph Schayes	18.5
1954	Minneapolis Lakers	George Mikan	18.1
1951	Rochester Royals	Arnie Risen	16.3
1948	Baltimore Bullets	Kleggie Hermsen	12.0

Only five teams in NBA history have lost a playoff game by 40 or more points and then won the next game in the series:

year	team	lost to	next game
1997	Suns	Sonics by 44 points	won by 7 points
1995	Celtics	Magic by 47 points	won by 7 points
1982	76ers	Celtics by 40 points	won by 8 points
1973	Warriors	Lakers by 56 points	won by 8 points
1956	Hawks	Lakers by 58 points	won by 1 point

for the record

:: The 1990/91 76ers hold the record for most overtime games in a season, with 14. The 76ers went 8-6, including a pair of double OT contests, in the regular season, then had an overtime victory against Milwaukee in Game 2 of the first round of the Eastern Conference playoffs.

:: Indiana's Butch Carter holds the record for most points in an overtime period, scoring 14 of the Pacers' 15 OT points in a 123-121 victory over the Celtics on March 20, 1984.

:: Only four players have scored 70 or more points in an NBA game: Wilt Chamberlain (six times), David Robinson (once), David Thompson (once) and Elgin Baylor (once).

:: Teams have tied for the best regular-season record only four times: 1997/98 (Bulls and Jazz), 1980/81 (Celtics and 76ers), 1974/75 (Celtics and Bullets) and 1954/55 (Nationals and Pistons).

:: The record for most blocked shots in a quarter is held by Manute Bol, with eight. Bol accomplished it twice: on December 12, 1985, and on February 26, 1987.

:: The record for highest field goal percentage by one team in a game is 70.7 percent, set by San Antonio on April 16, 1983. The Spurs hit 53 of 75 shots in the game.

:: The highest three-point field goal percentage in a season is .522, set by Miami's Jon Sundvold in 1988/89. Sundvold was 48-92 from long distance in the Heat's inaugural season.

:: Wilt Chamberlain needed just 236 games to score his first 10,000 points in the NBA. Michael Jordan reached 10,000 points the second fastest, in 303 games.

:: Wilt Chamberlain averaged a rookie record 46.4 minutes per game in his first NBA season with the Philadelphia Warriors in 1959/60.

:: More Wilt. In the 1961/62 season, Chamberlain had 40 or more points in 63 games.

:: The Lakers hold the record for consecutive winning seasons: 16 from 1976/77 to 1991/92.

:: The worst field goal percentage for a three-point shooting leader was 34.5 percent by Mike Dunleavy of San Antonio. That's the same Mike Dunleavy who coaches the Trail Blazers.

:: The last man to lead the NBA in assists while averaging fewer than nine per game was Don Buse of Indiana (8.5 assists per game) in 1976/77.

:: The only player to lead the NBA in free-throw percentage with an average below 80 percent was Washington's Bob Feerick in 1947/48 (78.8 percent).

:: The 1982/83 76ers have the best single-season winning percentage for one playoff year. Philadelphia went 12-1, good for a 92.3 winning percentage.

total access
fred "mad dog" carter   nba 2night

"I got my nickname when I was trying out for the Baltimore Bullets in 1970. As part of a defensive drill, rookies would have to defend against a whole line of veteran players coming at them, one after another. When it was 6-foot-9 Ray Scott's turn, somehow his shoulder wound up in my mouth. Okay, I bit him. He went back to the rest of guys muttering, 'He's worse than a mad dog.' It was nothing personal – I was just doing everything I could to make the team."

Q1

In 1998, Tim Duncan became the 10th No. 1 overall draft pick to take home Rookie of the Year honors.

level 1   *How many No. 2 picks have been named Rookie of the Year?*

level 2   *How many No. 1 picks went on to win both the Rookie of the Year and MVP awards in their careers? Name them.*

level 3   *How many No. 2 overall draft picks went on to win both the Rookie of the Year and MVP awards in their careers? Name them and the seasons in which they took both honors.*

question 1 answers

level 1   Nine

level 2   *a*   Two
          b   Kareem Abdul-Jabbar and David Robinson

level 3   *a*   Two
          b   Baltimore's Wes Unseld won both awards in the same season (1968/69), the only player to achieve that feat. Buffalo's Bob McAdoo won the 1973 Rookie of the Year and was named MVP. in 1975.

Q2

Pat Riley is third on the list of the NBA's all-time-winningest coaches.

level 1   *How many times has he won Coach of the Year honors?*

level 2   *Name the years and the teams he represented when he won.*

level 3   *Name the coaches who are first and second in career victories.*

question 2 answers

level 1   Three

level 2   *a*   1990 Lakers
          b   1993 Knicks
          c   1997 Heat

level 3   Lenny Wilkens is first (1,120 career victories). Red Auerbach is second (1,037 career victories).

michael jordan

- Michael Jordan was cut from his high school basketball team as a sophomore. When he asked if he could still accompany the Laney varsity squad to a district tournament, the coach agreed, on the condition that Jordan carry the players' uniforms.
- Despite a great three-year college career, he didn't hit the 2,000-point mark as a Tar Heel, leaving North Carolina with 1,788 points.
- Sidney Green was the Bulls' first round pick in 1983 (fifth overall). Chicago's first round pick in 1984? Jordan (third overall). What a difference a year makes.
- Only two players besides Jordan have led the NBA in scoring in the '90s: David Robinson (1994) and Shaquille O'Neal (1995).
- He has scored 50 or more points against 17 different NBA teams. His highest career-scoring average is against the Trail Blazers (35.3 ppg.), followed by the Jazz (34.8) and the Spurs (34.1). His lowest career average is against the Grizzlies (22.5 ppg.), the only team against which he averages fewer than 27 ppg.

- He ended the 1997/98 season with 840 consecutive games scoring in double figures.
- The last time he was held below 10 points was March 22, 1986, scoring just eight versus Cleveland.
- He has the highest scoring average in NBA All-Star Game history with 21.3 ppg. in 11 games. Oscar Robertson (20.5 ppg. in 12 games) is second, followed by Bob Pettit (20.4 ppg. in 11 games).
- On October 22, 1992, he testified during the drug and money laundering trial of golf shop owner Slim Bouler that he wrote a check for $57,000 to pay off golf gambling debts. Initially Jordan claimed it was a loan.
- As a member of the Birmingham Barons of the "AA" Southern League in 1994, Jordan hit .202 with three home runs, 46 runs scored, 51 RBI and 114 strikeouts in 436 official at-bats. He also stole 30 bases in 48 attempts and committed 11 errors in the outfield.
- According to statements made following his retirement from the NBA in 1993, Jordan is afraid of the water, can't swim and can't skate.

awards

-:- Damon Stoudamire, at 5 foot 10, is the shortest player to win the Rookie of the Year Award.

-:- The only two players besides Karl Malone and John Stockton (1998) to share the NBA All-Star Game MVP Award are St. Louis's Bob Pettit and Minneapolis's Elgin Baylor in 1959.

-:- Bill Walton is the only player to win the MVP Award (with the Trail Blazers in 1978) and the Sixth Man Award (with the Celtics in 1986).

-:- Buffalo's Bob McAdoo is the only North Carolina player other than Michael Jordan to win the NBA MVP Award. McAdoo, Jordan, Walter Davis and Phil Ford are the only four Tar Heels to win the Rookie of the Year honors.

-:- San Antonio's Alvin Robertson was the first winner of the Most Improved Player Award. He won it in his second season, 1985/86, after improving his scoring average from 9.2 to 17.0 points per game.

-:- Only two rookies have ever won the rebounding title: Fort Wayne's Larry Foust in 1951/52 and Philadelphia's Wilt Chamberlain in 1959/60.

-:- When Tim Duncan was named All-NBA First Team in 1997/98, it marked the first rookie to earn that honor since Larry Bird in 1980. Duncan, at age 22, was the second-youngest player to make All-NBA First Team. Max Zaslofsky was 21 years and four months old when he was honored in 1947.

-:- Duncan also had 57 double-doubles during his rookie year, 10 more than any other NBA player. Dikembe Mutombo and Antoine Walker were next, with 47.

-:- The only rookie to lead the NBA in free-throw shooting percentage was Buffalo's Ernie DiGregorio in 1973/74.

-:- The last team to have the regular-season field goal percentage and free-throw percentage leaders in the same season was the 1986/87 Celtics. Kevin McHale led in field goals, while Larry Bird led in free throws.

inside the numbers

Since 1980, more than half of the NBA champions have been led by the league's regular-season MVP:

year	champion	mvp
1998	Bulls	Michael Jordan
1996	Bulls	Michael Jordan
1994	Rockets	Hakeem Olajuwon
1992	Bulls	Michael Jordan
1991	Bulls	Michael Jordan
1987	Lakers	Magic Johnson
1986	Celtics	Larry Bird
1984	Celtics	Larry Bird
1983	76ers	Moses Malone
1980	Lakers	Kareem Abdul-Jabbar

Only seven times in NBA history has the league MVP averaged fewer than 20 points per game:

year	mvp	ppg.
1978	Bill Walton	18.9
1969	Wes Unseld	13.8
1965	Bill Russell	14.1
1963	Bill Russell	16.8
1962	Bill Russell	18.9
1961	Bill Russell	16.9
1958	Bill Russell	16.6

Q3

1997 marked the inaugural season of the WNBA.

level 1   *Name the league's first MVP.*

level 2   *Name the league's first champion and the team they defeated to win the WNBA title.*

level 3   *Name the six other original WNBA franchises.*

Q4

A second women's professional league, the ABL, also had a successful inaugural season in 1996/97.

level 1   *Name the league's first MVP.*

level 2   *Name the league's first champion and the team they defeated to win the ABL title.*

level 3   *Name the six other original ABL franchises.*

question 3 answers

level 1   Cynthia Cooper of the Houston Comets, who repeated as MVP in 1998.

level 2   Houston defeated the New York Liberty in the championship game 65-51, then repeated as champs in a three-game series over Phoenix in 1998.

level 3   a   Charlotte Sting
b   Cleveland Rockers
c   Los Angeles Sparks
d   Phoenix Mercury
e   Sacramento Monarchs
f   Utah Starzz

question 4 answers

level 1   Nikki McCray of the Columbus Quest

level 2   Columbus defeated the then-Richmond Rage, three games to two. The Quest became repeat champions in 1998, defeating the Long Beach StingRays, also by a 3-2 margin.

level 3   a   Atlanta Glory
b   Colorado Xplosion
c   New England Blizzard
d   Portland Power
e   San Jose Lasers
f   Seattle Reign

the gap gets bigger

Have you glanced at the bottom of the NBA standings lately?

∵ After playing 82 games apiece in the 1997/98 season, four different teams failed to achieve 20 victories: the L.A. Clippers, Vancouver, Denver and Toronto. The less said about the Clippers and the Grizzlies the better. The Nuggets, an established franchise with no particular excuse, managed only 11 wins. The Raptors won 16 games, five fewer than in 1995/96, their first season of existence.

∵ In recent seasons, the gap in the NBA between richer and poorer seems to be getting bigger, and perhaps Denver and Toronto are simply the most extreme examples.

∵ But are the have-nots really having fewer wins than ever?

∵ To check, we looked at the number of wins compiled by the top five and the bottom five teams in each season since the NBA absorbed the ABA in 1976. Rather than run all the data, we'll focus on three-year intervals, plus the last three seasons:

season	top five	bottom five	differential
1976/77	251	147	104
1979/80	291	124	167
1982/83	285	105	180
1985/86	290	138	152
1988/89	284	103	181
1991/92	291	107	184
1994/95	295	109	186
1995/96	310	105	205
1996/97	308	92	216
1997/98	304	82	222

∴ The 1995/96 season was the first in NBA history in which the top five teams combined for 300-plus wins. It's happened three consecutive seasons since.

∴ In 1997/98, four teams—Utah and Chicago (both 62-20), Seattle and the Los Angeles Lakers (both 61-21)—cleared the 60-victory hurdle. That had never happened before. In fact, in the 22 seasons since the merger, three teams had won 60-plus in a single season just three times.

∴ In both 1978/79 and 1983/84, the worst team in the NBA managed to win 26 games. These days, it's not uncommon for five or six teams to win fewer than 26.

∴ The smallest gap between rich and poor came in the first season after the merger, 1976/77, when the top five teams won 251 games, just 104 more than the bottom five (147). The next-smallest gap came two seasons later (252-146, 106), and then generally ranged between 160 and 180 until the '90s.

∴ What's going on? Maybe it's the Larry Bird Rule, which allows the teams with the best players to keep them with no regard to the supposed salary cap. Whatever the reason, the rich *are* getting richer, and the poor *are* getting poorer. Nuggets tickets, anyone? *rob neyer*

dubious distinctions

- Among players active during the 1997/98 season, Eddie Johnson scored the most points (19,190) without ever being chosen to play in the NBA All-Star Game.
- The Jazz was held to an NBA Finals record low 54 points in Game 3 of the 1998 championship round. Utah also set record lows for points in the second half (23), and that included a nine-point fourth quarter.
- The Pacers set a record for fewest points in a regular-season game since the shot clock was instituted. Indiana was held to 55 points by San Antonio on March 29, 1998 (Spurs won, 74-55).
- Olden Polynice was the player the Sonics acquired from the Bulls for Scottie Pippen on Draft Day in 1987. Polynice spent 3 1/2 seasons with Seattle before moving to the Clippers, Pistons and Kings.
- The Mavericks hold the record for scoring the fewest points in one quarter. Derek Harper hit a pair of free throws for Dallas's only two points in the third quarter versus the Lakers on April 6, 1997.
- Indiana's Rik Smits had spent the most seasons in the NBA (10) before making his first All-Star appearance in 1998. Three players—Calvin Murphy, Charles Oakley and Rickey Pierce—all made their first All-Star Game appearance in their ninth NBA season.
- The lowest-scoring game in NBA history took place on November 22, 1950, as the Fort Wayne Pistons edged the Minneapolis Lakers 19-18.
- The 1972/73 76ers posted the NBA's worst single-season win percentage (.110, 9-73) and tied the 1997/98 Nuggets and the 1992/93 Mavericks for the fewest wins (four) by the All-Star break.
- The Milwaukee Hawks and Minneapolis Lakers hold the record for the lowest combined field goal percentage in a game, 24.6 percent, set on November 6, 1954. The teams made only 48 of 195 attempts, with the Hawks' 22.9 percent shooting setting the all-time low mark for one team. And while there are no winners in a debacle like this, the final score was 79-67 Lakers.
- The franchise that has gone the longest since winning its last playoff series is the Clippers. They've been to the playoffs just three times since their last victory back in 1976, when the then-Buffalo Braves defeated the 76ers 2-1 in the first round before losing to Boston.

inside the numbers

Portland's 65-point loss to Indiana on February 27, 1998, is the second-largest margin of victory in NBA history. It's also the first time in NBA regular-season and playoff history that one opponent has at least doubled the score of the other:

year	winner	loser	final scores	margin
1991	Cavaliers	Heat	148-80	68
1998	Pacers	Trail Blazers	124-59	65
1992	Lakers	Warriors	162-99	63
1960	Nationals	Knicks	162-100	62
1991	Warriors	Kings	153-91	62

Q5

Kobe Bryant and Kevin Garnett made headlines when they jumped directly from high school to the pros.

level 1   *Name the first player to make the leap.*

level 2   *Who signed him and in what year?*

level 3   *What were the terms of his original contract?*

Q6

The 1997/98 Philadelphia 76ers had three No. 1 overall draft choices on their roster, but the 1986-89 Lakers had a record four.

level 1   *Name the four players.*

level 2   *Name their alma maters.*

level 3   *Name the No. 2 draft picks in the year that each was drafted.*

.✕. Zelmo Beaty has played the most conference finals games, 32, without appearing in an NBA championship series. (The Big Z did win a title with the Utah Stars of the ABA in 1970/71.) Derrick McKey and Al Bianchi are tied for second, with 27 games apiece.

.✕. Tom Van Arsdale played the most career games (922) without a playoff appearance. Vancouver's Lee Mayberry has the longest active futility streak (487 games), while Golden State's Clarence Weatherspoon is second (479 games).

.✕. The only active NBA No. 1 overall draft pick with at least five years experience who has never won an NBA playoff game is Chris Webber, who averaged 15.7 points and 8.3 rebounds in six losses (three with the Warriors and three with the Wizards).

.✕. The Hall of Fame players who were named to the fewest NBA All-Star Games during their careers are Dan Issel and Calvin Murphy, with one each.

.✕. The largest margin of defeat in an NBA overtime game is 17 points, when the Trail Blazers beat the Rockets on January 22, 1983, in a 113-96 victory.

.✕. The worst record for an NBA team following a championship season is 34-48 by the 1969/70 Celtics (under coach Tommy Heinsohn). The Celtics won the 1968/69 title under player/coach Bill Russell after a 48-34 season, then reversed their record in 1969/70 and never even reached the playoffs.

.✕. None of the NBA's Most Improved Players have made it to the Finals in the same season.

.✕. After losing to the Lakers in the first round of the 1997/98 playoffs, the Trail Blazers have not won a playoff series since 1991/92.

.✕. The Mavericks have not had a winning record since 1989/90, when they went 47-35.

.✕. Shawn Kemp averaged just 6.5 points per game as a rookie with Seattle in 1989/90.

.✕. Clyde Drexler averaged 7.7 points per game as a rookie with Portland in 1983/84.

.✕. Bob Lochmueller of the Syracuse Nationals fouled out of a playoff game against the Celtics in a record seven minutes on March 19, 1953.

.✕. The expansion Washington Mystics suffered the worst loss in the first two seasons of the WNBA, losing to the Houston Comets 110-65 on August 17, 1998.

.✕. In a 1984 exhibition game, the NBA All-Stars were defeated 97-82 by the U.S. men's Olympic basketball team. The Olympians, who included Patrick Ewing, Michael Jordan and Chris Mullen, went on to win gold.

inside the numbers

Karl Malone and Charles Barkley are the two active members on the list of all-time NBA leading scorers who have never won a championship:

player	career points	all-time rank
Karl Malone	27,782	4th
Dominique Wilkins	26,534	8th
Alex English	25,613	10th
Adrian Dantley	23,177	14th
Elgin Baylor	23,149	15th
Charles Barkley	22,792	16th

Q7

In 1998, Tim Duncan became the first rookie since 1979/80 to be named to the All-NBA First Team.

level 1   *Name the last rookie to make the All-NBA First Team.*

level 2   *How many times was he named to the All-NBA First Team in his career?*

level 3   *Name the other four members of the 1979/80 All-NBA First Team.*

question 7 answers

level 1   Larry Bird in 1979/80

level 2   Nine straight times

level 3   Julius Erving, Kareem Abdul-Jabbar, George Gervin and Paul Westphal

Q8

Wilt Chamberlain is the only NBA player to score 100 points in a game (36 field goals, 28 free throws).

level 1   *When and where was the game played?*

level 2   *Name the opponent.*

level 3   *What was the final score?*

question 8 answers

level 1   March 2, 1962, in Hershey, Pa.

level 2   New York Knicks

level 3   The Philadelphia Warriors won 169-147.

the draft

-:- You can make a pretty good All-Star team from former Atlanta first-round picks: Bob Cousy, Bill Russell, Lenny Wilkens, Pete Maravich and David Thompson.

-:- The Lakers can field a pretty good All-Star team from their former first-round picks: Jerry West, Magic Johnson, Elgin Baylor, James Worthy and Gale Goodrich.

-:- Pat Riley was a first-round pick (seventh overall) by San Diego in 1967.

-:- Dennis Rodman was a second-round pick (27th overall) by Detroit in 1986.

-:- Mark Price was a second-round pick (25th overall) by the Mavericks in 1986.

-:- Cedric Ceballos was a second-round pick (48th overall) by Phoenix in 1990.

-:- The Denver Nuggets of the ABA drafted Walt Frazier in the first round in 1967. Frazier ended up signing with the Knicks.

-:- As a member of the ABA, the New Jersey Nets used first-round draft choices on Kareem Abdul-Jabbar and Bob Lanier. Neither signed with them.

-:- Two players from the 1989 expansion draft played during the 1997/98 season: Tyrone Corbin and Rick Mahorn.

-:- The only two lottery selections to win titles with the teams that originally drafted them are Stacey King (drafted sixth overall by Chicago in 1989) and Robert Horry (drafted 11th by Houston in 1992).

-:- Since the NBA draft lottery's inception in 1985, Utah is the only team not to make a lottery selection.

-:- Lucy Harris became the first woman picked in the NBA draft when she was selected in the seventh round (137th overall) by the Jazz in 1977. She never played in the pros. The first woman signed to an NBA team was Ann Meyers, with the Pacers on September 5, 1979, but she was cut before she played a single game.

inside the numbers

Kevin Garnett (No. 5, Timberwolves) and Bryant Reeves (No. 6, Grizzlies) are the only top 10 selections in the 1995 NBA draft still playing for their original team:

player	draft position	drafted by	team entering 1998/99 season
Joe Smith	No. 1	Warriors	76ers
Antonio McDyess	No. 2	Nuggets	Suns
Jerry Stackhouse	No. 3	76ers	Pistons
Rasheed Wallace	No. 4	Bullets	Trail Blazers
Damon Stoudamire	No. 7	Raptors	Trail Blazers
Shawn Respert	No. 8	Bucks	free agent
Ed O'Bannon	No. 9	Nets	overseas
Kurt Thomas	No. 10	Heat	Mavericks

Q9

Only one player has led the NBA in scoring, rebounding and assists in a season, although he never led in all three categories in the same season.

level 1   *Name the player.*

level 2   *How many times did he lead the league in scoring, rebounds and assists?*

level 3   *When was his rookie season? How many points per game did he average that year?*

Q10

Scoring 50 or more points in a game is not an easy feat.

level 1   *Name the youngest player to score 50 points in an NBA game.*

level 2   *In what year did he do it?*

level 3   *How old was he when he hit the 50-point mark?*

question 9 answers

level 1   Wilt Chamberlain

level 2   He led in scoring seven times, in rebounds 11 times and in assists once (1967/68).

level 3   *a*   1959/60
         b   37.6 ppg.

question 10 answers

level 1   Rick Barry

level 2   1965

level 3   21 years, 261 days old. Allen Iverson was a bit older (yet still 21) when he scored 50 in 1997.

teammates

- The only player to be a teammate of Michael Jordan, Magic Johnson *and* Shaquille O'Neal is Corie Blount (Bulls 1993-95 and Lakers 1995-present).
- Two-time WNBA MVP Cynthia Cooper and Phoenix Mercury head coach Cheryl Miller were teammates on three USC women's teams that reached the Final Four. The 1983 and '84 teams won national championships, while the '86 team lost in the title game to Texas.
- The last NBA teammates to rank 1-2 in scoring are Denver's Alex English (28.4 ppg.) and Kiki Vandeweghe (26.7) in 1982/83.
- 1981/82 Celtics teammates Larry Bird and Danny Ainge are NBA head coaches going into the 1998/99 season. Another member of that team, M.L. Carr, coached Boston from 1995 to '97, while Chris Ford led the Bucks from 1996 to '98.
- Robert Horry, James Robinson, Jason Caffey and Roy Rogers were all teammates of Latrell Sprewell in Alabama.

inside the numbers

In 1997/98, Tim Duncan and David Robinson became the eighth set of teammates to each average more than 20 points and 10 rebounds a game in a season. The 1959/60 St. Louis Hawks are the only team to have three players in the 20/10 club:

season	team	teammates (points, rebounds)
1997/98	Spurs	Tim Duncan (21.1, 11.9), David Robinson (21.6, 10.6)
1992/93	Hornets	Alonzo Mourning (21.0, 10.3), Larry Johnson (22.1, 10.5)
1985/86	76ers	Moses Malone (23.8, 11.8), Charles Barkley (20.0, 12.8)
1984/85	Rockets	Hakeem Olajuwon (20.6, 11.9), Ralph Sampson (22.1, 10.4)
1968/69	Lakers	Wilt Chamberlain (20.5, 21.1), Elgin Baylor (24.8, 10.6)
1960/61	Hawks	Bob Pettit (27.9, 20.3), Clyde Lovellette (22.0, 10.1)
1959/60	Hawks	Bob Pettit (26.1, 17.0), Clyde Lovellette (20.8, 10.6), Cliff Hagan (24.8,10.7)
1958/59	Hawks	Bob Pettit (29.2, 16.4), Cliff Hagan (23.7, 10.9)

total access
rich eisen

"I was at the live auction at the 1998 Jimmy V Celebrity Golf Classic, which raises money for cancer research. Michael Jordan and Charles Barkley began bidding against each other on a Harley-Davidson Sportster, and the bidding went up in thousand-dollar increments until it quickly reached $20,000. Suddenly, they both hopped up onto the motorcycle together. Barkley joked to Jordan that he needed the bike more because *he* had made up his mind that he was retiring. Without missing a beat, M.J. replied, 'You have to play next year. You haven't won anything yet.' As usual, it was Jordan who came out on top, riding off with the Harley with a final bid of $30,000."

Q11

Isiah Thomas and Magic Johnson were friendly rivals over the years.

level 1   *They both attended Big Ten schools. Name the colleges they attended.*

level 2   *How many times did they meet in the NBA Finals?*

level 3   *Who won those match-ups?*

question 11 answers

level 1   Thomas went to Indiana, Johnson to Michigan State.

level 2   Twice

level 3   They split. The Lakers won in 1988, the Pistons won in 1989.

Q12

Michael Jordan had a memorable performance in Game 5 of the 1997 finals versus Utah, playing despite a virus.

level 1   *How many points did he score?*

level 2   *What did he shoot from the floor?*

level 3   *What was the final score of the game?*

question 12 answers

level 1   38 points

level 2   13 of 27

level 3   Chicago won 90-88.

streaks

---- The 1948 Washington Capitols and 1993 Houston Rockets share the best start to an NBA season: 15-0. The Capitols, coached by Red Auerbach, wound up falling to the Minneapolis Lakers in the NBA Finals, while the Rockets went on to win the first of their back-to-back NBA titles.

---- The last team the 1981/82 Cavaliers beat before beginning their record 24-game losing streak in 1981/82 was the San Diego Clippers. The now-L.A. Clippers are also the last team the Nuggets beat before embarking on their 23-game slide in 1997/98. Denver's slide ended with a win over the Clippers.

---- Kareem Abdul-Jabbar (then Lew Alcindor) topped the 30-point barrier in his first nine playoff games with the Bucks in 1970. No other rookie has notched even two consecutive 30-point playoff performances.

---- Elgin Baylor holds the record for the most consecutive playoff games with 30 or more points, 11 straight in 1962.

---- The team with the all-time record for the most consecutive playoff appearances is the Philadelphia Warriors, with 22 between 1949/50 and 1970/71. The Trail Blazers have the longest active playoff appearance streak, with 16 straight appearances.

---- The 76ers lost a record nine consecutive home playoff games from 1968 to '71.

---- The record for most overtime games won without a loss in a season is seven, held by the 1961/62 Lakers. Their postseason—and their record—came to an end with an overtime loss to the Celtics in Game 7 of the NBA Finals.

---- The record for the most triple-overtime games in a season is three, by the 1951/52 Lakers, including two on back-to-back nights.

---- Karl Malone finished in the top five in scoring for 11 straight years from 1987 to '98. However, the Mailman has never won a scoring title, finishing second five times, third twice, fourth twice and fifth twice.

---- The record for most consecutive complete games played—all 48 minutes—is 74, held by Wilt Chamberlain. Chamberlain set the record with the Philadelphia Warriors during the 1961/62 season. He also played in 1,045 NBA games without fouling out, another record.

---- The 1995/96 Bulls, who finished 72-10, had just one two-game losing streak all season (at Denver, February 4, 1996, and at Phoenix, February 6, 1996). The Bulls enjoyed an 18-game win streak (December 29, 1995-February 2, 1996) and a 12-game win streak (November 27-December 23, 1995).

did you know?

Besides being the first woman to play in a men's pro league (the USBL in 1986 and '87), WNBA playoffs analyst Nancy Lieberman-Cline was also the first WNBA player to be fined for fighting. Her 1997 dust-up with Los Angeles's Jamila Wideman cost her $500.

Q13

One of the ugliest moments in NBA history took place when Kermit Washington and Rudy Tomjanovich got into a fistfight.

level 1   *When did the brawl occur?*

level 2   *Name the teams they played for.*

level 3   *For how many games was Kermit Washington suspended?*

Q14

Only three players in NBA history have scored at least 20,000 points, grabbed 6,000 rebounds and dished 6,000 assists.

level 1   *Name the trio.*

level 2   *Name the colleges this exceptional trio attended.*

level 3   *Michael Jordan is not on this list. Which category does he fall short in?*

question 13 answers

level 1   December 9, 1977

level 2   Washington played for the Lakers, Tomjanovich for the Rockets.

level 3   Washington received a 26-game suspension.

question 14 answers

level 1   *a* John Havlicek
           b Oscar Robertson
           c Clyde Drexler

level 2   *a* Ohio State
           b Cincinnati
           c Houston

level 3   Assists (5,012 as of the end of the 1997/98 season)

personal files

-:- Chuck Connors, better known as the star of TV's *The Rifleman*, is the first NBA player credited with shattering a backboard. The then-Celtic did it during warm-ups on November 5, 1946.

-:- Joe "Jellybean" Bryant, Kobe's father, spent eight seasons in the NBA, averaging 8.7 ppg.

-:- Pacers guard Jalen Rose's father is Jimmy Walker, the first overall pick in the 1967 draft (by Detroit).

-:- Pat Riley's father, Leon, was catcher with the Philadelphia Phillies in 1944.

-:- The Van Arsdale brothers were drafted back-to-back in 1965: the Knicks chose Dick 15th overall, while the Pistons tabbed Tom 16th.

-:- Keeping up with the Joneses: brothers Caldwell, Charles, Major and Wil Jones all played in the NBA.

-:- Sacramento Monarchs guard Ruthie Bolton-Holifield is a first lieutenant in the Army Reserves.

-:- Kareem Abdul-Jabbar led the team that broke the Harlem Globetrotters' 24-year, 8,829-game winning streak in 1985. The then-48-year-old Abdul-Jabbar made 15 of 16 shots from the field in a 91-90 victory.

-:- Dell Curry was drafted by the Baltimore Orioles in the 14th round of the MLB draft in 1985.

-:- Kevin Johnson was drafted by the Oakland Athletics in the 23rd round of the MLB draft in 1986.

-:- K.C. Jones was drafted by the Los Angeles Rams as a defensive back in the 30th round of the 1955 NFL draft.

-:- John Havlicek was chosen as a wide receiver by the Cleveland Browns in the seventh round of the 1962 NFL draft.

-:- Celtic Rick Fox's given name is Ulrich Alexander Fox.

-:- B.J. Armstrong's given name is Benjamin Roy Armstrong Jr.

-:- Chris Webber's given name is Mayce Edward Christopher Webber III.

-:- Jack Haley appeared in the video for Aerosmith's "Love in an Elevator."

-:- Dunbar High School in Baltimore produced NBA players Muggsy Bogues, Sam Cassell, David Wingate and Reggie Williams.

-:- On June 21, 1997, New York's Rhonda Blades made the first three-point shot in the WNBA.

-:- On January 25, 1988, Jazz guard Rickey Green scored the NBA's five millionth point, as part of a 119-96 win over Cleveland.

inside the numbers

In 1997/98, San Antonio's Tim Duncan became the fifth rookie since 1984/85 to average at least 20 ppg. and 10 rpg.:

rookie	season	ppg.	rpg.
Tim Duncan	1997/98	21.1	11.9
Shaquille O'Neal	1992/93	23.4	13.9
Alonzo Mourning	1992/93	21.0	10.3
David Robinson	1989/90	24.3	12.0
Hakeem Olajuwon	1984/85	20.6	11.9

Q 15

P.J. Carlesimo has had a noteworthy coaching career beyond his stormy relationship with Latrell Sprewell.

level 1   *Name the college he led to the NCAA championship game and the year.*

level 2   *Name the two current NBA players who played for Carlesimo at Seton Hall.*

level 3   *Which NBA franchise did he coach before joining the Golden State Warriors in 1997?*

question 15 answers

level 1   Seton Hall, 1989

level 2   Phoenix's Mark Bryant (1984-88) and Sacramento's Terry Dehere (1989-93)

level 3   Portland Trail Blazers

Q 16

In 1998, Larry Bird was named Coach of the Year in his rookie season.

level 1   *Name the only other men who were named Coach of the Year in their rookie season.*

level 2   *Name the Coach of the Year in Bird's rookie season as a player.*

level 3   *Name the only other Pacers coach to win the Coach of the Year Award.*

question 16 answers

level 1   *a*   Harry Gallatin (1962/63)
       b   Johnny Kerr (1966/67)
       c   Mike Schuler (1986/87)

level 2   Boston's Bill Fitch

level 3   No, it's not Jack Ramsay or Larry Brown. Jack McKinney took the honors in 1981, after leading the Pacers to their first 40-win season and their first playoff appearance.

the coaches

⊹ Only two men have won Rookie of the Year and Coach of the Year honors: Larry Bird (1980, 1998) and Tom Heinsohn (1957 and 1973). Both coached their teams to a franchise-record number of wins. Bird went 58-24 in his rookie year with the Pacers, while Heinsohn established the 68-14 in his fourth season with the Celtics.

⊹ Tom Heinsohn is also the only former Rookie of the Year to coach a Rookie of the Year (Dave Cowens/Celtics, 1971).

⊹ Utah's Jerry Sloan, with a postseason record of 64-56, has the most playoff victories without winning a title.

⊹ The coach with the most regular-season wins without winning a title is Don Nelson. Nellie has won 867 games in 21 seasons but is just 51-61 in the postseason.

⊹ The last NBA head coach/general manager to lead a team to a title was Red Holzman with the 1973 Knicks. Holzman has a retired number, 613, hanging at the Madison Square Garden and signifying his win total with the team.

⊹ Portland coach Mike Dunleavy was a player/coach for the Carolina Lightning of the All-American Basketball Association in 1977/78.

⊹ Scotty Robertson, the first coach of the New Orleans (now Utah) Jazz, lasted just 15 games in his first season, going 1-14.

⊹ Red Auerbach, known for his outstanding record with the Celtics, spent three seasons coaching the Washington Capitols (1946-49).

⊹ Three of the NBA's 50 Greatest Players, Clyde Drexler, Bob Cousy and Willis Reed, went on to coach Division I men's college basketball. Drexler was hired by his alma mater, the University of Houston, following his retirement after the 1997/98 season. Cousy was with Boston College for six seasons, winning 75 percent of his games. Reed spent four seasons at Creighton, posting a career record under .500 but winning 20 games in his final season.

⊹ Dick Motta is the only person in NBA history to coach two different teams to four consecutive seasons of improved wins. He did it with the Bulls from 1968/69 to 1971/72, and with the Mavericks from 1980/81 to 1983/84.

⊹ Coaching the Baltimore Bullets, Clair Bee posted the NBA's worst winning percentage (minimum 100 losses). From 1952 to '54, Bee went 34-116, a .227 winning percentage.

⊹ Former Bulls coach Phil Jackson wasn't always a Zen master. Jackson committed 360 personal fouls as a player in 1974/75, tying Bob Dandridge for the NBA lead that season.

⊹ The quickest coaching change in NBA history occurred when Dolph Schayes was fired as head coach of the Buffalo Braves after the first game of the 1971/72 season.

Q

At the 1998 draft, two teams had an NBA-high three first-round picks.

level 1   *Name the teams.*

level 2   *Name the team that had the most first-round picks in a single NBA draft and the year of that draft.*

level 3   *Name the players and the overall position in which each was drafted.*

question 17 answers

level 1   Rockets and Magic

level 2   Kings, 1990

level 3   *a*   Lionel Simmons (7th)
                 b   Travis Mays (14th)
                 c   Duane Causwell (18th)
                 d   Anthony Bonner (23rd)

Q

Only Kareem Abdul-Jabbar has been named NBA MVP more often than Bill Russell, a key element in the Celtics dynasty.

level 1   *How many times was Russell named NBA MVP? List the years.*

level 2   *How many championships did he win as player-coach with the Celtics? List the years.*

level 3   *What was his career scoring average?*

question 18 answers

level 1   Five: 1958, '61, '62, '63, '65

level 2   Two: 1968, '69

level 3   15.1 ppg.

franchise history

- The first two expansion teams in WNBA history were the Detroit Shock and Washington Mystics.
- The two teams that have met the most often in NBA history are the Knicks and Celtics, with Boston having the edge (237-155).
- The WNBA averaged 9,669 fans per game during its first season, 1997.
- On February 13, 1990, Rony Seikaly became the only Heat player to score 40 points against the Bulls. Miami still lost to Chicago, 107-95.
- Only three players have spent at least 10 seasons with the Phoenix Suns: Alvan Adams (13), Walter Davis (11) and Kevin Johnson (11).
- The New York Knicks have not lost a first-round playoff series since 1990/91.
- The 1974/75 Celtics and 1967/68 Knicks are the only teams with winning records to win more games on the road than at home during the regular season.
- The Rockets have lost both games in which Hakeem Olajuwon scored more than 50 points: April 19, 1990, against Denver and December 18, 1995, against Boston.
- San Antonio enjoyed the greatest one-season improvement in NBA history. The Spurs went from 21-61 in 1988/89 to 56-26 in 1989/90, posting 35 more wins.

inside the numbers

In 1997/98, the Sonics became one of only three franchises to win at least 55 games for six or more consecutive seasons. But Seattle is the only team never to have won at least one title during that stretch:

team	no. of seasons with 55+ wins	titles
1980-88 Celtics	9	3
1985-91 Lakers	7	3
1960-65 Celtics	6	6
1993-98 Sonics	6	0

total access
andrea kremer

"In 1994, when Toni Kukoc took that controversial final shot in Game 5 of the Bulls/Knicks series instead of Scottie Pippen, no one knew what had happened–except me and my cameraman. We'd been focusing on Pippen during the timeout and got the heated exchange between the disgruntled guard and Phil Jackson on tape. Pippen refused to enter the game, and everyone wanted to get the real story from Jackson, who wasn't talking to anybody. Well, I had just spent the past 10 days getting him to commit to doing ESPN's Sunday Conversation the very next morning. Setting up with the crew at the Bulls practice facility, I passed Phil and Jerry Krause in the stairwell. 'What's she doing here?' the Bulls G.M. growled. My heart sank. 'She had an interview scheduled,' Phil said. 'I gave her my word I'd talk to her, and I'm going to keep it.' He did–and we got the exclusive."

Q19

The Big O, Oscar Robertson, always excelled in All-Star competition.

level 1 *How many times was he voted All-Star Game MVP?*

level 2 *In which years did he win that honor?*

level 3 *What was his All-Star Game scoring average?*

question 19 answers

level 1 Three
level 2 1961, '64, '69
level 3 20.5 ppg.

Q20

The short-lived ABA played its first All-Star Game on January 9, 1968.

level 1 *Which city hosted the game?*

level 2 *Which team and conference did Connie Hawkins represent?*

level 3 *Name the game's MVP, who is currently an NBA coach.*

question 20 answers

level 1 Indianapolis
level 2 Hawkins played for the East as a member of the Pittsburgh Pipers.
level 3 Larry Brown

the last time

∴ The last time the regular-season champions from both the NBA and NHL won their respective postseason championships was 1989, when the bad boy Pistons won the first of their two NBA titles and the Calgary Flames won their first Stanley Cup.

∴ The last Rookie of the Year to play on an NBA championship team was Keith Wilkes of the Warriors in 1975. Wilkes went on to win three more titles with the Lakers. Tom Heinsohn is the only other Rookie of the Year to play on a champion team.

∴ The last player to lead the NBA in minutes while averaging under 40 minutes per game is Rodney McCray (39.5 in 1989/90).

∴ The last team to come back from 2-0 down in the NBA Finals and win the championship was the 1977 Trail Blazers. Coached by ESPN's Dr. Jack Ramsay, Portland came back to defeat the 76ers. The only other team to rally from a 2-0 deficit in the Finals was the '69 Celtics, who beat the Lakers.

inside the numbers

When Boston retired Robert Parish's number on January 18, 1997, the Chief's 00 became the 20th Celtics number to hang in the rafters, the most of any pro sports franchise.

franchise	sport	retired numbers
Celtics	NBA	20
Yankees	MLB*	15
Bears	NFL	13
Dodgers	MLB*	11
Giants	NFL	9
Canadiens	NHL	7
Bruins	NHL	7

*Includes Jackie Robinson's 42

did you know?

Fred Carter was defending against Pete Maravich the night Pistol Pete scored 50 points against the 76ers on January 16, 1972: 18 free throws and 14 field goals, for 25 points in the first half and 25 in the second. "In the locker room at half-time, my teammates said I looked like a guy on a race track just flagging the cars through," Carter says.

Q21

Michael Jordan holds the NBA record for points scored in a playoff game.

level 1   *Who was the opponent?*
When was the game?

level 2   *How many points did Jordan score?*

level 3   *How many field goals and free throws did he make? What was the final score?*

question 21 answers

level 1   Boston Celtics on April 20, 1986
level 2   63 points
level 3   22 field goals and 19 free throws in a 135-131 double overtime loss

Q22

Michael Jordan's career regular-season high, as well as the Bulls' all-time single game high, occurred on March 28, 1990.

level 1   *Name the team the Bulls were playing.*

level 2   *How many field goals and free throws did Jordan make?*
What was the final score?

level 3   *Name the highest-scoring player on the opposing team. How many points did he contribute?*

question 22 answers

level 1   Cleveland Cavaliers
level 2   He contributed 23 field goals and 21 free throws for 69 points in a 117-113 Bulls victory.
level 3   Craig Ehlo, with 26 points

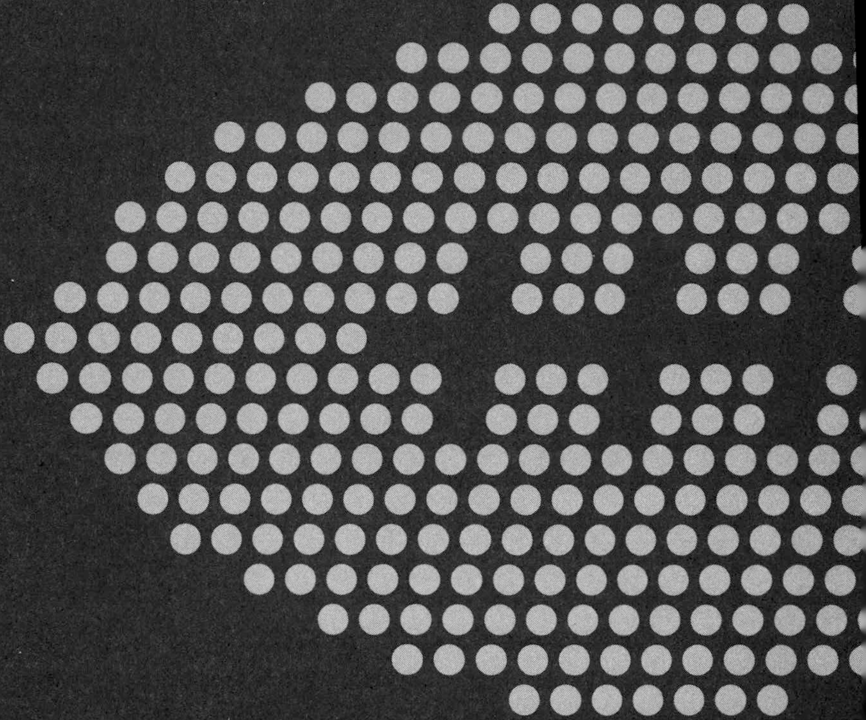

**do not remove
tag under
penalty of law**

Stats are good up to the
start of the 1998 season.

did you know?

SUNDAY NFL COUNTDOWN analyst Jim Kelly had six games
of 30 or more points as a high school basketball player at
East Brady High School in Pennsylvania. Recruited as a LB
by Joe Paterno, he was the winning QB when Miami upset
then-No. 1 Penn State, 17-14, on October 31, 1981.

the super bowl

-:- The three years that the Broncos started a season 6-0, they have gone on to play in the Super Bowl.
Denver lost to the Cowboys in Super Bowl XII and the Giants in Super Bowl XXI before beating the Packers in
Super Bowl XXXII.

-:- In five Super Bowl appearances (all victories), no 49ers quarterback (including reserves) has ever thrown an
interception, while starters Joe Montana and Steve Young combined for 17 touchdown passes.

-:- While no club has ever won three consecutive Super Bowls, the Packers are the only team to win three
straight championships. They turned the trick twice, 1929-31 and 1965-67.

-:- The Packers and Redskins each won three Super Bowls without having a 1,000-yard rusher in any of their
title seasons.

-:- The only player to play in the Super Bowl for three different teams is Preston Pearson
(1969 Colts, 1975 Steelers, 1976 Cowboys). Matt Millen (Raiders, 49ers, Redskins) and Jeff Rutledge
(Rams, Giants, Redskins) were both on three Super Bowl teams but didn't play in every Super Bowl game.

-:- The only two teams to play in the Hall of Fame Game and reach the Super Bowl in the same season are the
1988 Bengals and the 1994 Chargers. The Bengals beat the L.A. Rams 14-7 in the Hall of Fame Game and
later went on to Super Bowl XXIII, which they lost to the 49ers 20-16. The Chargers lost to the Falcons
21-17 in the Hall of Fame Game, then lost Super Bowl XXIX to the 49ers 49-26.

-:- While the Broncos are the sixth team to go to at least five Super Bowls, they are the only club in that group
to meet a different foe (Cowboys, Giants, Redskins, 49ers, Packers) in each contest.

-:- New Orleans hosted the first Super Bowl under a dome (Louisiana Superdome) in 1978, Super Bowl XII.
Dallas beat Denver 27-10 as the Cowboys intercepted four Craig Morton passes.

-:- Of the last 12 Super Bowl MVPs, only one played defense (Dallas's Larry Brown, Super Bowl XXX).

-:- The only championship game in which no interceptions were thrown was Super Bowl XXV (Giants-Bills).

-:- The Steelers and Cowboys hold the Super Bowl record for fewest penalties: two, in Super Bowl X.

inside the numbers

Wonder why Joe Montana was so revered? Here are the top four performances by a QB in the Super Bowl:

quarterback	super bowl	yards	comp-att.	td-int.	outcome
Joe Montana	XXIII	357	23-36	2-0	won 20-16
Doug Williams	XXII	340	18-29	4-1	won 42-10
Joe Montana	XIX	331	24-35	3-0	won 38-16
Steve Young	XXIX	325	24-36	6-0	won 49-26

You again! Here's how teams who met in the Super Bowl fared in their first rematch the following season:

super bowl	result	rematch result
IV 1970	Chiefs 23, Vikings 7	Vikings 27, Chiefs 10
XI 1977	Raiders 32, Vikings 14	Raiders 35, Vikings 13
XIII 1979	Steelers 35, Cowboys 31	Steelers 14, Cowboys 3
XXVII 1993	Cowboys 52, Bills 17	Bills 13, Cowboys 10
XXXI 1997	Packers 35, Patriots 21	Packers 28, Patriots 10

Nine times, the team that led the NFL in scoring defense won the Super Bowl the same season:

season	team	ppg. allowed
1996	Packers	13.1
1990	Giants	13.2
1985	Bears	12.4
1984	49ers	14.2
1982	Redskins	14.2
1978	Steelers	12.2
1973	Dolphins	10.7
1972	Dolphins	12.2
1966	Packers	11.6

the playoffs

-⊹- 1996 was the first time that all four teams in the conference championship games (Cowboys and Packers in the NFC; Steelers and Colts in the AFC) were previous Super Bowl winners. It was also the first time that two teams from the original NFL met in the AFC championship game. The Colts, when they were located in Baltimore, were part of the NFL from 1950 to '69. The Steelers played in the NFL from 1933 to '69.

-⊹- The Packers are 12-0 at home in postseason games (10-0 at Lambeau Field, 2-0 at Milwaukee), including 5-0 in championship games (4-0 at Lambeau Field, 1-0 at Milwaukee). In those games, Green Bay has outscored the opposition 329-128.

-⊹- Since the merger, the AFC and NFC championship games have both been decided by a touchdown or less in the same year just once. In 1987, Denver defeated Cleveland 38-33 to win the AFC, while Washington took the NFC crown from Minnesota 17-10.

-⊹- The only team to win a division title after having that year's No. 1 overall draft selection is the 1968 Vikings. The Vikings chose tackle Ron Yary out of USC and won the Central Division title, followed by a conference championship loss to the Baltimore Colts. The only other teams to reach the playoffs after having the No.1 draft pick are the 1991 Cowboys, the 1982 Patriots (who benefited from a strike-shortened season) and the 1978 Oilers.

-⊹- In the playoffs, the only time a team has defeated the same opponent two years in a row on the road is Washington at Chicago, 1986 and '87.

-⊹- Only three teams (1969 Chiefs, 1980 Raiders and 1997 Broncos) have won two road playoff games and then gone on to win the Super Bowl. The 1998 Patriots won three straight road playoff games, but lost Super Bowl XX to the Bears 46-10.

-⊹- Only four 0-3 teams—1981 Jets (0-3), 1982 Buccaneers (0-3), 1992 Chargers (0-4) and the 1995 Lions (0-3)—have rebounded to make the playoffs.

-⊹- The Browns are the only team to make the playoffs twice with a non-winning record: they went to the 1982 playoffs with a 4-5 mark and won the AFC Central in 1985 with an 8-8 record.

-⊹- Both road teams have won conference championship games on three occasions: Dallas and Buffalo in 1992, Green Bay and Kansas City in 1966, and Green Bay and Denver in 1998.

-⊹- The Jaguars are the only expansion team to make the playoffs in two of their first three seasons.

total access
andrea kremer

"I grew up totally devoted to the Miami Dolphins. When Bob Griese broke his leg, I sent him a Get Well card. When the Dolphins' record 1972 winning streak finally came to an end with a loss to Oakland the next season, I wrote Don Shula a condolence letter. I even named my two-year-old Border collie, Zonk, after my favorite player. Some little girls had Barbie. I had Larry Csonka."

inside the numbers

Wild card teams have had pretty solid records at times (since 1978):

year	team vs. team	winner
1980	Rams 11-5 at Cowboys 12-4	Rams, 24-17
1984	Raiders 11-5 at Seahawks 12-4	Seahawks, 13-7
1990	Chiefs 11-5 at Dolphins 12-4	Dolphins, 17-16
1992	Eagles 11-5 at Saints 12-4	Eagles, 36-20
1997	Jaguars 11-5 at Broncos 12-4	Broncos, 42-17

During playoffs is the wrong time to see the offense struggle. Here are the lowest-scoring playoff games (1966-97):

points	final score	year	game
5	Cowboys 5, Lions 0	1970	NFC Divisional Playoffs
9	Rams 9, Buccaneers 0	1979	NFC Championship
13	Steelers 7, Patriots 6	1997	AFC Divisional Playoffs
14	49ers 14, Eagles 0	1996	NFC Wild Card Game
14	Dolphins 14, Jets 0	1982	AFC Championship Game

These teams have been the most dominant within their divisions:

team	division	years	titles
Rams	NFC West	1973-79	7
Steelers	AFC Central	1974-79	6
Vikings	NFC Central	1973-78	6
Cowboys	NFC East	1992-96	5
49ers	NFC West	1986-90	5
Bears	NFC Central	1984-88	5
Raiders	AFC West	1972-76	5

May **10**

1955 Chris Berman is born.
1969 The NFL is born when the National Football League
merges with the American Football League.

.⋅: Chicago Cardinals star Ernie Nevers set the record for points in an NFL game with 40 (six touchdowns, four extra points), set November 28, 1929, versus the Bears. That mark has held for almost 70 years.

.⋅: Jim Brown holds the record for most seasons leading the league in rushing (eight). He is also the only player to finish his NFL career with more touchdowns than games played, retiring in 1965 with 126 TDs in 118 games.

.⋅: Sammy Baugh holds the NFL record for most seasons leading the league in passing (six). The former Redskin QB and defensive end is also the only player to pass for four touchdowns and intercept four passes (November 14, 1943, in a 42-20 victory over the Lions).

.⋅: The single-season record for highest average gain per carry is 8.4 yards, set by Chicago's Beattie Feathers in 1934, who rushed for 1,004 yards on 119 attempts. In 1997, his best season, Barry Sanders averaged 6.1 yards per carry, rushing for 2,053 yards in 335 attempts.

.⋅: The 1972 Dolphins are the only NFL team to finish a season unbeaten and untied and win the title. The first NFL team to finish without a loss and win the championship was the 1922 Canton Bulldogs, who went 10-0 with two ties.

.⋅: Since regular-season overtime was instituted in 1974, the Steelers' 14-5-1 overtime record, including a 3-0 record in 1997, is the NFL's best.

.⋅: O.J. Simpson set the record for best opening game performance by a running back. On September 16, 1973, Simpson rushed for 250 yards on 29 carries, including an 80-yard run, and had two TDs against the Patriots.

.⋅: Vikings wide receiver Anthony Carter holds the record for receiving yards in a playoff game, with 227 against the Niners on January 9, 1988.

.⋅: Morten Andersen has the mark for most field goals of 50 or more yards (eight) in one season, set in 1995.

.⋅: Rams receiver Tom Fears caught a record 18 passes versus the Packers on December 3, 1950.

.⋅: The Packers' franchise record for interceptions in one season is 10, set by Irv Comp in 1943.

.⋅: The only man to run and pass for 1,000 or more yards in the same season was Orban Sanders of the New York Yankees of the AAFC in 1947. He passed for 1,442 yards and ran for 1,432.

.⋅: The NFL's longest non-touchdown pass was 98 yards, completed on December 10, 1972, from Cardinals quarterback Jim Hart to Ahmad Rashad (then known as Bobby Moore). St. Louis beat the Rams 24-14, only one of two home wins in 1972.

inside the numbers

Dan Marino and John Elway share the NFL record for career 3,000-yard passing seasons:

player	number of 3,000-yard passing seasons
Dan Marino	12
John Elway	12
Warren Moon	9
Joe Montana	8
Jim Kelly	8

Q1

The 32 Super Bowl championships have been won by a total of 18 head coaches.

level 1 *Name the only head coach to win four Super Bowl championships.*

level 2 *Name the only head coaches to take two different franchises to the Super Bowl.*

level 3 *Name the only head coaches to win a college national championship and a Super Bowl.*

question 1 answers

level 1   Chuck Noll

level 2   Don Shula and Bill Parcells

level 3   Jimmy Johnson and Barry Switzer

Q2

Football is a team game, but there have been some singular accomplishments attached to the Super Bowl.

level 1 *Name the only player to win three Super Bowl MVP awards.*

level 2 *Name the only coach to win three Super Bowls with three different quarterbacks. Name the quarterbacks.*

level 3 *Name the only player to win three consecutive Super Bowl titles.*

question 2 answers

level 1   Joe Montana with the 49ers in XVI, XIX and XXIV

level 2   Joe Gibbs with the Redskins
     a   Joe Theismann-XVII
     b   Doug Williams-XXII
     c   Mark Rypien-XXVI

level 3   Ken Norton Jr. won with the Cowboys in XXVII and XXVIII and with the 49ers in XXIX.

jerry rice

- ❖ Jerry Rice picked up the nickname All World at Mississippi Valley State, where he set NCAA career records for receptions (301) and receiving yards (4,693), catching 50 touchdown passes.
- ❖ He was the No. 1 overall pick by the Birmingham Stallions in the 1985 USFL draft. That's the same league that helped develop his future 49ers quarterback, Steve Young, who played two seasons for the L.A. Express.
- ❖ He was the first pick by the 49ers in the 1985 NFL draft. Fifteen players were drafted ahead of him, including two other wide receivers who are no longer active (Al Toon of the Jets, 10th overall, and Eddie Brown of the Bengals, 13th overall).
- ❖ He didn't catch his first TD pass as a pro until his fifth career game, a 25-yard pass from Joe Montana in the final quarter against the Falcons on October 6, 1985.
- ❖ Both his career highs in receptions (140) and touchdowns (22) also came against the Falcons.
- ❖ He had just three touchdown receptions in his first season, but he has been making up for it ever since.
- ❖ He has scored at least one touchdown against every NFL franchise he has faced.

⁙ Talk about establishing benchmarks. Here are some of the league records achieved by the only non-kicker to score 1,000 career points in the NFL. He has the most:

Career receptions: 1,057	100-catch seasons: 4
Yards receiving: 16,455	Yards receiving in a season: 1,848 (1995)
Touchdowns: 166	Touchdown receptions in a season: 22 (1987)
Touchdown receptions: 155	Consecutive games with a touchdown: 13
Games with at least 100 yards receiving: 61	Consecutive 100-catch seasons: 3
1,000-yard receiving seasons: 11	Seasons with 50 or more catches: 11

⁙ Rice also holds 10 Super Bowl records, including most career receptions (28), most receptions in a game (11, tied with Bengals TE Dan Ross), most career points (42), most points in a game (18), most career touchdowns (seven) and most touchdown receptions (seven). He also has the most points in a Super Bowl (18), the most career yards receiving (512), the most yards receiving in a game (215) and the most touchdowns in a game (three, tied with three others).

⁙ Watch out, Michael Jordan and Mario Lemieux. Rice made the cut at the 1997 AT&T Pebble Beach PGA event.

awards

❖ Since the merger, the only player to be named Pro Bowl MVP from a Super Bowl-winning team is Dolphin Garo Yepremian. In 1974 Miami won Super Bowl VIII 24-7 over the Vikings (Larry Csonka won MVP). In the Pro Bowl, Yepremian kicked five field goals to contribute all the AFC points in a 15-13 victory, including a 42-yard game winner with 21 seconds left.

❖ Cal Hubbard is the only member of both the Pro Football and Baseball Halls of Fame. Hubbard's football career included stints with the Giants(1929-33, '36) and the Packers (1935). He played with the Pittsburgh Pirates (1936), then became an umpire from 1936 to '51. He was inducted into Canton in 1963 and into Cooperstown in 1978.

❖ The first Heisman Trophy winner to win a Pro Football MVP Award was Frank Sinkwich in 1944. Sinkwich had won the Heisman at the University of Georgia in 1942.

❖ Eight Heisman Trophy winners have played for the Lions: Frank Sinkwich, Doak Walker, Leon Hart, Howard "Hopalong" Cassady, Steve Owens, Billy Sims, Barry Sanders and Andre Ware. Another Heisman winner, Gino Torretta, was on the practice squad but never played.

❖ Pro Football Hall of Fame linebackers Willie Lanier (1966) and Jack Lambert (1972) were both MVPs of the Florida Citrus Bowl (formerly the Tangerine Bowl).

❖ The first NFL Rookie of the Year was Alan Ameche of Baltimore in 1955. He was better known for scoring the winning touchdown in the 1958 NFL championship game.

❖ Johnny Unitas was voted Most Outstanding Back in the Pro Bowl in consecutive years (1960-61).

❖ Dallas's Chuck Howley is the only player on a losing team—as well as the only linebacker—to earn Super Bowl MVP honors (Super Bowl V).

total access
kenny mayne

"I knew I had no hope of making the Seahawks – my plan was to stick around long enough to make enough of a name for a USFL signing. (What the hell, they gave me free sweats.) One day in my little free agent tryout, I ran up against Kenny Easley in a passing drill. Mark McGrath was running the route for me, a deep curl at about 18, and Easley had it covered. McGrath came back … and came back some more. Easley was on him like a new layer of skin, but we completed the pass. Okay, there was no rush, I had seven seconds to throw the ball, that 18-yard curl ended up being a five-yard curl, and McGrath had to have the ball removed by the jaws of life. Still, Kenny Mayne beat Kenny Easley on a route."

Q**3**

The NFL instituted regular-season overtime in 1974.

level 1   *Who played in the first regular-season overtime game in 1974?*

level 2   *Who won the first regular-season overtime game in 1974?*

level 3   *Name the team that played in an NFL-record five overtime games in one season. Name the season.*

question 3 answers

level 1   Steelers and Broncos
          (ended in a 35-35 tie)

level 2   Jets over Giants 26-20

level 3   Packers in 1983

Q4

ABC's *Monday Night Football* kicked off its 29th season in 1998.

level 1   *Name the teams that played in the first ABC Monday Night Football game.*

level 2   *Who won the game?*

level 3   *Name the team that has played in the most ABC Monday Night Football games.*

question 4 answers

level 1   Browns and Jets

level 2   Browns 31-21

level 3   The Dolphins have appeared 57 times.

the underestimated rusher

When you think Herschel Walker, do you also think Hall of Fame?

∴ Probably not. But consider that in the long history of professional football, no man has accounted for more yardage than Herschel Walker.

∴ Here are the all-time leaders in combined (or all-purpose) yardage, which includes rushing, receiving, punt return, kickoff return and—in the CFL—missed-field-goal return yardage.

player	combined yardage	leagues – seasons
Herschel Walker*	25,283	USFL-1, NFL-12
Michael Clemons*	22,291	CFL-11
Henry Williams*	21,928	USFL-1, NFL-1, CFL-10
Walter Payton	21,803	NFL-13
George Reed	20,051	CFL-13
Rufus Crawford	19,331	NFL-1, CFL-7
Leo Lewis	18,576	CFL-12
Marcus Allen	17,648	NFL-16
Jerry Rice*	17,075	NFL-13
Tony Dorsett	16,326	NFL-12

*Active. Combined yardage for Clemons and Williams include the first eight games of the 1998 CFL season, while stats for Walker and Rice are through the 1997 season.

Of the 10 players on the list, half spent the majority of their careers in the CFL, including current Michael "Pinball" Clemons and Henry "Gizmo" Williams. Of the other five, two are in the Hall of Fame (Walter Payton and Tony Dorsett), and two more are virtual locks for eventual enshrinement (Marcus Allen and Jerry Rice). And then there's Herschel Walker, right up there on top.

∴ Walker will be remembered for a lot of things that have nothing to do with how good a player he is: a stupid trade by the Vikings, an alleged (by some members of the press) suicide attempt, his dalliance with world-class bobsledding and his legendary workout regimen (which helped keep him in the NFL long past the age at which most running backs retire).

∴ Walker *should* be remembered as an unselfish football player, one who readily volunteered for special-teams duties late in his career, one who, for a five-year stretch, was perhaps the most talented runner on the planet. Does a stint in the USFL, clearly a lesser league, mean he should be denied his place in Canton? I don't think so. Say we take out those three USFL seasons. Walker plummets all the way to ... *second* on the NFL's all-time, all-purpose yardage list, ahead of Allen and Dorsett. And after all, it is called the *Professional* Football Hall of Fame, not the *National* Football Hall of Fame. *rob neyer*

inside the numbers

Entering the 1998 season, these teams* have gone the longest without a 1,000-yard rusher:

season	team	last 1000-yard rusher	total yardage
1989	Saints	Dalton Hilliard	1,262
1991	Chiefs	Christian Okoye	1,031
1994	Rams	Jerome Bettis	1,025
1994	Chargers	Natrone Means	1,350

*The Ravens and Jaguars have never had a 1,000-yard rusher, while the Cleveland Browns last had two in 1985 (Kevin Mack and Earnest Byner).

Players with the most 1,000-yard rushing seasons:

player	no. of seasons	years
Walter Payton	10	1976-81, 1983-86
Barry Sanders	9	1989-97
Franco Harris	8	1972, 1974-79, '83
Tony Dorsett	8	1977-81, 1983-85
Thurman Thomas	8	1989-96

.∵. The Patriots are the oldest existing franchise in any major sport to have never won a championship. New England entered the AFL in 1960 and is winless in two Super Bowl trips.

.∵. The Buccaneers have returned 1,323 kickoffs in their 22-year history, yet have never scored a touchdown on a kickoff return.

.∵. The coldest game played was on January 10, 1992, when the temperature dropped to minus 59 degrees as the hometown Bengals beat the Chargers 27-7.

.∵. The most lopsided NFL game took place on December 8, 1940, when the Bears won the Super Bowl with a 73-0 rout of the Redskins.

.∵. On November 4, 1979, the Seahawks set the NFL record for worst offensive performance, with minus seven total yards in a 24-0 loss to the Rams.

.∵. Following both of their Super Bowl championship campaigns (XXI and XXV), the Giants failed to make the playoffs. They are the only franchise to manage that feat twice.

.∵. The Lions lost both the highest-scoring postseason tilt in NFL history—58-37 to the Eagles in the 1995 wild card game—and the lowest scoring—5-0, to Dallas in the 1970 NFC divisional playoffs.

.∵. Detroit's 30-7 loss to the Redskins at Jack Kent Cooke Stadium in 1997 dropped the Lions' lifetime record in Washington (including playoffs) to 0-19.

.∵. In 1974, Denver hosted the NFL's first, and most futile, regular-season overtime game. After five quarters, the Broncos and Steelers remained tied 35-35.

.∵. The Jets have not had a quarterback lead or share in the NFL race for most touchdown passes since Joe Namath had 19 in 1972.

.∵. Bert Jones and Warren Moon were sacked the most times in a game, 12. On October 26, 1980, Jones was taken down 12 times by the Cardinals, who won 17-10.
Moon, then a member of the Oilers, was leveled by the Cowboys on September 29, 1985 (Dallas won, 17-10).

.∵. The most rushing yards gained in a losing effort is 273, by O.J. Simpson against the Lions on Thanksgiving Day 1976. The Bills somehow managed to lose 27-14 despite Simpson's efforts.

.∵. For all their Super Bowl success (5-0), the 49ers are the only team to have twice been eliminated in the playoffs by the same team in three straight years: the Cowboys (1970-72) and the Packers (1995-97).

.∵. The team that has gone the longest without a 10-win season is the Cardinals, who went 10-4 under Don Coryell in 1976. The Cardinals haven't had a winning season since 1984.

.∵. The only division winner to have a losing division record is the 1971 49ers. San Francisco finished 2-4 within the NFC West (9-5 overall) before losing to Dallas in the NFC championship game.

.∵. The last NFL team to fail to complete a pass in a game was the Bills on September 29, 1974, versus the Jets. High winds and rain left Joe Ferguson with an 0-2 day. O.J. Simpson took over for 117 yards on 31 carries as the Bills won 16-12. Joe Namath finished 2-13, not getting his first completion until there was only 1:50 left.

.∵. The most points allowed in a season is 533, by the Baltimore Colts in 1981.

.Х: The record for fewest touchdowns in one season is three, established by the expansion Cincinnati Reds in 1933.

.Х: Adrian Murrell of the Jets joined Dick Bass of the 1962 Rams and Gale Sayers of the 1969 Bears as the only NFL players to rush for 1,000 yards for a team with one win.

.Х: The 1996 Steelers are the only Super Bowl team to lose to a first-year expansion team that same season. The Jaguars beat the Steelers 20-16 in Week 6.

.Х: The last time a Bears quarterback led the NFL in touchdown passes was 1949. Johnny Lujack, the 1947 Heisman winner from Notre Dame, threw 23 touchdown passes in 1949, helping the Bears go 9-3, although they didn't make the playoffs.

inside the numbers

Some teams believe in finishing even-steven (since 1970; excluding nine-game strike season in 1982):

year	team	record	pts. for / against
1994	Eagles	7-9	308 / 308
1986	Falcons	7-8-1	280 / 280
1984	Bengals	8-8	339 / 339
1984	Cowboys	9-7	308 / 308

One is the loneliest number, especially if you finish 1-15 (since 1978):

year	team	lone victory
1980	Saints	at Jets, 21-20
1989	Cowboys	at Redskins, 13-3
1990	Patriots	at Colts, 16-14
1991	Colts	at Jets, 28-27
1996	Jets	at Cardinals, 31-21

andre aldridge

total access
espnews

"Marcus Allen and I were Little League teammates in San Diego, members of the dominating Encanto Braves. I played second, Marcus played shortstop, but I don't remember him making many outs. His older brother, Harold, was the catcher and his dad, Red, was our coach. Two other Braves, Ty and Kevin Waller, both went on to play pro ball (Ty with the Cubs and Astros and Kevin in the Braves organization)."

humble beginnings

- Brett Favre started his career in Atlanta, playing two games for the Falcons in 1991. He attempted just five passes in those two outings, and his only two completions were to members of the opposition (interceptions).
- Cris Carter had five receptions in nine games as a rookie with the Eagles in 1987. Not many for a guy who has had 122 receptions in two different seasons.
- Steve Young began his pro football career with the USFL's Los Angeles Express in 1984. He played 25 games for the Express, throwing 16 touchdowns and 22 interceptions.
- Jay Novacek began his career with the St. Louis Cardinals. He had just one catch in 16 games his first season.
- Pro Bowl guard Nate Newton started his pro career as an undrafted free agent with the Redskins. He was cut before his first regular-season game.
- Vikings wide receiver Jake Reed had 11 receptions in his first 27 NFL games (1991-93). He then made 85 receptions in 1994.
- All-Pro wide receiver Herman Moore made just 11 catches during his rookie season.
- Warren Moon made more interceptions than touchdowns in each of his first three NFL seasons (1984-12 TD, 14 INT; 1985-15 TD, 19 INT; 1986-13 TD, and a league-high 26 INT).
- Hall of Fame wide receiver Fred Biletnikoff didn't have a touchdown catch among his 24 receptions as a rookie with the Raiders in 1965.
- Hall of Fame quarterback Len Dawson threw just 45 passes (21 completions, two touchdowns, five interceptions) from 1957 to '61.
- Terry Bradshaw threw 24 interceptions and a mere six touchdown passes as a rookie with the Steelers in 1970.
- Charlie Joiner, who finished his career with 750 receptions, made just seven as a rookie with the Oilers in 1969.
- Johnny Unitas made nine touchdown passes and 10 interceptions in 12 games as a rookie with the Baltimore Colts in 1956.

did you know?

Sterling Sharpe still holds the University of South Carolina records for single-season receptions (74 in 1986), receiving yards (1,106 in 1986), and career marks for receptions (169) and receiving yards (2,497). He played with the Gamecocks in 1983, 1985-87. On October 12, 1985, he returned a kickoff 104 yards for a touchdown versus Duke.

Q5

Dan Marino and Jerry Rice have played in a record 32 *Monday Night Football* games.

level 1   *Name the player who scored the first touchdown on* Monday Night Football.

level 2   *Name the players who connected for the longest pass in* Monday Night Football *history.*

level 3   *Name the player who owns the record for the most rushing yards in a* Monday Night Football *game.*

question 5 answers

level 1   Browns WR Gary Collins
8-yard TD pass from QB Bill Nelson

level 2   Packers QB Brett Favre and
WR Robert Brooks
99 yards at Chicago in 1995

level 3   L.A. Raiders RB Bo Jackson
221 yards at Seattle in 1997

Q6

There were no division titles awarded in 1982 due to the players' strike.

level 1   *Name the team that has won the most division titles since 1970.*

level 2   *Name the only team to win their division without a winning record.*
What was the year?

level 3   *Name the only division whose champion has posted a minimum of 10 wins each year.*

question 6 answers

level 1   49ers, 16 titles
level 2   The 1985 Browns won the AFC
Central with an 8-8 mark.
level 3   NFC East

-:- Bart Starr was the lowest-drafted future Super Bowl MVP, selected by the Packers in the 17th round of the 1956 draft.

-:- The defensive back selected highest in the NFL draft is Colorado A&M's Gary Glick. He was selected No.1 overall by Pittsburgh in the 1956 NFL draft, and played seven seasons with the Steelers, Redskins and Chargers.

-:- In the 1971 NFL draft, the first three picks were quarterbacks: Jim Plunkett, Archie Manning and Dan Pastorini.

-:- Not a single quarterback was picked in the first round of the 1988 draft. The first QB chosen was Chris Chandler in Round 3 (76th overall) by the Colts.

-:- Before Orlando Pace was taken first overall by the Rams in 1997, the last offensive lineman to be selected No. 1 overall was Ron Yary by the Vikings in 1968.

-:- Two running backs were selected ahead of Marcus Allen (10th overall by the Raiders) in the 1982 draft. USC's Allen wasn't even the top back chosen from the Pac-10 that year. That honor went to Stanford's Darrin Nelson (seventh, Vikings) and Arizona State's Gerald Riggs (ninth, Falcons).

-:- Curtis Martin was the 10th running back chosen in the 1995 draft, selected by the Patriots (74th overall).

-:- In 1965, the Bears drafted both Dick Butkus and Gale Sayers in the first round.

-:- The Bills have fared well on offense with stars coming after the first round. Thurman Thomas was the 40th overall pick in the 1988 draft, while Andre Reed was a fourth-round pick in the 1985 draft, selected 86th overall.

-:- All-Pro linebacker/defensive lineman Kevin Greene was the 113th overall selection in the 1985 draft, selected by the Rams.

-:- Former 49ers tight end Brent Jones was a fifth-round pick in the 1986 draft, selected 135th overall by the Steelers.

-:- Bengals QB Jeff Blake was a sixth-round pick in 1992, selected 166th overall by the Jets.

-:- Jaguars wide receiver Keenan McCardell was a 12th-round pick in the 1991 draft, selected 326th overall by the Redskins.

-:- The initial first-round draft pick of the Kansas City Chiefs (formerly the Dallas Texans) was quarterback Don Meredith (in 1960).

-:- The Rams selected quarterback Roman Gabriel and defensive tackle Merlin Olsen in the first round of the same NFL draft (1962).

inside the numbers

Here are top rushing performances in a single game by a rookie:

yards	player	team vs. opponent	year
246	Corey Dillon	Bengals vs. Oilers	1997
237	Jim Brown	Browns vs. Rams	1957
223	Tom Wilson	Rams vs. Packers	1956
221	Bo Jackson	L.A. Raiders vs. Seahawks	1987
212	Jerome Bettis	Rams vs. Saints	1993

Q 7

Five wild card teams have made it to the Super Bowl.

level 1   *Name the first wild card team to make it to the Super Bowl.*

level 2   *Name the first wild card team to win the Super Bowl.*

level 3   *Before wild card berths were awarded, what non-division winner won the Super Bowl?*

question 7 answers

level 1   Cowboys in Super Bowl X

level 2   Raiders in Super Bowl XV

level 3   Chiefs in Super Bowl IV

Q8

The NFC/NFL owns a 19-13 advantage in the 32 Super Bowls.

level 1   *Name the only current division where all five franchises have appeared in a Super Bowl.*

level 2   *Name the only NFL franchise to represent the NFL and the AFC in a Super Bowl.*

level 3   *Name the only team to win a Super Bowl a year after posting a losing record.*

question 8 answers

level 1   AFC East

level 2   Baltimore Colts
NFL in Super Bowl III
AFC in Super Bowl V

level 3   The Super Bowl XVI champion 49ers were 6-10 in 1980.

- Vikings All-Pro defensive lineman John Randle was not drafted. However, his brother, Ervin, was taken in the fifth round of the 1985 NFL draft by Tampa Bay.
- Franco Harris and Irving Fryar attended the same New Jersey high school, Rancocas Valley.
- Vikings wide receiver Jake Reed is the brother of Chiefs cornerback Dale Carter.
- Cowboys 1998 draft pick Flozell Adams is a cousin of Seattle Sonics guard Hersey Hawkins.
- Bears running back Bam Morris's cousin is boxer Terry Norris.
- Four Browner brothers played in the NFL: defensive back Jim (Bengals), defensive back Joey (Vikings, Bucs), linebacker Keith (Chargers, Raiders, 49ers, Bucs) and defensive end Ross (Bengals, Packers).
- Like father, like son rang true for the Buddes: Ed Budde was a Kansas City guard from 1963 to '76, earning Pro Bowl honors seven times. Son Brad was a Chiefs guard from 1980 to '86.

inside the numbers

While 1995 No. 1 overall draft pick Ki-Jana Carter has struggled to make an impact in the pros, these running backs had standout rookie seasons:

rookie	team	year	total rushing yardage
Eric Dickerson	Rams	1983	1,808
George Rogers	Saints	1981	1,674
Ottis Anderson	Cardinals	1979	1,605
Curtis Martin	Patriots	1995	1,487
Barry Sanders	Lions	1989	1,470
Earl Campbell	Oilers	1978	1,450
Curt Warner	Seahawks	1983	1,449
Jerome Bettis	Rams	1993	1,429
Eddie George	Oilers	1996	1,368
Rueben Mayes	Saints	1986	1,353

did you know?

Tom Jackson was a two-time Missouri Valley Conference
Player of the Year at Louisville (1970-72), where his coach
was ESPN's Lee Corso.

Q9

A bad start usually adds up to a bad season...but sometimes it doesn't.

level 1   *How many games did the Buccaneers lose before posting their first-ever victory?*

level 2   *Name the only two teams to advance to the Super Bowl following an 0-2 start.*

level 3   *Name the only team to advance to the playoffs following an 0-4 start.*

question 9 answers

level 1   26

level 2   Cowboys, in Super Bowl XXVIII, and Patriots, in Super Bowl XXXI

level 3   Chargers, in 1992

Q10

The Carolina Panthers and Jacksonville Jaguars joined the NFL in 1995.

level 1   *What year did the Buccaneers and Seahawks join the NFL?*

level 2   *What team did Seattle beat in 1976 for their first-ever victory?*

level 3   *What divisions housed the Buccaneers and Seahawks during their first seasons in the NFL?*

question 10 answers

level 1   1976

level 2   Tampa Bay 13-10

level 3   *a*   AFC West Buccaneers
         b   NFC West Seahawks

streaks

- The Cowboys lost their 10th scheduled game for 10 consecutive years from 1986 to '95. The streak ended when the Cowboys won at San Francisco 20-17 in overtime on November 10, 1996.
- Barry Sanders holds the NFL record for most consecutive 100-yard rushing games with 14 for the Lions in 1997.
- The 1997 Tennessee Oilers became the first NFL team to go without an interception in their first six games.
- Only Eric Dickerson and Terry Allen have rushed for more than 1,000 yards in consecutive seasons with two different teams. Dickerson rushed for 1,821 yards with the Rams in 1986 and 1,011 with the Colts in 1987 after a midseason trade. Allen rushed for 1,031 yards with the Vikings in 1994 and 1,309 with the Redskins in 1995. New Seahawk Ricky Watters could also join that list after gaining 1,000 yards in three straight seasons with the Eagles.
- Joe Montana has started in seven conference championship games, the most of any quarterback since the merger in 1970. Terry Bradshaw and Roger Staubach each made six starts, while John Elway has made five.
- Led by Don Coryell, the 1980-83 Cardinals offense was the only one to lead the NFL in first downs for four consecutive seasons.
- In the 28-year history of Three Rivers Stadium (1970-97), the Steelers have never had a losing season at home.
- The Dolphins hold the NFL record for consecutive victories at home, with 27 from 1971 to 1974.
- Only two teams have beaten the same opponent in the playoffs three seasons in a row. Green Bay defeated San Francisco in 1998, '97 and '96. The Cowboys pulled off the hat trick twice, defeating Green Bay in 1993, '94 and '95, and San Francisco in 1970, '71, and '72.
- The only player to catch 15 touchdown passes in a Division I-A season and 10 in an NFL season is Henry Ellard. Ellard caught 15 TD passes for Fresno State in 1982 and 10 for the L.A. Rams in 1988.
- Vikings defensive end Jim Marshall is the NFL's Iron Man, playing in 282 consecutive games from 1961 to '79.
- The Rams won an NFL-record seven straight (outright) NFC West titles from 1973 to '79.
- Florida has the longest consecutive streak of producing at least one NFL first-round pick: nine years (1983-1991).
- In 1996, the Vikings lost their sixth straight playoff game, tying the NFL record. Minnesota ended the streak by upsetting the N.Y. Giants in the 1997 playoffs 23-22. Before the Vikings, Cleveland was the last team to lose six straight postseason games (1969-1985).
- Miami holds the record for most consecutive wins against one opponent, with 20 victories over Buffalo (1970-79).
- The record for scoring in the most consecutive games is 222, held by Morten Andersen (1982-current).
- Tom Morrow intercepted passes in a record eight straight games from 1962 to '63.
- Tampa Bay is 0-17 when the game-time temperature is 40 degrees or lower.
- The Redskins haven't made the playoffs during a Democratic presidency since 1945. Washington's last postseason appearance was in 1992 shortly before Bill Clinton was sworn into office.

did you know?

Joe Theismann still holds the Notre Dame single-season passing yardage record (2,429 yards in 1970). His Irish mark for single-season completions (155 in 1970) was shattered by Ron Powlus in 1997 (182).

Q11

Warren Moon, Seattle's 41-year-old starting QB, was one of the most interesting late bloomers in NFL history.

level 1 *In what round was he drafted?*

level 2 *What was his age at the start of his first NFL season?*

level 3 *What is his greatest single-season passing yardage total?*

question 11 answers

level 1   He wasn't drafted by any NFL team. His pro career started with the Edmonton Eskimos in the CFL, where he won five Grey Cups between 1978 and '82.

level 2   He was 27.

level 3   In 1991, he passed for 4,690 yards.

Q12

Certain football teammates stay friends after their playing days are over. Playing in college and the NFL together can form a bond. That was the case on a historic Friday night in 1994.

level 1 *Name the former Bills teammate who drove O.J. Simpson in the white Bronco around Los Angeles while police trailed them, live coverage of which was broadcast during Game 5 of the 1994 Rockets/Knicks NBA championship series?*

level 2 *When and in what position were the pair drafted?*

level 3 *How many different franchises did that driver play for? Name the teams and years.*

question 12 answers

level 1   Former DL Al Cowlings, known as A.C. They were also college teammates at USC.

level 2   In 1969 and '70, the Bills chose Simpson and Cowlings, as their first-round draft picks (first and fifth overall respectively).

level 3
   a   Bills (1970-72)
   b   Oilers (1973-74)
   c   Rams (1975, '77)
   d   Seahawks (1976)
   e   49ers (1979)

the baseball connection

-:- Deion Sanders was originally drafted by the Royals in the sixth round of the 1985 MLB draft; he did not sign with them. Sanders eventually played in the majors with the Yankees (1989-90), Atlanta (1991-94), Cincinnati (1994-95, '97) and San Francisco (1995).

Ken Stabler was a pitcher at Foley High School in Alabama. He handed Baseball Hall of Fame pitcher Don Sutton his only loss in high school. Stabler also turned down a signing bonus offer from the Mets, opting instead for football.

-:- In the 1979 MLB draft, Kansas City selected Dan Marino in the fourth round (99th overall pick) and John Elway in the 18th round. Among players who were picked and signed after Marino and Elway that season were Don Mattingly (19th round) and Brett Butler (23rd round).

-:- John Elway played in the Yankees organization as an outfielder for the Class "A" Oneonta (N.Y.) Yankees in 1982. He batted .318 that season.

-:- Eagles quarterback Rodney Peete was also a 14th-round pick by Oakland in the 1988 MLB draft.

-:- Giants quarterback Danny Kanell was drafted by Milwaukee in 1992 and the Yankees in 1995.

-:- Tampa Bay safety John Lynch was a second-round choice by the Marlins in 1992. He finished the 1992 season with a 2.13 ERA with Erie of the "A" New York-Penn League.

-:- George Halas was an outfielder for the 1919 Yankees, batting .091 in 12 games.

-:- Bo Jackson played for three different MLB teams (Royals, White Sox and Angels).

inside the numbers

Entering 1998, the Marino-to-Clayton tandem had the most touchdown passes, just ahead of Young to Rice:

passer / receiver	touchdowns
Dan Marino / Mark Clayton	79
Steve Young / Jerry Rice	75
Jim Kelly / Andre Reed	65
Johnny Unitas / Raymond Berry	63
John Hadl / Lance Alworth	56

total access
nfl 2night
anthony muñoz

"Did you know that a recent inductee to the Pro Football Hall of Fame was undefeated as a pitcher at USC? Yes, that's me. I was 1-0 pitching for the Trojans! And going back to my high school baseball team, one of my teammates at Chaffey H.S. was current NL umpire Dana DeMuth."

Q

Winning a Heisman Trophy and earning Super Bowl MVP honors is a difficult double.

level 1   *How many times has it been done?*
level 2   *Name the players who have accomplished that feat.*
level 3   *In which Heisman years and Super Bowls did they win?*

question 13 answers

level 1		Four
level 2	*a*	Roger Staubach
	b	Jim Plunkett
	c	Marcus Allen
	d	Desmond Howard
level 3	*a*	1961-Heisman SB VI
	b	1970-Heisman SB XV
	c	1981-Heisman SB XVIII
	d	1991-Heisman SB XXXI

Q

Charles Haley was a money player whose teams fared well over the years.

level 1   *How many Super Bowls did he play in?*
level 2   *For how many different franchises did he play in the Super Bowl?*
level 3   *Name the teams and the number of times he played in the Super Bowl for them.*

question 14 answers

level 1		Five
level 2		Two
level 3	*a*	Cowboys 3
	b	49ers 2

the coaches

❖ Before Dick Vermeil ended his hiatus (sidelined from 1983-96) by signing with the Rams in 1997, Ted Marchibroda had the longest tenure between NFL coaching stints: 13 years, from 1979 to '92.

❖ The coach with the longest NFL career without a winning record is Marion Campbell, who coached the Falcons and Eagles for nine losing seasons. His best season was 1984, when the Eagles went 6-9-1.

❖ Mike Ditka and Tom Flores are the only two people who have played and coached on Super Bowl-winning teams. Ditka played for the champion Cowboys in Super Bowl VI and coached the Bears in Super Bowl XX. He also got a ring as an assistant with Dallas at Super Bowl XII. Flores was on the Chiefs' Super Bowl IV squad and coached the Raiders in Super Bowl XVIII.

❖ Before every home game in 1988, then-Houston Oilers coach Jerry Glanville left tickets at the gate for Elvis Presley, James Dean, Buddy Holly, Loni Anderson and the Phantom of the Opera.

❖ The coach with the most wins without reaching the Super Bowl is Chuck Knox, who won 193 games with the Rams, Bills and Seahawks but never took a team to the big game.

❖ The man who coached the most seasons without ever appearing in the playoffs is Norm Van Brocklin. In 13 seasons with the Vikings and Falcons, Van Brocklin went 66-100-7. As a player, however, the Hall of Fame quarterback led the Eagles to a Super Bowl victory in 1960.

❖ Don Shula was involved in the largest trade in NFL history. On March 25, 1953, the then-defensive back was traded from Cleveland to Baltimore in 1953 in a 15-player deal, as one of 10 players the expansion Colts acquired from the Browns.

❖ Packers coach Mike Holmgren was a quarterback at USC (1966-69). He was drafted by the St. Louis Cardinals in the eighth round of the 1970 NFL draft.

❖ Hall of Fame coach Vince Lombardi was one of the famed "Seven Blocks of Granite" as a player at Fordham University.

❖ Weeb Ewbank is the only coach to win the championship in both the NFL and AFL. He won with the Colts in 1958 and '59, and the Jets in '68. He is the only NFL coach to lead teams in each league to the championships: the NFL Colts in 1958 and 1959 and the AFL Jets in 1969.

❖ Vikings coach Dennis Green and Lions coach Bobby Ross coached against each other in the 1991 Aloha Bowl. Ross's Georgia Tech team edged Green's Stanford squad 18-17.

❖ The only member of both the Canadian and U.S. Pro Football Halls of Fame is Bud Grant, the only coach to win 100 games in both leagues. Grant coached the Vikings to four Super Bowl appearances and the Winnipeg Blue Bombers to four Grey Cup championships.

Q15

Jerry Rice is the only player in Super Bowl history with over 200 yards in receptions in one game.

level 1   *Name the opponent and Super Bowl number.*

level 2   *Where was the game played?*

level 3   *How many yards did Rice finish with?*

question 15 answers

level 1   Bengals, Super Bowl XXIII

level 2   (Then known as) Joe Robbie Stadium in Miami.

level 3   He caught 11 passes for 215 yards.

Q16

Entering the 1998 season, the NFL's 40,000-yard passing club was relatively exclusive.

level 1   *How many players had 40,000 or more career passing yards?*

level 2   *Name them.*

level 3   *How many were active entering the 1998 campaign?*

question 16 answers

level 1   Seven

level 2   a   Dan Marino
       b   John Elway
       c   Warren Moon
       d   Fran Tarkenton
       e   Dan Fouts
       f   Joe Montana
       g   Johnny Unitas

level 3   Three: Marino, Elway and Moon

personal files

- Deion Sanders threw for 839 yards and rushed for 499 more as a senior at North Fort Myers High School in 1984. Sanders was the left-handed option quarterback for the Red Knights. He also played on the defensive side of the ball and picked off four passes in his senior year.
- The following star NFL quarterbacks were all born in February: Fran Tarkenton (Feb. 3, 1940), Bob Griese (Feb. 3, 1945), Roger Staubach (Feb. 5, 1942), Jim Kelly (Feb. 14, 1960) and Drew Bledsoe (Feb. 14, 1972).
- The only other NFL player besides Joe Montana to have No. 16 retired is Kansas City's Len Dawson, which was why Montana couldn't wear his usual number when he joined the Chiefs in 1993. The most frequent retired NFL numbers are 12, 14, 40 and 7 (in descending order).
- NFL commissioner Paul Tagliabue played college basketball at Georgetown.
- The first president of the NFL was Jim Thorpe, who took the post in 1920.
- Former Supreme Court justice Byron "Whizzer" White was an All-League selection in 1940, leading the Lions in passing, rushing and scoring.
- Three former USC assistant football coaches are in the Pro Football Hall of Fame: Raiders owner Al Davis, former Redskins coach Joe Gibbs and former Giants center Mel Hein.
- In 1966, Baltimore drafted Michigan State's Bubba Smith. He was popular there, as the Bullets picked him in Round 11 of the 1967 NBA draft.
- Warren Sapp averaged 43.5 yards as a punter for Apopka High School in Florida.
- Hall of Fame Bears running back Gale Sayers is a Green Bay Packers shareholder.
- Giants wide receiver Homer Jones is credited with inventing the high-five.
- The face with the eye patch in the Raiders logo was modeled after actor Randolph Scott.
- Viking kicker Fred Cox (1963-77) holds the patent for the Nerf football.

did you know?

Mark Malone shares the Steelers record for the longest pass reception in team history. In 1981, Terry Bradshaw hit Malone for a 90-yard touchdown versus the Seahawks. The record was matched in 1990 when Bubby Brister hit Dwight Stone for 90 yards against the Broncos.

Q17

Super Bowl I started a great tradition.

level 1   *Who played in that game?*

level 2   *Where was the game played?*

level 3   *Who scored the first touchdown?*

question 17 answers

level 1   Packers versus Chiefs

level 2   Memorial Coliseum, Los Angeles

level 3   Max McGee caught a 37-yard touchdown pass from Bart Starr.

Q18

George Halas was one of football's true greats.

level 1   *How many years did he coach the Bears?*

level 2   *How many NFL titles did he win?*

level 3   *In 1920, Halas was a player-coach. Name the team.*

question 18 answers

level 1   40

level 2   Seven

level 3   The Decatur Staleys

monday night football

::: September 21, 1970, marked the first *Monday Night Football* game, brought to Cleveland by Art Modell, a leading member of the NFL's television committee. The largest crowd ever for a Browns game (85,703) saw the home team beat Joe Namath and the Jets 31-21.

::: The Falcons have played four *Monday Night Football* games at the Georgia Dome, losing all four by a combined score of 161-47.

::: After the Raiders' last-second loss in Week 2 in 1997 dropped their *Monday Night Football* win percentage to .684, the Seahawks were left with the best *MNF* win percentage at .688 (11-5).

::: The 1998 season marks the first time since *Monday Night Football* began in 1970 that the Raiders do not appear on Monday night. No other team can claim such a streak.

::: The Steelers have won 10 of 11 *Monday Night Football* games under Bill Cowher and are 25-16 overall for a win percentage of .610.

inside the numbers

Divisional dominance (since 1970):

team	division	years	titles
Rams	NFC West	1973-79	7
Steelers	AFC Central	1974-79	6
Vikings	NFC Central	1973-78	6
Cowboys	NFC East	1992-96	5
49ers	NFC West	1986-90	5
Bears	NFC Central	1984-88	5
Raiders	AFC West	1972-76	5

did you know?

ESPN draft guru Mel Kiper Jr. played on the same sandlot baseball team with NFL All-Pro punter Sean Landeta. They were on the same side of the Loch Raven Optimist infield: Landeta played third and Kiper played shortstop.

Q

Rushing for 1,500 yards in a season is impressive.

level 1   *What was the most times it was done in one season?*

level 2   *Name the players who did it that season.*

level 3   *Who led the NFL in rushing that season?*

question 19 answers

level 1   Four times, in 1979

level 2   *a*   Earl Campbell
          b   Walter Payton
          c   Ottis Anderson
          d   Wilbert Montgomery

level 3   Campbell, with 1,697 yards

Q 20

The 1995 season was a great one for receivers.

level 1   *Who led the NFL in receptions that season?*

level 2   *How many receivers had 100 or more catches?*

level 3   *Name those players.*

question 20 answers

level 1   Herman Moore, with 123 catches

level 2   Nine players had 100 or more receptions.

level 3   *a*   Herman Moore
          b   Jerry Rice
          c   Cris Carter
          d   Isaac Bruce
          e   Michael Irvin
          f   Brett Perriman
          g   Eric Metcalf
          h   Robert Brooks
          i   Larry Centers

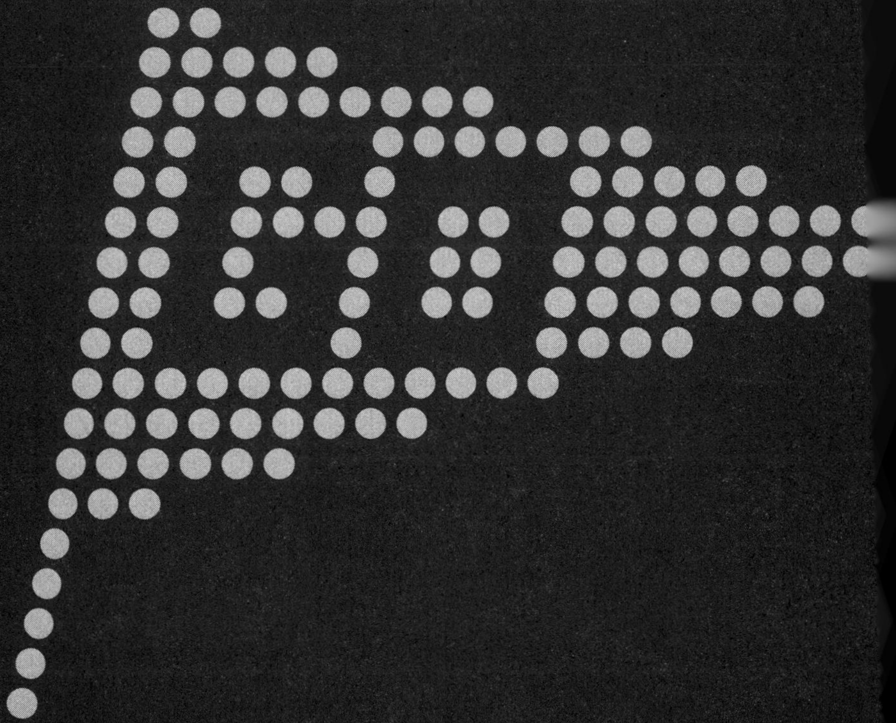

do not immerse in water
Stats are good up to
September 15, 1998.

the majors

- On April 13, 1986, 46-year-old Jack Nicklaus became the oldest player to win The Masters. In 1997, Tiger Woods, at 21 years, three months and 14 days, became the youngest Masters winner. Woods shot a 40 on the front nine on Day 1, and 230 for the final 63 holes.
- The largest third-round deficit overcome to win The Masters is eight strokes, by Jack Burke Jr. in 1956.
- Only two golfers in the last 23 Masters have held the lead outright after the first round and gone on to win the green jacket: Ray Floyd in 1976 and Ben Crenshaw in 1984.
- The lowest round by a first-year amateur in The Masters is 67, shot by Jodie Mudd in the third round of the 1982 tournament. Mudd finished 6 over par as the low amateur and tied for 20th overall.
- Since the first Masters in 1934, only two players have won back-to-back titles: Jack Nicklaus (1965-66) and Nick Faldo (1989-90).
- The best opening round shot by a British Open champion was 66: Peter Thomson (1958), Nick Faldo (1992) and Greg Norman (1993).
- Tom Lehman is the last person to lead the British Open outright in every round (1996). The tournament has seen wire-to-wire winners 10 times.
- Greg Norman has the record for the best finishing round for a British Open champion: 64 at Royal St. George's in 1993.
- The lowest score after 36 holes at the British Open is 130 (66-64), shot by Nick Faldo in 1992. Faldo went on to win the 1992 title at Muirfield, the third of his three British Open championships. In 1998, Tiger Woods or John Huston could have matched the record by repeating their first-round 65s. Instead, Woods shot a 3 over 73, and Huston ballooned to +2 with a 77.
- Since 1920, the highest fourth-round score for a British Open Champion is 79, shot by Henry Cotton in 1934. Helping Cotton's cause was his second-round 65, which helped him establish a record 10-stroke lead after three rounds.
- The last man to win back-to-back British Open Golf tournaments was Tom Watson (1982-83).
- Ben Hogan was the first to win three major tournaments in one year. In 1953, he won The Masters (his second), the U.S. Open and the British Open.
- In winning the 1998 U.S. Open, Se Ri Pak saw her score go up in each of the first four rounds: 69-70-75-76.
- Only four golfers have ever won The Masters and the U.S. Open in the same year, with Jack Nicklaus being the last to accomplish it, in 1972. Arnold Palmer pulled off the double feat in 1960, Ben Hogan did it twice in 1951 and '53 and Craig Wood achieved it in 1941.
- The last amateur to win the U.S. Open was John Goodman in 1933. At least one amateur has made the cut in all but six U.S. Opens, but three of those six have come in the last four years.
- Since the first U.S. Open in 1895, a player won back-to-back titles just six times: Curtis Strange (1988-89), Ben Hogan (1950-51), Ralph Guldahl (1937-38), Bobby Jones (1929-30), John McDermott (1911-12) and Willie Anderson (1903-05). Anderson is the only golfer to win three straight U.S. Open Championships (1903-05). The last repeat U.S. Open champion was Strange in 1988-89, but before him, you have to go back to 1950-51 to find the next repeat winner (Hogan).
- The last player to successfully defend his PGA championship was Denny Shute, who won back-to-back titles in 1936 and '37. Shute had to defeat six players in match play to win the titles, which earned him just $9,200 for each victory. The 1998 winner, Vijay Singh, pocketed $540,000.

did you know?

Jimmy Roberts was recruited to play for the then-NCAA
champion University of Maryland lacrosse team, but got
cut and immediately started his broadcasting career by
calling Terps games on the radio.

inside the numbers

*While Tiger Woods is the youngest golfer to win The Masters, he's the
oldest of the four youngest players to win a Major:*

tournament	player	age at victory
1968 British Open	Young Tom Morris	17 years, 5 months
1911 U.S. Open	John J. McDermott	19 years, 10 months
1922 PGA	Gene Sarazen	20 years, 5 months
1997 Masters	Tiger Woods	21 years, 3 months

*Sam Snead is the oldest winner in PGA history, winning the Greater Greensboro
at 52 years, 10 months in 1965. Jack Nicklaus won The Masters at 46 years, two
months in 1986. Here are the five oldest PGA winners in the '90s:*

golfer	age	tournament
Ray Floyd	49 years, 6 months	1992 Doral
Hale Irwin	48 years, 9 months	1994 MCI
Tom Watson	48 years, 8 months	1998 Colonial
Ed Dougherty	47 years, 7 months	1995 Deposit
Tom Watson	46 years, 9 months	1996 Memorial

championships

- Jack Nicklaus went 17 straight years with at least one PGA Tour win (1962-78).
- Byron Nelson went 113 straight tournaments in the 1940s without missing the cut.
- Sam Snead holds the record for most career PGA Tour wins with 81. The only major tournament he never won was the U.S. Open.
- Sam Snead holds the PGA record for most wins at a single event, winning the Greater Greensboro Open eight times.
- Kathy Whitworth has the most LPGA Tour wins with 88. She was the leading money winner on the LPGA Tour eight times.
- At the 1949 Motor City Open, Cary Middlecoff and Lloyd Mangrum were tied through 11 holes of sudden death before they were declared co-winners by mutual agreement.
- The Nike Tour alumnus with the most career PGA Tour victories is Ernie Els, with six.
- The largest margin of victory in LPGA history is 14 strokes. Louise Suggs won the 1949 U.S. Open by 14 shots, and Cindy Mackey won the 1986 Mastercard International Pro-Am by the same margin. In 1998, Se Ri Pak won the Jamie Farr Kroger Classic by nine strokes.
- Other than Nick Faldo's six major titles, his only PGA Tour wins have come at the 1984 Heritage Classic, the 1995 Doral-Ryder Open and the '97 Nissan Open.
- Tom Kite holds the Pebble Beach record, shooting a 62 in the 1983 Bing Crosby National Pro-Am.
- Phil Mickelson is the only lefty to win the U.S. Amateur event (1990).

total access
linda cohn

"During Nancy Lopez's miraculous rookie season in 1978 when she won five straight LPGA tournaments, she hit a spectator in the head with her approach shot at the par 4, 10th hole in the first round at the Rochester Invitational. 'If this guy's dead,' a distraught Lopez said, 'I'm quitting right now.' Well, the fan, an optometrist named Dr. Jerry Messolella, was fine, Lopez went on to make double bogey and eventually win the tournament, and the two became friends (she invited him to her first wedding). But can you imagine what the LPGA Tour would have been like without Nancy Lopez?"

Q1

Three-time U.S. Amateur champion Tiger Woods made an immediate impact on the PGA Tour.

level 1   *When and at what tournament did he turn pro?*

level 2   *How many tournaments did he win in his first 30 pro events?*

level 3   *What were his earnings over those first 30 pro events?*

question 1 answers

level 1   August 27, 1996, at the Greater Milwaukee Open

level 2   Seven wins

level 3 $2.91 million

Q2

Jack Nicklaus has won a record six Masters championships.

level 1   *When was his last Masters championship?*

level 2   *Who was the runner-up that year?*

level 3   *How many times did he win the U. S. Amateur championship.*
Name the year(s).

question 2 answers

level 1   1986

level 2   Greg Norman

level 3   Twice
1959 and '61

championships

-:- John Huston was 16 under par through two rounds of the 1998 Hawaiian Open, tied with a handful of golfers for the lowest two-round total. Steve Jones was a record 16 under par after two rounds of the 1997 Phoenix Open; John Cook (1996 St. Jude), Rick Fehr (1996 Las Vegas), Paul Azinger (1989 Texas Open) and Tommy Bolt (1954 Virginia Beach Open) for the lowest opening two rounds of any tournament (126).

-:- When John Huston finished the 1998 Hawaiian Open at 28 under par, he shattered the 43-year old record of Mike Souchak, who was 27-under at the 1955 Texas Open. Huston also set the mark for most birdies in a 72-hole tournament: 31.

-:- Jack Nicklaus barely ranks in the top 30 on the PGA Tour career money list with $5.6 million, despite having won the most Majors and the second-most PGA Tour events (70). Greg Norman is No. 1 on the money list with $12 million in earnings as of July 8, 1998. It comes down to when you win, not how many you win: The Golden Bear earned a total of $637,650 for his 18 major wins, while Lee Janzen got $535,000 for his 1998 U.S. Open victory. The most Nicklaus won for any single major was $144,000 for the 1986 Masters.

-:- In 1996, Karrie Webb became the first rookie, either LPGA or PGA Tour, to reach $1 million in earnings.

-:- The last time a PGA Championship was decided in a match-play format was 1957, when Lionel Hebert defeated Dow Finsterwald 3 and 1 in a 36-hole final to win the title. Hebert's first-prize check for winning that five-day endurance test? $8,000. When the PGA Championship went to a four-day, 72-hole stroke play format in 1958, Finsterwald won the title.

-:- The leading money winner on the men's golf tour in 1936 was Horton Smith, with $7,682. The leading PGA money winner in 1997, Tiger Woods, earned $2,066,833 in prize money.

total access
mike tirico

"When John Huston smashed the PGA record for most shots under par at the 1998 Hawaiian Open, not too many people know that he was playing for the first time with a replacement caddy: his sister. It would be their first and only professional outing, but what a team!"

Q3

South Korean phenom Se Ri Pak won two majors early in the 1998 LPGA season.

level 1   *Name the tournaments.*

level 2   *What were her par scores in those two events?*

level 3   *In the nine LPGA events before her first major win, what was her best finish?*

Q4

The Ryder Cup, which takes place every two years, is golf's most prestigious team trophy in golf.

level 1   *When did the Ryder Cup competition begin?*

level 2   *What was the result of the 1998 Ryder Cup?*

level 3   *Which team has the overall edge in the competition and by what margin?*

question 3 answers

level 1   *a*   LPGA Championship
          b   U.S. Women's Open

level 2   *a*   -11
             b   +6 before beating Jenny Chuasiriporn in a playoff round

level 3   11th at the Long's Drugs Challenge

question 4 answers

level 1   1927

level 2   Europe defeated the U.S.A. 14 ½-13 ½

level 3   U.S.A. leads 23-7-2.

- Hale Irwin was a two-time All-Big Eight defensive back at Colorado.
- Esteban Toledo had a 12-1 record as a pro boxer fighting out of the lightweight division
- Chris Perry is the son of former major league pitcher Jim Perry.
- Lee Janzen played Little League baseball as a youngster in Maryland.
- Fred Funk was the golf coach at the University of Maryland from 1982 to '88. He won the Deposit Guarantee event in 1998.
- Amy Alcott has served as a part-time short order cook at the Los Angeles-based Butterfly Bakery.
- David Duval, who won three PGA Tour events in 1997, saw his father, Bob, join the Senior PGA Tour that year.

did you know?

Bob Stevens would have been a four-year letter winner on his high school golf team, but the team was disbanded his senior year (hence the career change). He then went on to the University of Tulsa, where his classmates included two Hall of Famers, the NFL's Steve Largent and the LPGA's Nancy Lopez.

total access
jimmy roberts

"In preparation for a story on presidential golf, I once teed it up with George Bush at his home course in Maine, Cape Arundel. The former President insisted on playing for a dollar a side, and while Bush (who self-deprecatingly referred to himself as Mr. Smooth due to a balky putting stroke) had a very un-Presidential day, I had the round of my life, a best-ever 83. I was too embarrassed to ask the former leader of the free world to autograph my earnings, but a staff intermediary assured me that it wouldn't break any laws to sign a dollar bill. That trophy, along with the scorecard, is now proudly framed and displayed in my office."

Q5

Nancy Lopez was inducted to the LPGA Hall of Fame in 1987.

level 1   *When did she win Rookie of the Year?*

level 2   *How many years did she lead the LPGA in money earnings?*

level 3   *In 1978, how many tournaments did she win, and what was her longest tournament win streak that year?*

question 5 answers

level 1   1978
level 2   Three
level 3   Nine wins, including five in a row

Q6

Byron Nelson has his name all over golf's record books.

level 1   *He owns the record for the most wins in a calendar year. What was the year and how many PGA victories did he post?*

level 2   *He owns the record for most events without missing a cut. How many consecutive PGA events did he play in?*

level 3   *He owns the record for consecutive tournaments won. How many did he win?*

question 6 answers

level 1   1945, 18 victories
level 2   113
level 3   11

did you know?

Analyst Betsy Nagelsen played 23 consecutive years at Wimbledon between 1974 and '96, surpassed by only Virginia Wade and Martina Navratilova. A superb athlete, while in the seventh grade she threw a softball 210 feet, a Florida state record that still stands.

australian open

: Ken Rosewall is both the oldest (37 years, two months in 1972) and the youngest (18 years, two months in 1953) Australian Open men's champion. Rosewall also won titles in 1955 and 1971.

: Half of Roy Emerson's 12 Grand Slam singles titles (six) came at the Australian Open. He won in 1961 and '63 through '67.

: The last unseeded woman to win a Grand Slam event was Chris O'Neil in the 1978 Australian Open.

: The last man to win consecutive Australian Open men's tennis singles titles was Jim Courier (1992-93).

french open

: Since the turn of the century, the best finals record in any men's Grand Slam event is 6-0, set by Bjorn Borg in the French Open. The all-time record at a Grand Slam is 7-0, established by Richard Sears, who won the first seven U.S. Opens (1881-87).

: The oldest French Open men's singles champion was Spain's Andres Gimeno, 34 years and 10 months in 1972.

: At the 1997 French Open, Gustavo Kuerten became the first player to earn his first career singles title at a Grand Slam since Mats Wilander did it at the '82 French.

: The only Grand Slam singles title Jimmy Connors didn't win was the French Open.

inside the numbers

By winning the 1998 French Open, Arantxa Sanchez Vicario tied Monica Seles for fourth on the list of career French Open women's titles in the open era (1969 to the present). Her career record at Roland Garros is 62-9, and she is a three-time runner-up, including twice to Steffi Graf:

player	french open titles
Chris Evert	7 1974, '75, '79, '80, '83, '85, '86
Steffi Graf	5 1987, '88, '93, '95, '96
Margaret Court	5 1962, '64, '69, '70, '73
Arantxa Sanchez Vicario	3 1989, '94, '95
Monica Seles	3 1990, '91, '92

In 1997, Gustavo Kuerten became one of only three unseeded players to win the men's title at the French Open. Mats Wildander (1988) and Marcel Bernard (1946) are the others. Here are the lowest men's seeds to win the French Open:

year	winner	seed
1989	Michael Chang	15th
1998	Carlos Moya	12th
1993	Sergi Bruguera	10th
1991	Jim Courier	9th
1970	Jan Kodes	7th
1950	Budge Patty	7th
1939	William McNeill	7th

wimbledon

- The first Wimbledon took place in 1877 and 22 men competed for the singles crown. There are now 128 men in the main draw.
- The last time a Wimbledon women's final featured players with a combined age of over 60 years was in 1977, when Virginia Wade, 31, defeated Betty Stove, 32, in three sets. Jana Novotna and Nathalie Tauziat just missed in 1998.
- Bobby Riggs is the only player to win the triple crown at Wimbledon in his first appearance. In 1939, the 21-year-old won the men's singles, doubles and mixed doubles at the All-England Club, then followed up by winning the U.S. Open.
- Boris Becker is the only unseeded man to win the Wimbledon singles title (1985). Two unseeded men have made the singles final there in the '90s: MaliVai Washington (1996) and Cedric Pioline (1997).
- There has never been an unseeded women's singles champion at Wimbledon. The last unseeded woman to make the Wimbledon finals was Billie Jean Moffitt, better known as Billie Jean King later on (1963).
- Billie Jean King won a record 20 Wimbledon titles. Her first All-England championship came in 1961, and her last in 1979 (includes singles and doubles matches).

total access

chris mckendry

"I learned to play tennis through the Arthur Ashe Youth Tennis Center in Philadelphia. The Center was instrumental in helping me earn a scholarship to Drexel University, which was Ashe's plan for young players. In 1968, the year I was born, Arthur Ashe won the U.S. Amateur and U.S. Open championships, the first and only time a player has won both in the same year. However, since he was an amateur at the Open, the runner-up, pro Tom Okker, went home with the first place prize money. Ashe received only his expense money, then $28 dollars a day."

Q1

Martina Hingis became the youngest player to win a Grand Slam singles title in the open era (since 1968).

level 1   *Which Grand Slam did she win?*

level 2   *What year did it happen?*

level 3   *How old was she when she won?*

question 1 answers

level 1   Australian Open

level 2   1997

level 3   16 years, three months and 26 days

Q2

Pete Sampras has dominated men's tennis in the '90s.

level 1   *From 1993 to '98, how many Wimbledon men's singles titles did he win?*

level 2   *When was his first Grand Slam singles appearance?*

level 3   *How did he fare in that first Grand Slam singles appearance?*

question 2 answers

level 1   He won five times over that six-year span.

level 2   1988, at the U.S. Open

level 3   He lost in the first round to Jaime Yzaga.

martina navratilova

- Her given name at birth was Martina Subertova. She later took the name of her stepfather, Mirek Navratil.
- Her birth father committed suicide when Navratilova was eight. She didn't know the true story until she was 23. Her mother had claimed he died during a stomach operation.
- She made $6,100 in her first year on the WTA Tour (1973).
- She held the No. 1 ranking on the WTA Tour for a total of 381 weeks, over seven years.
- She won 167 WTA Tour singles championships, the most tour titles, male or female.
- She captured 18 Grand Slam singles titles and 37 Grand Slam doubles titles. Her first Grand Slam singles title was at Wimbledon in 1978; her last was at Wimbledon in 1990.
- From 1988 to '94, she won just one Grand Slam singles title (1990 Wimbledon).
- It took Navratilova nine years to reach her first U.S. Open singles final and 11 years to win her first U.S. Open women's singles championship.
- She collaborated with Liz Nickles on three mystery novels: The Total Zone (1994), Breaking Point (1996) and Killer Instinct (1997).

Q3

Steffi Graf has the longest consecutive reign ranked No. 1 in women's tennis.

level 1   *How many times has Graf won each of the four Grand Slam tournaments ?*

level 2   *Helping Graf maintain her No.1 ranking was the reason a German fan gave for stabbing Monica Seles during a match. When did the stabbing occur and at what tournament?*

level 3   *How many straight weeks was Graf ranked No. 1?*

question 3 answers

level 1   a   Australian Open, four times
      b   French Open, five times
      c   Wimbledon, seven times
      d   U.S. Open, five times

level 2   1993 Citizen Cup in Hamburg

level 3   186 weeks between August 1987-March 1991

Q4

Jimmy Connors had one of the greatest careers in tennis history.

level 1   *How many overall championships did he win?*

level 2   *How many times did he win the U.S. Open singles championship?*

level 3   *What year did he turn pro?*

question 4 answers

level 1   He won 109 titles, a record for men's tennis.

level 2   Five times. Bill Larned, Richard Sears and Bill Tilden each won the U.S. Open a record seven times.

level 3   1972

did you know?

Analyst Fred Stolle is one of only three unseeded men who
have won the U.S. Open singles title: Mal Anderson in 1957,
Stolle in 1966 and Andre Agassi in 1994. Agassi knocked
off five seeded players en route to the title: Michael Stich
(4), Michael Chang (6), Todd Martin (9), Wayne Ferreira
(12) and Thomas Muster (13).

the u.s. open

∴ The youngest U.S. Open women's tennis champion is Tracy Austin, who won in 1979 at 16
years, 8 months, 28 days. Austin beat Chris Evert in '79, then won a second U.S. Open title in
1981, her only two Grand Slam titles.

∴ John McEnroe's first Grand Slam singles title was at the 1979 U.S. Open; his last was at the
1984 U.S. Open.

∴ By winning the 1998 U. S. Open women's doubles title (with Jana Novotna), Martina Hingis
became the fourth woman to sweep all four Grand Slam doubles in one year. Hingis won the
Australian with Mirjana Lucic and the rest with Novotna. Martina Navratilova and Pam Shriver
won all four as a team in 1984, while Maria Bueno swept with two different partners in 1960.

∴ No defending U.S. Open men's champion has ever lost in the first round the ensuing year.
Three have lost in the second round: Stefan Edberg to Karel Novacek in 1993, Mats Wilander
to Pete Sampras in 1989 and Ilie Nastase to Andrew Pattison in 1973.

∴ The earliest a defending U.S. Open women's singles champion lost in the ensuing year
was Round 2. Maria Bueno had to default with tendinitis in her right arm in 1967.

∴ In 1976, Raul Ramirez was the top money winner in men's tennis with $484,343, which is
$215,657 less than the 1998 U.S. Open champion received.

∴ In 1971, the total prize money on the women's tennis tour was $250,000, which is $450,000
less than the 1998 U.S. Open winner received.

∴ In 1969, F. D. Robbins beat Dick Dell in a first-round match at the U.S. Open. It lasted a record
100 games (22-20, 9-7, 6-8, 8-10, 6-4). There is a fifth-set tiebreaker now.

inside the numbers

Since 1960, only three people have won the triple crown at the U.S. Open–singles, doubles and mixed doubles:

year	player	doubles partner	mixed doubles partner
1960	Neale Fraser	Roy Emerson	Margaret duPont
1967	Billie Jean King	Rosie Casals	Owen Davidson
1970	Margaret Court	Judy Dalton	Marty Riessen
1987	Martina Navratilova	Pam Shriver	Emilio Sanchez

Q5

Rod Laver is the only man to win the Grand Slam twice.

level 1   *What years did he accomplish this feat?*

level 2   *To capture the second Grand Slam,*
Laver had to beat four different opponents
in the four finals.
Name them.

level 3   *After winning his second Grand Slam, how*
many Grand Slam tournaments did he win
during the rest of his career?

Q6

The U.S. Open honored Arthur Ashe in 1997 by naming its renovated tennis stadium after him.

level 1   *How many Grand Slam singles titles did*
he win?

level 2   *Name the only Grand Slam tournament he*
never won.

level 3   *What was his best finish in that*
Grand Slam?

question 5 answers

level 1   1962, 1969

level 2   *a*   Andres Gimeno/Australian Open
b   Ken Rosewell/French Open
c   John Newcombe/Wimbledon
d   Tony Roche/U.S. Open

level 3   None

question 6 answers

level 1   Three

level 2   French Open

level 3   Quarterfinalist

did you know?

ESPNEWS anchor Michael Kim's grandfather was a national collegiate tennis champion in Korea.

grand slams

··· Fred Perry, known as "Mr. Tennis," was the first man to win the Grand Slam and the last Englishman to win the singles title at Wimbledon (1936).

··· Bjorn Borg never won the Australian Open or the U.S. Open, where he was a finalist four times. His combined singles match record at the French Open and Wimbledon was 100-6.

··· After winning the Grand Slam in 1969, Rod Laver never got past the quarterfinals at any other Grand Slam event. His best post-'69 showing was an appearance in the Wimbledon quarterfinals in 1971. In 1969, when Laver won the men's Grand Slam, his total prize money for the year was $124,000.

··· Pete Sampras has never lost twice in the same year to the same opponent in Grand Slam singles events. He avenged his 1998 Australian Open defeat to Karol Kucera at the U.S. Open.

personal files

··· Monica Seles rang the bell at the Stock Market on August 31, 1998, the first day of the U.S. Open. The market went down 512 points that day.

··· John McEnroe participated in the Davis Cup for the U.S. team for 12 years, playing in 49 singles matches and winning a record 41.

··· Chris Evert once held a 125-match win streak on clay (August 1973-May 1979). She was finally defeated by Tracy Austin in the semifinals of the Italian Open, 6-4, 2-6, 7-6.

··· Pete Sampras's older sister, Stella, won the NCAA women's doubles championship playing for UCLA in 1988.

··· At 16 years, one month and 10 days, Martina Hingis became the youngest player, male or female, to earn $1 million in prize money.

··· Andre Agassi's first pro championship came when he was a wild card entry in 1987 (at Itaparica).

··· Andre Agassi's father, Mike, was a boxer at the 1952 Olympics.

··· Gabriela Sabatini won the Orange Bowl juniors tournament, age 18 division, at age 13 in 1983.

··· Future broadcasters John McEnroe and Mary Carillo teamed up to win the French Open mixed doubles championship in 1977.

··· In 1973, then 29-year-old Billie Jean King beat 55-year-old Bobby Riggs 6-4, 6-3, 6-3 in straight sets in the Battle of the Sexes at the Houston Astrodome. But she wasn't the first woman to beat a man in a professional tennis match. In 1933, seven-time Wimbledon champ Helen Willis Moody defeated Phil Neer.

Q7

In her debut at the 1997 U.S. Open, Venus Williams became the first woman to reach the finals there since 1978.

level 1   *Name the person who defeated Williams in the final.*

level 2   *Who was the 1978 finalist who played in the championship match in her debut?*

level 3   *Name the player who won the 1978 U.S. Open.*

question 7 answers

level 1   Martina Hingis
level 2   Pam Shriver
level 3   Chris Evert

Q8

Andre Agassi has been around the pro tour for over a decade.

level 1   *When was his first career Grand Slam singles appearance and how old was he?*

level 2   *In his first four Grand Slam singles appearances, what was his best finish?*

level 3   *Name the player he beat to win his first Grand Slam. When and where did it take place?*

question 8 answers

level 1   1986 U.S. Open, 16 years old
level 2   Second round of the 1987 French Open
level 3   Goran Ivanisevic at Wimbledon in 1992

the main event

- In the first heavyweight championship fight ever, James J. Corbett knocked out John L. Sullivan in the 21st round in New Orleans (September 7, 1892).
- The 1984 U.S. Olympic boxing team produced six world champions: Meldrick Taylor, Pernell Whitaker, Mark Breland, Frank Tate, Virgil Hill and Evander Holyfield. Future champs Mike Tyson and Michael Nunn failed to make the team.
- Mike Tyson had four pro knockouts inside of 40 seconds. His fastest was a 30-second KO of Marvis Frazier in July 1986.
- Roy Jones Jr. didn't have to go 10 rounds as a pro until his 18th bout.
- The late middleweight champion Carlos Monzon fought 102 pro bouts in his 13-year career, retiring at 98-3 with one no-contest.
- Archie Moore's pro boxing career spanned 27 years and 229 fights. (Moore's real name is Archibald Lee Wright.)
- Muhammad Ali's final pro fight was a 10-round loss to Trevor Berbick in 1981.
- Jess Willard's 1915 upset over Jack Johnson for the heavyweight title was a 26th-round knockout.
- Ray Leonard won titles in five different weight classes: WBC Welterweight, WBA Junior Middleweight, WBC Middleweight, WBC Super Middleweight and WBC Light Heavyweight.
- Only Evander Holyfield, Muhammad Ali and Floyd Patterson have regained the heavyweight title in rematches with the champions who won it from them.
- Lorenzo Boyd is the only boxer to face both Mike Tyson and Peter McNeeley. Boyd stepped into the ring July 11, 1986, and went down in Round 2 (a Tyson KO). After losing to Tyson, he went 2-15-0 before being KO'd by Hurricane Pete in the first round on November 11, 1994.
- Rocky Marciano went 49-0 with 43 KOs in his pro career (1947-56). Not bad for a man who worked as a gardener, delivery boy and leather tanner in a shoe factory before making it to boxing's big time.
- Buster Douglas was a 42-1 underdog when he upset Mike Tyson on February 11, 1990. Tyson was 37-0 entering the bout.
- Five of the most famous heavyweight champs were born in January: Floyd Patterson (January 4, 1935), Muhammad Ali (January 17, 1942), Joe Frazier (January 12, 1944), George Foreman (January 22, 1948) and Jersey Joe Walcott (January 31, 1914).

September **15**

1950 Al Bernstein is born.
1978 Muhammad Ali regains the heavyweight championship for the third time, in a 15-round decision over Leon Spinks.

inside the numbers

When Mike Tyson was busy, he was at his best. In his first two years as a pro, he fought 28 times. From 1987 on, he has had just 20 pro bouts, and while he had 15 fights his first year and 13 the next, he's never had more than four in any other year:

year	fights	record	
1985	15	15-0, 15	KO
1986	13	13-0, 11	KO
1987	4	4-0, 2	KO
1988	3	3-0, 3	KO
1989	2	2-0, 2	KO
1990	3	2-1, 2	KO
1991	2	2-0, 1	KO
1992-94	0	Inactive	
1995	2	2-0, 1	KO
1996	3	2-1, 2	KO
1997	1	0-1	
1998	0	License revoked	

Five men have gone the distance with Mike Tyson in his pro career. Iron Mike won all five decisions: *

date	opponent	rounds
May 3, 1986	James Tillis	10
May 20, 1986	Mitch "Blood" Green	10
March 7, 1987	James "Bonecrusher" Smith	12
August 1, 1987	Tony Tucker	12
June 28, 1991	Donovan "Razor" Ruddock	12

*Both Buster Douglas and Evander Holyfield (twice) beat Tyson in KOs.

the first time

- In his first pro fight on November 15, 1984, Evander Holyfield weighed just 177 pounds. It wasn't until his 19th pro fight that he entered the ring weighing more than 190 pounds.
- Muhammad Ali weighed 186 in his pro debut (October 1960).
- Larry Holmes's first pro fight was in March of 1973. He won a four-round decision.
- George Foreman's first pro fight was in June of 1969. He won a third-round TKO and fought at 219 pounds.
- Joe Frazier went five rounds or less in each of his first 10 pro fights.
- Joe Louis fought 23 times in his first full calendar year as a pro, going undefeated. His first pro loss came in his 28th fight, when Max Schmeling stunned him in 1936.
- Jack Johnson had his first pro fight at age 19. He was 50 when he finally quit the sport.
- Sugar Ray Leonard earned $40,000 for his first pro fight, a decision over Luis Vega on February 5, 1977. Leonard's first world title came less than three years after his pro debut, November 30, 1979. He beat Wilfred Benitez for the WBC Welterweight title.

total access
charley steiner

"My first overseas assignment became somewhat of an international incident. It took place in 1981 inside the press room at Wimbledon, in a year when the British tabloids were particularly unmerciful about John McEnroe's rumored break-up with his then-girlfriend, Stacy Margolin. After a week of relentless postmatch badgering about whether he and Margolin were indeed splitsville, McEnroe cursed out the offending British gossip columnist. An overly cramped and undersized press room became the site of a spontaneous combustion. I was confronted by a British writer, who started a fight with me. A fight! At a tennis match! On international television! I am pleased to report I retired as a fighter unbloodied, undefeated and a dubious footnote in the history of the All-England Lawn Tennis and Croquet Club."

Q

Let's bite off a few questions about Evander Holyfield and Mike Tyson.

level 1   *In the first meeting, which Holyfield won on an 11th-round TKO, who was ahead on the scorecards when the bout was stopped?*

level 2   *When was Tyson-Holyfield originally scheduled to be fought?*

level 3   *Besides Holyfield, name the only two other opponents Tyson has faced twice as a pro since 1986.*

Q

Muhammad Ali had many memorable fights, but in 1974, he showed his ability to stun the so-called experts, winning the match known as the Rumble in the Jungle against George Foreman.

level 1   *What country was the fight held in?*

level 2   *In which round did Ali knock out Foreman?*

level 3   *What is the name of the Academy Award-winning documentary about that fight?*

goooal!

- When the World Cup began in 1930, only 13 nations participated. In 1998, 172 countries participated in various qualifying matches until 32 countries vied for world supremacy.
- The best performance ever by an American World Cup team was in 1930, when the Americans reached the semifinals. Using a squad of Scottish immigrants, the U.S.A. defeated both Belgium and Paraguay to win its group and advance to the semifinals, where they lost to Argentina 6-1. Uruguay went on to win the first of its two World Cup titles, defeating Argentina in the Final on their home soil.
- The record for most goals by two teams in a World Cup Final is 12 (Austria 7, Switzerland 5 in 1954).
- The oldest player to score a goal in a World Cup final round match is Cameroon's Roger Milla, who was 42 when he scored a goal against Russia in 1994.
- English goalkeeper Gordon Banks enjoyed a streak of seven straight shutouts in World Cup play (1966).
- Just Fontaine of France holds the World Cup Final record for goals, scoring 13 in 1958.
- The last team to win back-to-back World Cup championships was Brazil (1958, '62).
- Brazil has won the World Cup four times, and each time Mario Zagallo played a major role: in 1958 and 1962 as a player, in 1970 as a coach and in 1994 as assistant coach. With Zagallo back as coach in 1998, the Brazilians reached the Final, but lost to France 3-0. Only one other man has won the World Cup as both a player and coach: Franz Beckenbauer, The Kaiser, captained West Germany to the championship in 1974 and coached a united German team to the championship in 1990.
- Ticket sales accounted for 50 percent of the organizational costs of World Cup '98.
- According to the Organizing Committee, the '98 World Cup event saw 1,925 goals in 644 games (qualifying through to championship), a worldwide audience of 37 billion people viewing 5,760 hours of match coverage, and 1,768 boys and girls employed to chase balls that went out of bounds.
- The '98 World Cup event was insured for up to $355 million in damages.
- At the '98 World Cup, from the second round on to the finals (15 games), 11 contests were decided by one goal or on penalty kicks.
- The last time both teams scored in the World Cup Final was 1986, when Argentina beat West Germany 3-2. The last three Finals have seen at least one team shut out.

total access
jeremy schaap

"Joe Gaetjens scored the biggest goal in U.S. soccer history, the only goal in America's stunning upset of England in the 1950 World Cup. Columbia's Andres Escobar scored the second-biggest goal in U.S. soccer history, when he kicked the ball into his own net in 1994 to give the U.S. its first World Cup win since the England upset. Did you know that both Gaetjens and Escobar were later murdered? Gaetjens was killed by the Tonton Macoutes, the secret police in his native Haiti, in 1964. Escobar was gunned down in Columbia, just days after the goal, by unforgiving fans."

Q1

The U.S. soccer team was disappointing in the 1998 World Cup, scoring just one goal in its three losses.

level 1   *Name the U.S. coach who left after the World Cup.*

level 2   *Name the three countries that beat the Americans.*

level 3   *Who scored the lone U.S. goal and against which opponent?*

question 1 answers

level 1   Steve Sampson

level 2   Germany, Iran and Yugoslavia

level 3   Brian McBride against Iran

Q2

France won the 1998 World Cup as a host nation.

level 1   *Name the country the French beat in the championship game.*
What was the final score?

level 2   *How many other countries have won the World Cup as host?*

level 3   *Name those winners and the years they won.*

question 2 answers

level 1   Brazil 3-0

level 2   Five

level 3   *a*   Uruguay 1930
b   Italy 1934
c   England 1966
d   West Germany 1974
e   Argentina 1978

victory laps

::: Where you start the Indianapolis 500 does make a big difference in where you finish the race. Fifty-one winners of the Indy 500 have come out of the first two rows, including 15 from the pole position. The highest position from which a driver has ever started and gone on to win is 28th (done by Ray Harroun in 1991 and Louis Meyer in 1936). No one has ever won from positions 29, 30, 31, 32 or 33.

::: In 1998, Eddie Cheever became the second person to win the Indy 500 from the 17th position.

::: Andre Ribeiro won the inaugural Rio 400 in his native Argentina in 1996.

::: Since 1979, John Andretti is the only driver to win both a Winston Cup and a CART race. Andretti won his first and only CART race in Australia in 1991. His only Winston Cup win is the 1997 Pepsi 400.

::: In 1990, Arie Luyendyk set the Indy 500 race record with an average speed of 185.981 mph, beating Bobby Rahal's record of 170.722 mph, set in 1986. It was Rahal's only Indianapolis win and the closest 1-2-3 finish in Indy 500 history (Kevin Cogan finished second, Rick Mears third).

::: In 1993, Nigel Mansell became the first non-Andretti to drive for Newman-Haas racing. Mansell teamed with Mario while Michael competed in Formula One, and went on to win the PPG Cup title that year. Since then, Paul Tracy, Christian Fittipaldi and Roberto Moreno have also driven for Newman-Haas.

::: Jeff Gordon and David Pearson are the only two Winston Cup drivers to win the first two races of a season. Gordon won the Daytona 500 and Goodwrench 500 in 1997, while Pearson won the L.A. Times 500 and Daytona 500 in 1976.

::: Davey Allison is the only driver to win consecutive titles at The Winston (1991, '92). Allison started from the pole each time (his only two poles in this event). He also finished third in 1988 and fifth in 1990.

::: In 1957, Buck Baker became the first Chevy driver to win a Winston Cup championship. Chevy drivers have won the last five Winston Cup titles, 19 overall.

::: Dale Earnhardt is the only driver to win Rookie of the Year and Winston Cup titles in consecutive years (1979 and 1980). He would go on to win six more Winston Cup titles. Jeff Gordon won the Rookie of the Year Award in 1993 and his first Winston Cup title two years later in 1995.

::: Al Unser Jr. and Michael Andretti share the CART record for most wins in a single season: eight. Unser won eight in his championship season of 1994, while Andretti did it in 1991 when he won the title. Little Al also shares (Alex Zanardi tied it in 1998) the record for most consecutive wins in a season: four, in 1990.

::: Bill Elliott has won the Most Popular Driver Award 12 of the past 14 years, including seven straight years from 1991 to '97. Darrell Waltrip took the honors in 1989 and 1990.

::: The only non-American to win Winston Cup Rookie of the Year was Canadian Earl Ross in 1974.

::: The last driver to win a Winston Cup race the same season he won Rookie of the Year was Davey Allison in 1987.

did you know?

Until Bobby Allison won the 1978 Daytona 500 after
starting 33rd, Benny Parsons held the record for winning
Daytona from the worst starting position: 32nd. They
remain the only two drivers to win from outside Row 10.

inside the numbers

*Since 1979, Bobby Rahal leads all drivers with 259 starts, and his 24 career wins rank fourth
on the all-time CART list:*

driver	starts	ppg cups		career wins
Bobby Rahal	259	3	1986, '87, '92	24
Al Unser Jr.	251	2	1990, '94	31
Michael Andretti	225	1	1991	37
Mario Andretti	209	1	1984	19
Emerson Fittipaldi	195	1	1989	22

*Consistency. That's the ticket on the Winston Cup
circuit. Here are the top winners over two seasons:*

driver	two seasons	wins
Darrell Waltrip	1981, '82	24
Jeff Gordon	1996, '97	20
Jeff Gordon	1997, '98	19 through Sept. 3
Rusty Wallace	1993, '94	18*
Darrell Waltrip	1982, '83	18
Jeff Gordon	1995, '96	17
D. Waltrip	1980, '81	17

*Wallace did not win the Winston Cup championship
in either season.

*Only six drivers have won a Twin 125 race
and the Daytona 500 in the same year since
the Daytona 500 began in 1959:*

driver	year
Dale Earnhardt	1998
Sterling Marlin	1995
Bobby Allison	1988
Bill Elliott	1985
Cale Yarborough	1977, '84
Fireball Roberts	1962

richard petty

- Richard Petty hitchhiked home with his family to Level Cross from Charlotte in 1949 after the very first Winston Cup race ever. He was 11 years old and his father, Lee, had wrecked the family car competing.
- His first win, at the Lakewood Speedway in 1959, was taken away because his father, who'd come in second, filed a protest with the scorers. Lee Petty later said that he just wanted to teach his son a lesson, but he was in a championship chase with Cotton Owens and needed the points. The senior Petty won the title that year.
- He made 61 starts before he won his first Winston Cup title in 1964.
- The most money he ever earned in a season was $531,292 (1979). In 1967, when the King won his record 27 races and 18 poles, his earnings were only $130,000.
- After 546 starts, in 1971 Petty finally became NASCAR's first million-dollar driver.
- The King won his 200th race in Daytona on July 4, 1984, in a car not owned by Petty Enterprises. From 1983 to 1986, he drove for a Nashville country music producer,

Mike Curb. Richard left Petty Enterprises to give his son, Kyle, a chance to emerge from his shadow. It didn't work out. Kyle feuded with his grandfather and oleft to join the Petty family's archrivals, the Wood Brothers.

- ✦ The Pettys are the only family to have four generations win in the same sport. Lee Petty was the first to win 50 Winston Cup races, a record broken by his son, who holds the all-time winning record. Richard's son, Kyle, has eight victories. And in June 1998, Kyle's son, Adam, won an ASA race at the 1-70 Speedway in Missouri.
- ✦ Junior Johnson used to keep a photo of Petty, whom he disliked intensely, taped to the urinal of his race shop.
- ✦ Possibly the most prolific autograph signer ever, he was once asked to sign a duck. He can sign for hours because he pushes the pen with his arm, not his fingers, a habit that he learned in business school in 1956.
- ✦ Jeff Gordon's first Winston Cup race, in November 1992, was Petty's last. It didn't end well for the King. His car caught fire, and he was overheard on ESPN saying, "Get me the h___ outta here."

victory laps

::: Junior Johnson is the only owner to win three straight Winston Cup championships with the same driver (Cale Yarborough, 1976-78). Johnson also won three titles as Darrell Waltrip's owner in 1981, '82 and '85. Rick Hendrick is the only owner to win three consecutive Winston Cups with more than one driver (Jeff Gordon in 1995 and '97 and Terry Labonte in 1996).

::: Only three drivers have won both the BGN and Winston Cup Rookie of the Year awards: Johnny Benson (1994 and '96), Ricky Craven (1992 and '95) and Jeff Gordon (1991 and '93). Gordon is the only one to win the BGN Rookie of the Year and a Winston Cup championship.

::: The last time a NASCAR driver lost his points lead at the season finale was in 1992. Heading into the Hooters 500 in Atlanta, Davey Allison led Alan Kulwicki by 30 points but finished 27th and ended up third in the standings behind Kulwicki and Bill Elliott. Kulwicki won the title because he received the five extra bonus points for leading the most laps in that race and nipped Elliott by 10 points, the closest margin in NASCAR history.

::: Mark Martin is the only Winston Cup driver in the '90s to finish in the top 10 each year without winning a title.

inside the numbers

In 1998, Dale Earnhardt won his first Daytona 500 at 46 years, nine months, a tremendous accomplishment but not a record. The oldest winner of the Great American Race is Bobby Allison, who won his third Daytona 500 in 1988 at 50 years, two months:

driver	daytona 500 win	age
Bobby Allison	1988	50
Dale Earnhardt	1998	46
Lee Petty	1959	44
Bobby Allison	1982	44
Richard Petty	1981	43
Cale Yarborough	1984	43

total access
john kernan   rpm 2 night

"When Dale Jarrett won his first Winston Cup race at Michigan in the great battle with Davey Allison in 1991, I was covering his pit. His crew chief, Eddie Wood, who is a friend of mine, asked me if I knew how Davey's car was handling. We had reported a few minutes earlier on the air that it was tight, so I didn't see the harm in telling him. He immediately radioed D.J. and told him. When Dale held off Davey by a fender to win the race, Eddie jumped from the pit wall onto me and hugged me. After that I felt somewhat responsible for helping D.J. win his first race. However, I don't tell crew chiefs about other cars now, even if they ask."

Q 1

Dale Earnhardt has been a star on the NASCAR circuit for many years.

level 1   *What is his nickname?*

level 2   *When was his first NASCAR season?*

level 3   *How many times has he won the Daytona 500?*

question 1 answers

level 1   The Intimidator

level 2   1975

level 3   Once. He won his first Daytona 500 in 1998 after 18 unsuccessful attempts.

Q2

Texas Motor Speedway has also become a popular spot in a short time.

level 1   *When did the site first host a NASCAR event?*

level 2   *Who won the first NASCAR race there?*

level 3   *What city is this track located in?*

question 2 answers

level 1   1997

level 2   Jeff Burton

level 3   Fort Worth, Tex.

family secrets

- In 1998, Terry and Bobby Labonte became the first brothers to start 1-2 at the Daytona 500. Terry finished 13th and Bobby finished second. Before that, the last time brothers started 1-2 for a Winston Cup race was at North Wilkesboro. Brett Bodine had the pole and Geoff started second for the 1993 First Union 400. Brett finished 17th and Geoff finished 28th.
- The Labontes are also the last brothers to finish 1-2 in a Winston Cup race. On August 20, 1995, at the Goodwrench Dealer 400, Bobby finished first, while Terry came in second—for the second time in the same season. On May 28, the Labontes finished 1-2 (Bobby won again) at the Coca-Cola 600.
- Kenny and Rusty Wallace are the only set of NASCAR racing brothers who have not won poles at Michigan Speedway (Rusty got one in 1987). Ward and Jeff Burton each have one. Terry Labonte has two, while Bobby has one. Geoff Bodine has two, Brett has one. Darrell and Michael Waltrip each have one.
- Davey Allison finished second when father Bobby won the 1988 Daytona 500.
- In 1997, Cruz and Tony Pedregon met in the finals of the Slick 50 Nationals, the first professional final round between brothers in NHRA history. Tony won.

inside the numbers

In 1998, Michael Andretti became the fourth driver to win back-to-back season opening races. His father did it twice in the '80s:

driver	race	season opening victories
Michael Andretti	Homestead	1997, '98
Rick Mears	Phoenix	1989, '90
Mario Andretti	Long Beach/Phoenix	1987, '88
Mario Andretti	Long Beach	1984, '85
Johnny Rutherford	Ontario/Phoenix	1980, '81

total access
rece davis

"Wrecks are not unusual on the track at Talladega. And with well over a hundred thousand fans driving to the track, fender benders outside the Speedway aren't uncommon either–but rarely do the two happen at once. While I was covering the race in July, 1993, Jimmy Horton was exiting Turn 1 when his car left the speedway, rolled down a hill and came to rest outside the track, the first time anyone had ever stopped that far afield. Said Horton, who was uninjured, 'I knew it wasn't good when the first guy to get to me had a beer in his hand.'"

Q3

The Brickyard 400 is one of the most popular NASCAR races.

level 1 *When did the race debut?*

level 2 *Who won the first Brickyard 400?*

level 3 *Who is the only driver to win it twice?*

Q4

Let's see what you know about Formula One.

level 1 *Name the driver with the most career wins.*

level 2 *In 1994 and '95, Michael Schumacher led in total wins. How many races did he win?*

level 3 *How many world driving championships did Jackie Stewart win and in what years?*

question 3 answers

level 1 1994

level 2 Jeff Gordon

level 3 Jeff Gordon

question 4 answers

level 1 Alain Prost with 51

level 2 17

level 3 Three
1969, '71 and '73

summer games

- Rafer Johnson, who won the decathlon in Rome in 1960, was walking through the kitchen of the Ambassador Hotel with Robert Kennedy when the senator was assassinated on June 5, 1968.
- Jackie Robinson's brother Mack won the silver medal in the 200-meters in Berlin in 1936, coming second to Jesse Owens.
- Mildred "Babe" Didrikson got her nickname when, as a young girl, she hit so many home runs she was compared to Babe Ruth (Didrikson later carried a .400 batting average in a Dallas softball league). In 1934, she pitched a hitless inning in an exhibition game for the Philadelphia Athletics against the St. Louis Cardinals.
- Jackie Joyner-Kersee was named by her grandmother after then-First Lady Jacqueline Kennedy.
- When Stella Walsh, who won gold in the 100-meters in 1932, was shot during a robbery attempt in 1980, an autopsy revealed that she was a he.
- In 1988, Canada's Ben Johnson became the 43rd Olympic athlete to be disqualified for testing positive for banned drugs since testing began in 1968. Third-place sprinter Linford Christie also tested positive for banned substances, although the levels were so small that he wasn't punished.
- Only two Americans have ever won gold medals in boxing's bantamweight class: Oliver Kirk in 1904 and Kennedy McKinney in 1988.
- Evander Holyfield had to beat Ricky Womack twice in the Olympic box-offs to even earn a spot on the 1984 squad. He settled for a bronze when he was disqualified for hitting New Zealand's Kevin Barry while being instructed by the referee to break when the fighters were tied up. The Holyfield-Barry fight was in the Olympic semifinals.
- When Cassius Clay (later Muhammad Ali) won a gold medal in 1960, he fought as a light heavyweight (178-pound weight maximum).
- No American male gymnast has ever won a gold medal in the Individual All-Around competition.
- The first women's throwing event in track and field in the modern games was the discus throw (1928).
- The 1984 silver-medal-winning U.S. baseball team included Mark McGwire, Barry Larkin, Will Clark and Bill Swift. The '88 squad included Robin Ventura, Andy Benes, Tino Martinez, Charles Nagy and Jim Abbott.
- U.S. fencer Peter Westbrook competed on six different Olympic teams, including the '96 squad in Atlanta.
- Michael Johnson got fame and fortune for winning both the 200 and 400 meters at the '96 Olympics. Marie-Jose Perec of France accomplished the same feat on the women's side.

inside the numbers

Since the 1980 U.S. boycott of the Summer Olympics, the growth of the games has been evident. Look at the number of participating countries:

year	number of countries
1980	81
1984	140
1988	160
1992	172
1996	197

Q1

Americans have traditionally excelled in the decathlon, with 10 winning gold medals between 1904 and 1996.

level 1 *Name the only American decathlete to win the gold medal in consecutive Olympics.*

level 2 *Name the future professional football and baseball player who won in 1912, the movie that was made of his life story and the actor who played him.*

level 3 *List the 10 events that make up the decathlon.*

Q2

The U.S.A. men's basketball team entered the 1972 Olympics 62-0 in Olympic competition, but lost the final game in one of the most controversial incidents in international sporting history.

level 1 *Name the team that beat the Americans to take gold.*

level 2 *What was the final score?*

level 3 *The controversy centered around whether the opposing team could call a timeout before or after an American went to the free throw line in the last six seconds. Name the future NBA coach who sank two free throws to give Team USA what they thought was a victory.*

question 1 answers

level 1 Robert Mathias 1948, '52

level 2 Burt Lancaster played Jim Thorpe in 1951's *Jim Thorpe-All American.*

level 3 *a* Discus throw
b 100-meter dash
c 400-meter run
d 110-meter hurdles
e Pole vault
f High jump
g Javelin throw
h 1500-meter run
i Long jump
j Shot put

question 2 answers

level 1 The Soviet Union

level 2 51-50

level 3 Doug Collins

winter games

: The youngest competitor to win a gold medal at the Winter Olympics was Kim Yoon-Mi of North Korea. She was 13 years, 83 days old when she won the women's short track relay (speed skating) at the 1994 Games in Lillehammer.

: The youngest woman to win a world figure skating championship was Tara Lipinski, who was 14 years and nine months old when she won the world crown in 1997.

: Norway's Sonja Henie won 10 consecutive world championships between 1927 and 1936. She won her third gold medal at the age of 23 (1936).

: In 1998, Tara Lipinski became the youngest woman to win an individual figure skating gold medal. She was 15 years and two months old, younger than Henie when the Norwegian phenom won the first of her record three consecutive gold medals in 1928.

: Nancy Kerrigan was injured when she was attacked by Shane Stant on January 6, 1994, at an ice rink in Detroit. Kerrigan resumed practicing just 10 days later.

: Despite making headlines in the Kerrigan affair, Tonya Harding finished eighth in the '94 Olympics figure skating.

: The only active NHL players who participated on the U.S. '84 Olympic hockey team are Chris Chelios and Ed Olczyk. They are now teammates again, playing for the NHL Blackhawks.

: American brothers won Olympic gold medals in figure skating in 1956 and '60. Hayes Alan Jenkins won in '56, while his younger brother, David, won four years later.

: According to the '98 Nagano Olympic Committee, there was an operating surplus of $32 million and operating costs in excess of $840 million.

: In 1998, the U.S. was shut out of short track speed skating medals for the first time ever.

: The U.S. has earned one medal in men's cross country skiing: Bill Koch gained a silver in 1976.

: Bonnie Blair won six gold medals and one bronze in speedskating from 1988 to '94.

: Peter Forsberg of the Colorado Avalanche scored the game-winning goal for Sweden in a shootout win over Team Canada at the '94 Olympics.

: Bjorn Dahlie has won more gold medals (eight) than any other athlete in Winter Olympics history. He also has four silvers. Dahlie won the 10-kilometer cross country skiing event in the '98 Olympics with a time of 27:24.5. The last-place finisher, Philip Boit of Kenya, was more than 20 minutes behind (47:25.5).

total access
jeremy schaap

"At the 1988 Winter Olympics in Lillehammer, I was a writer for the prime time telecast hosted by former ESPN anchor Greg Gumbel. The first evening of the ladies' figure skating competition–featuring Nancy Kerrigan and Tonya Harding–was the second-most-watched show in American history. Only the final episode of M∗A∗S∗H was seen in more homes."

Q3

Four Olympians have played Tarzan in the movies.

level 1 *Name the swimmer who starred in* Tarzan, the Ape Man, *opposite Margaret O'Sullivan.*

level 2 *How many gold medals did he win in his Olympics career?*

level 3 *Name the other Olympians who played Tarzan.*

question 3 answers

level 1   Johnny Weissmuller

level 2   Five, four in 1924 and one in 1928

level 3   *a*   Buster Crabbe
gold in the 400-meter freestyle
(1932)

      b   Herman Brix

      c   Glenn Morris
gold in the decathlon
(1936)

Q4

Babe Didrikson was voted the greatest female athlete of the half-century by Associated Press.

level 1 *In 1932, despite qualifying in five Olympic events, she was only allowed to compete in three. Which three did she choose, and how did she perform in each?*

level 2 *Her greatest post-Olympics success came as a professional golfer. How many U.S. Opens did she win?*

level 3 *Actress Susan Clark won an Emmy for her portrayal of Didrikson in the 1975 TV movie* Babe. *Name the NFL Hall of Fame athlete who played Didrikson's husband, wrestler George Zaharias.*

question 4 answers

level 1   *a*   80-meter hurdles
gold, world record

      b   Javelin
gold

      c   High jump
silver, shared world record

level 2   Three

level 3   Alex Karras, who would later marry Clark and star with her in the sitcom *Webster*

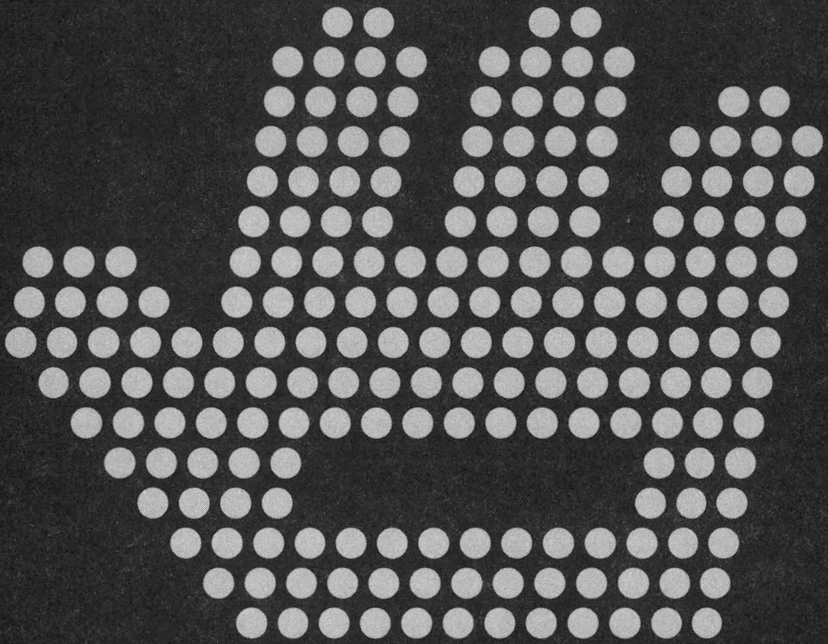

chapter 7 *baseball*

did you know?

Joe Morgan is the only second baseman to win NL MVP twice.
He is also one of four players since 1960 to win the NL MVP in
consecutive years: Morgan (1975-76), Mike Schmidt (1980-
81), Dale Murphy (1982-83) and Barry Bonds (1992-93).

for the record

- Cy Young holds the major league record for number of seasons pitching 300 or more innings: 16.
- Longest home run ever? Mickey Mantle hit one 643 feet in Detroit against the Tigers on September 10, 1960.
- The 1943 Red Sox hold the record for the most extra-inning games in a season: 31.
- The record for most strikeouts in a major league debut is 15, shared by Brooklyn Dodger Karl Spooner (1954) and Astro J.R. Richard (1971).
- The major league record for most consecutive innings pitched without a walk in a season is 84 ⅓, set by Kansas City's Bill Fischer in 1962.
- The record for most combined shutouts in both leagues in one day is eight (five in AL; three in NL) on June 4, 1972.
- The record for the best single season home unbeaten record is 13-0, shared by Tex Hughson (Red Sox, 1944) and Boo Ferriss (Red Sox, 1946).
- The Red Sox hit a record four consecutive triples against the Tigers on May 6, 1934.
- The record for most NL games played in one day this century is 12. All 12 NL teams played two on September 7, 1970.
- The major league record for home runs in a game is 10, set by Toronto on September 14, 1987.
- The modern-day record for the most hits by one team in a game is 31, shared by the 1901 New York Giants in 1901 and the 1992 Milwaukee Brewers.
- The record for most career wins versus one team by a pitcher is 70, by Grover Cleveland Alexander, who picked up 70 wins over the Reds from 1911 to '30.
- The record for most multi-home-run games in one season is 11, set by Hank Greenberg in 1938 and Sammy Sosa in 1998.
- The record for the most career wins by a relief pitcher is 124 by Hoyt Wilhelm.
- Tom Seaver holds the record for the most consecutive years with 200 or more strikeouts, with nine from 1968 to '76 with the Mets. Nolan Ryan has the ML record for the most 200-K seasons, with 15 between both leagues.
- The record for the most two-out runs scored by one team in one inning is 13, shared by the '73 Indians and the '56 Kansas City Athletics.
- The fastest nine-inning game in baseball history took 51 minutes. The New York Giants beat Philadelphia 6-1 in the first game of a doubleheader on September 28, 1919.

inside the numbers

Mark McGwire was pretty consistent in his record-breaking 70-home-run season. He tied the mark for most home runs at the All-Star break, then shattered the single-season mark:

player	season	HRs at break	season total
Mark McGwire	1998	37	70
Reggie Jackson	1969	37	47
Frank Howard	1969	34	48
Ken Griffey Jr.	1994	33	40
Matt Williams	1994	33	43
Mark McGwire	1987	33	49
Roger Maris	1961	33	61

Since Roger Maris established his home-run record in 1961, five teams have slugged 61 or fewer in a season (not including 1981, the strike year):

year	team	total team HRs
1979	Astros	49
1975	Angels	55
1972	Rangers	56
1986	Cardinals	58
1980	Mets	61

April **9**

1945 Peter Gammons is born.
1974 The San Diego Chicken is born, as Ted Giannoulas dons the big bird suit for the first time in a 9-5 Padres loss to the Astros.

home runs

-:- All four members of the 60-home-run club played for other teams before they had their 60-HR seasons. Mark McGwire was originally drafted by the Expos in the eighth round in 1981. He signed instead with the A's, who later traded him to the Cardinals for Blake Stein, T.J. Mathews and Eric Ludwick. Sammy Sosa was traded twice: in 1989, from Texas to the White Sox as part of the Harold Baines deal, then to the Cubs for George Bell in 1992. Babe Ruth played for the Red Sox from 1914 to 1919 before going to the Yankees. Roger Maris was with the Indians from 1957 to 1958, then the Royals in 1958 and 1959 before joining the Yankees.

-:- Roger Maris did not receive a single intentional walk in 1961, the year Mickey Mantle, who finished with 54 home runs, hit behind him.

-:- The record for most home runs by a pitcher in a season is nine, set by Cleveland's Wes Ferrell in 1931.

-:- The record for the most at-bats in one season without a home run is 672 , set by Rabbit Maranville in 1922. The shortstop hit just 28 HRs in a 23-year Hall of Fame career.

-:- The only pinch hitters to hit home runs in both games of a doubleheader were Expo Hal Breeden (1973) and Red Sox Joe Cronin (1943).

-:- Before Babe Ruth, the single-season home run record-holder was Chicago White Stocking Ned Williamson, who hit 27 home runs in 1884.

-:- The top three home-run hitters of all time both started and finished their careers with different teams in the same city: Henry Aaron (Milwaukee Braves-Brewers); Babe Ruth (Boston Red Sox-Braves) and Willie Mays (New York Giants-Mets).

-:- The only players with 300 career home runs and no 30-homer seasons are Harold Baines and Al Kaline. Kaline has the most home runs of the pair, hitting 399 in 22 campaigns with the Tigers, twice knocking out 29. Baines had one 29-home-run season.

-:- The only player to hit a pinch home run in his first major league at-bat and never homer again is Detroit's Bill Roman (September 30, 1964).

-:- The last player to lead either league in home runs with fewer than 40 was Fred McGriff ('92 NL-35 HRs, '89 AL-36 HRs).

-:- The most home runs in a five-year span is 256, hit by Babe Ruth from 1926 to '30. Mark McGwire hit 228 from 1994 to '98.

-:- The closest a player has ever come to hitting more home runs than his team had wins was Ralph Kiner, with 37 HRs for the 1952 Pirates (42-112). The Pirates finished last in the NL, 54 ½ games behind the Brooklyn Dodgers. In 1998, Mark McGwire hit 70 while the Cardinals won 83 games.

total access
tim kurkjian   espn: the magazine

"Mark McGwire told me about the 75 specially tagged balls used during his home run chase, and how he hit No. 60 with ball No. 3, chosen at random. 'No. 3, that was Babe Ruth's number,' McGwire said. 'And I'm the third guy to hit 60.' 'You hit No. 60 on the third pitch,' I added. He looked to the heavens. 'I believe in things like that,' he said."

ans outfielder Manny Ramirez tied a major league record when he hit six home runs in a three-game
n (September 15-17, 1998). He was the first major leaguer to do that since Mike Schmidt in 1976 and
first AL player since Gus Zernial of the Philadelphia Athletics in 1951.

lies pitcher Rick Wise hit two home runs during his 4-0 no-hitter against the Reds on June 23, 1971.

1884 Chicago White Stockings are the only team to have the top four home run hitters in one year: Ned
iamson (27), Fred "Fritz" Pfeffer (25), Abner Dalrymple (22) and Cap Anson (21). The White Stockings
ved in Lake Front Park, which featured the shortest-ever outfield distances, only 180 feet down the left-
d line, 196 down the right-field line.

rk McGwire is the only player to compete on two different teams and finish with 50 home runs in a
son (Athletics/Cardinals in 1997).

ry Aaron hit just 13 home runs in 468 at-bats as a rookie with Milwaukee in 1954. Later, while with the
ves, he and teammate Eddie Mathews homered in the same game a record 75 times.

ee sets of teammates have combined to hit 100 or more home runs in a season. Yankees Roger Maris
Mickey Mantle totaled 115 in 1961 and Babe Ruth and Lou Gehrig had 107 in 1927. Cardinals Mark
Gwire and Ray Lankford combined for 101 in 1998. (Ken Griffey Jr. and Jay Buhner fell just short in
7, with 96.)

y-five of Mark McGwire's 70 home runs came versus right-handed pitchers, 38 were hit at home and 37
e solo shots. The most home runs hit against any team was seven (Cubs and Marlins). Sixty-five pitchers
ved up those home run balls. McGwire's favorite inning was the fourth (13 HRs). Tuesday was his favorite
(16 HRs) and May, his favorite month (16 HRs). His 70 homers were more than the number of wins for
teams in 1998.

998 Greg Vaughn (50 homers) and Mo Vaughn (40 homers) combined for 90 HRs in a season, the most
r by two players with the same last name.

inside the numbers

In 1998, Nomar Garciaparra became the fifth
MLB player to have 30 or more home runs in
each of his first two seasons:

player	seasons
Nomar Garciaparra	1997-98
Mark McGwire	1987-88
Jose Canseco	1986-87
Ron Kittle	1983-84
Rudy York	1937-38

pitching

- Five players pitched to both Roger Maris and Mark McGwire in their major league careers: Joe Niekro, Phil Niekro, Tommy John, Nolan Ryan and Don Sutton.
- The pitcher against whom Mark McGwire has the most career at-bats without a HR is Bret Saberhagen with 34. Sammy Sosa is also homerless versus Saberhagen in 10 career at-bats.
- Tom Glavine has had more 20-win seasons in the '90s than any other major league pitcher: four.
- On May 6, 1998, 20-year-old Kerry Wood became the first pitcher to match his age in strikeouts since 17-year-old Bob Feller had 17 Ks against the Philadelphia A's on September 13, 1936.
- The most consecutive wins by a pitcher in a single season this century is 19, by Rube Marquard of the N.Y. Giants. He finished the 1913 season with 26 wins, 11 losses with an ERA of 2.57.
- Philadelphia's Ken Brett has the record for home runs hit in consecutive games by a pitcher: four
- In 1992, the White Sox had three different pitchers with 10 or more saves: Bobby Thigpen (22), Scott Radinsky (15) and Roberto Hernandez (13).
- Cy Young is the only player to win 200 games in both leagues.
- The most hits allowed in a complete-game shutout is 14, shared by Cub Larry Cheney (defeated the N.Y. Giants 7-0 on September 14, 1913) and Senator Milt Gaston (defeated the Indians 9-0 on July 10, 1928).
- Gaylord Perry is the only pitcher to win the Cy Young Award in both leagues (1972, Indians; 1978, Padres).
- Cleveland's Addie Joss is the only pitcher to no-hit the same team twice during his career (the White Sox on October 2, 1908, and April 20, 1910).
- Christy Mathewson and Walter Johnson are the only managers in major league history to have pitched no-hitters and managed no-hitters.
- On May 2, 1917, the Reds' Fred Toney pitched a no-hitter against the Cubs. Hippo Vaughn, who had pitched 9 ⅓ hitless innings himself, finally gave up two hits in the 10th. The Reds won 1-0 on Jim Thorpe's RBI single.
- The only no-hitter to be thrown on Opening Day was pitched by Bob Feller in 1940.
- On May 27, 1998, Eddie PRIEST made his first start for the Reds. The Cincinnati registry also has these other pitchers: Howie NUNN (1961-62), Bubba CHURCH (1952-53), Randy SAINT Claire (1988) and Bill CHAPPELLE (1909). Pity Jim ABBOTT and PREACHER Roe never pitched for the Reds.

inside the numbers

In 1998, Kerry Wood set the record for most strikeouts in consecutive games. He did it in fewer innings than any of the men who struck out 32 in two games, accomplishing the feat in the fifth and sixth starts of his career:

pitcher	year	Ks (game 1, game 2)	innings pitched
Kerry Wood	1998	33 (20, 13)	16
Randy Johnson	1997	32 (19, 13)	17
Dwight Gooden	1984	32 (16, 16)	17
Nolan Ryan	1974	32 (13, 19)	17.2
Luis Tiant	1968	32 (13, 19)	19

Q1

Mark McGwire was the first of two players to break Roger Maris's single-season home run record. McGwire belted his 62nd of the season on September 8, 1998. He finished the season with 70.

level 1   *Name the team he hit No. 62 against.*

level 2   *Name the pitcher who served up No. 62.*

level 3   *What number game was it for the Cardinals when he hit the famed 62nd?*

Q2

The New York Yankees enjoyed a stellar 1998.

level 1   *When did the Yankees clinch the AL East title (date and game number)?*

level 2   *Only one team since the start of divisional play clinched earlier than New York. Name the team and year.*

level 3   *What was the Yankees' record at the All-Star break (through 81 games)?*

cal ripken jr.

- A MLB player who didn't miss a game for 16 straight seasons (multiply by 162 games) would have played in 2,592 straight games and still be 41 short of breaking Cal Ripken Jr.'s record of 2,632 consecutive starts.
- Ripken and Lou Gehrig are the only two players in major league history to play more than 2,000 straight games. Everett Scott, third on the all-time list, is more than 800 games behind Gehrig's 2,130 games.
- All 2,632 games were starts. Ripken never pinch hit or pinch ran to extend the streak.
- The day before Ripken's streak began, May 29, 1982, Floyd Rayford started at third base for Baltimore in the second game of a doubleheader. The next day, Hall of Famer Jim Palmer was the Orioles starting pitcher. Nobody from the Blue Jays or Orioles starting lineup is active in major league baseball today.
- His overall stats during the streak: .277 batting average, 2,832 hits, 381 home runs and 1,494 RBI, two MVP awards (1983 and '91), two Gold Gloves (1991-92), the Rookie of the Year award (1982) and a World Series ring (1983).
- Ripken played for eight different Oriole managers during the streak.

- "Ebony and Ivory" by Stevie Wonder and Paul McCartney was the No. 1 single when the streak started. "Hill Street Blues" won the Emmy for top TV drama, while Gandhi won the Oscar for best picture. Ronald Reagan was president.
- When the streak ended on September 20, 1998, Ripken had played in more consecutive games than the next 17 active players on the list. (Albert Belle took over active leadership and finished the 1998 regular season at 327 straight games.)
- The man who replaced Ripken at third base when the streak ended is the same Ryan Minor who was Big Eight Player of the Year in basketball as a junior at Oklahoma.
- Six ballparks that were around when Ripken started the streak not longer exist, including Baltimore's Memorial Stadium.
- Brady Anderson played the most games of any Oriole teammate during the streak: 1,330.
- The Orioles changed the logo on their caps three times during the streak.
- Ripken is one of 14 players in Orioles history to wear No. 8. He will certainly be the last.

streaks

- Tony Gwynn and Honus Wagner are the only eight-time winners of the NL batting title, tied for second behind Ty Cobb's 12 titles overall. Gwynn, Wagner and Cobb are three of six players to win four straight batting crowns (the rest are Rogers Hornsby, Wade Boggs and Rod Carew. Gwynn and Cobb are the only ones with two streaks of three straight titles.
- Only three men have had 500 home runs and 3,000 hits during their careers: Henry Aaron (755 HRs, 3,771 hits), Willie Mays (660, 3,283) and Eddie Murray (504, 3,255). All three are employed by their primary teams: Aaron is senior vice-president of the Braves, Mays is special assistant to the president of the Giants and Murray is a coach with the Orioles.
- Jimmie Foxx has the record for consecutive seasons with 30 or more home runs: 12 (1929-40).
- Since expansion in 1969, the Orioles are the only team to win 100 or more games in three straight seasons (1969-71).
- During Joe DiMaggio's record 56-game hit streak in 1941, he had just one hit in 34 of those games.
- The only players to lead the majors in HRs for three consecutive seasons are Gavvy Cravath, Babe Ruth, Ralph Kiner, Mike Schmidt and Mark McGwire.
- The record for most career games pitched with one club is 802, shared by Walter Johnson and Elroy Face. Hall of Famer Johnson pitched all 21 of his big-league seasons for the original Washington Senators, while Face spent 15 years with the Pirates in the '50s and '60s.
- The longest hitting streak by a player who did not finish with a .300 batting average that season is 33 games, set by Hal Chase in 1907 (.287).
- The major league record for consecutive at-bats without a home run is 3,347 (Tommy Thevenow, 1926-38).
- The 1963 Mets lost a modern-era record 22 consecutive road games from June 16 to July 28.
- The major league record for longest road winning streak is 17 games, shared by the Giants and the 1984 Tigers.
- The record for the most individual winning streaks of 10 or more games is five, set by Walter Johnson. The Big Train won 16 games, 14 games, 13 games and 10 games twice in a career totaling 417 wins for the Washington Senators from 1907-27.
- The only team never to have been shut out over an entire season (minimum 150 games) was the 1932 Yankees, part of a record 308 no-shutout streak that lasted one day short of exactly two years from 1931 to '33.

inside the numbers

Only six players in major league history have played in more games than Cal Ripken Jr.'s consecutive starts streak ran:

player	total games played
Ty Cobb	2,935
Brooks Robinson	2,870
Willie Mays	2,842
Hank Aaron	2,760
Tris Speaker	2,698
Eddie Collins	2,650

Q3

The Atlanta Braves remained dominant by winning the NL East.

level 1   *How many consecutive division titles have the Braves won?*

level 2   *Who finished second in the NL East?*

level 3   *When was the last time Atlanta had a losing record? What was the W-L record?*

question 3 answers

level 1   Seven
level 2   New York Mets
level 3   A 65-97 record in 1990.

Q4

The Indians completed 1998 with their fifth straight winning season.

level 1   *Before the '98 campaign, when was the last time the Tribe enjoyed five consecutive winning seasons?*

level 2   *What is the club record for most wins in a season?*

level 3   *When did Cleveland set that record?*

question 4 answers

level 1   1952 to '56
level 2   111 wins
level 3   1954

he did it

We all saw him do it. But *how* did Mark McGwire hit 70 home runs? And, for that matter, how did Sammy Sosa—who had never before hit more than 40 home runs—wallop 66?

∴ Not many baseball pundits were that surprised to see McGwire make history in 1998. If not for injuries, he might well have broken Roger Maris's record in 1995 or '96. If you look at McGwire's home runs in the regular season over the past four seasons, it's clear that the ability has always been there:

year	games played	regular-season HRs	HRs projected per 162 games
1995	104	39	61
1996	130	52	65
1997	156	58	60
1998	155	70	73

The key was staying healthy and, after years of lingering ailments, McGwire finally played in 156 games in 1997, then 155 in 1998. But does this completely explain McGwire obliterating Maris's 37-year-old mark?

∴ Could the full explanation lie elsewhere? Home runs are up all over. The ball is juiced. The hitters are bulked up on Creatine and weight machines. All the ballparks are bandboxes. Well, some or all of those things may be true—except for the first assertion. In fact, home runs were *not* appreciably up in 1998, when the average major league game included 2.09 HRs. From 1994 through '97, the ratios were 2.07, 2.02, 2.19 and 2.05. That means the '98 homer rate was only about two percent higher than the '97 rate and significantly lower than in '96, when no one seriously threatened any records.

∴ Before 1996, the best home-run season was 1987, when the hitters averaged 2.11 HRs per game, obviously close to the '98 rate. Yet in '87, not a single player reached the 50-homer plateau: Andre Dawson and a rookie named Mark McGwire co-led the majors with 49 big flies apiece. In 1998, *four* major leaguers topped 50 home runs, and two of them topped 65.

∴ The difference is even more dramatic if we look at the 40-homer barrier. In 1987, four hitters reached that mark: Dawson, McGwire, George Bell and Dale Murphy. In 1998, 13 major league hitters topped 40 dingers, and the great majority of them did it with plenty of room to spare.

∴ At first glance, this doesn't make a lot of sense. If the overall rates in those two seasons were virtually the same, why would the best power hitters hit so many more homers in 1998? Are today's sluggers that much better than their brethren of just over a decade ago?

∴ Probably not. Actually, what all this suggests is what science writer Stephen Jay Gould might call "an increase in variation." While the *average* remains approximately the same, the *extremes* at the ends of the scale are exaggerated. In 1911, American League hitters batted .273 as a group. However, Ty Cobb batted .420 and Shoeless Joe Jackson batted .408. In 1950, American League hitters batted .271, but the top two hitters averaged just .354 and .340. Though the league batting average in those two seasons was virtually identical, the top hitters in 1911 performed at a significantly higher level than the top hitters of 1950. Simply put, there was more variation in 1911, more players further above and below the league average.

∴ For most of baseball history, variation has been decreasing, which is why we haven't seen a .400 hitter since 1941. But things are different now, probably because of expansion and the popularity of other sports among America's youth. It seems that after a steady decline throughout this century, variation is now increasing. Whether this is good for baseball in the long run is debatable, but it certainly makes for good TV. *–rob neyer*

batting

:: On August 4, 1982, Joel Youngblood became the only player to get two hits for two different teams (Mets and Expos) in two different cities on the same day.

:: Only one player in major league history has struck out over 2,000 times, Reggie Jackson, who had 18 seasons of 100 or more strikeouts.

:: When Ted Williams hit .406 in 1941, he went hitless in only 29 out of 143 games.

:: The most strikeouts by a batting champion is 107, set by Pittsburgh's Dave Parker in 1977. The other players to win a batting title with 100-plus Ks are Alex Rodriguez (104 in 1996), Willie McGee (104 in 1990) and Roberto Clemente (103 in 1967).

:: Pete Rose's 4,000th hit came on April 13, 1984, exactly 21 years after his first major league hit.

:: Rob Deer had 64 RBI despite batting .179 in 1991. No other player has had as many RBI when batting below .200 in a season.

:: The most RBI in a three-year span is 509, by Lou Gehrig from 1930 to '32 (the Iron Horse batted .356 with 121 HRs).

:: Seattle's Edgar Martinez is the only player to win the batting title primarily as a designated hitter (.356 in 1995).

:: The player with the most career homers without winning a league home run title is Stan Musial with 475. Eddie Murray (504 HRs) tied for the AL-lead in the strike year of 1981.

:: The last team to hit .300 for a season was the 1950 Red Sox. Led by Billy Goodman's major league best .354, Boston hit .302 and finished four games behind the eventual World Series champion Yankees.

:: The only team to have three players hit for the cycle in one year is the 1933 Philadelphia Athletics. Mickey Cochrane, Pinky Higgins and Jimmie Foxx all hit for the cycle in August, three of eight hit that year (four in each league).

:: Since 1900, only two players have had 50 doubles and 50 stolen bases in the same season: Tris Speaker of the 1912 Red Sox (53 doubles, 52 steals) and Craig Biggio of the 1998 Astros (51 doubles, 50 steals).

inside the numbers

In 1998, Alex Rodriguez became the third player to join the exclusive 40-40 club (40 homers and 40 stolen bases):

year	player	team	HR	SB
1998	Alex Rodriguez	Mariners	42	46
1996	Barry Bonds	Giants	42	40
1988	Jose Canseco	Athletics	42	40

grand slams ⟶ Since 1900, the only player to hit a grand slam in his first major league game was Bobby Bonds. Barry's dad did it in his third at-bat for the Giants against the Dodgers on June 25, 1968. (Philadelphia's Bill Duggleby hit a grand slam in his first at-bat in 1898.)

⟶ On August 14, 1998, Baltimore's Chris Hoiles became the ninth player to hit two grand slams in one game.

⟶ Only three players have retired with more than 150 HRs and no grand slams: Glenn Davis (190), Ron Kittle (176) and Claudell Washington (164).

⟶ The single-season record for grand slams is six, set by Don Mattingly in 1987.

⟶ The only time four pitchers hit grand slams in the same year was 1950. In 1995, three pitchers, Jeff Juden, Chris Hammond and Denny Neagle hit grand slams.

inside the numbers

While Pittsburgh Pirates catcher Jason Kendall had a terrific season in 1998 (.327 batting average), he was still far off from the top batting averages for catchers:

batting average	catcher	year*
.362	Bill Dickey, NYY	1936
.362	Mike Piazza, LA	1997
.358	Chief Meyers, NYG	1912
.357	Mickey Cochrane, PHI-AL	1930
.354	Gaby Hartnett, CUBS	1937

*minimum 100 games caught

did you know?

Between 1980 and 1996, only three players won the AL stolen base title: Rickey Henderson (1980-86, '88-91), Kenny Lofton (1992-96) and ESPN's Harold Reynolds, who stole 60 bases for the Mariners in 1987.

world series

- The first official game between the AL and the NL was on October 1, 1903, Game 1 of the 1903 World Series between Boston and Pittsburgh.
- The Fall Classic has ended on a home run just twice: in 1960 Pirate Bill Mazerowski homered to beat the Yankees, and in 1993 Joe Carter accomplished the same heroic feat to help the Blue Jays defeat the Phillies.
- The last time the AL and NL home-run leaders met in the World Series was in 1956, when Mickey Mantle's Yankees defeated Duke Snider's Brooklyn Dodgers 4-3.
- The fewest runs scored by a team in the World Series is two, set by the 1966 Dodgers, who lost four straight to Baltimore.
- The only stadiums to host both the World Series and the Super Bowl are Miami's Pro Player Stadium (formerly Joe Robbie Stadium), the Los Angeles Coliseum, Qualcomm Stadium (formerly Jack Murphy Stadium) in San Diego and Minneapolis's Metrodome.
- The 1997 Indians were the first team since the 1977 Yankees to host both the World Series and the All-Star game in the same year.
- The oldest current franchises never to have reached the World Series are the Angels and Rangers, major league baseball's first expansion teams.
  (The Rangers were known as the Washington Senators when they began play in 1961.)
- The only two players to lead the majors in saves and win a World Series title in the same season were Cincinnati's Rawly Eastwick (1976) and St. Louis's Bruce Sutter (1982).
- The last AL MVP to play on a World Series championship team was pitcher Willie Hernandez of the 1984 Tigers.
- Since 1950, only Ralph Houk, Billy Martin, (both with the Yankees) and Red Schoendienst (Cardinals) have won the World Series title as a player and manager with the same team.
- Carl Yastrzemski holds the record for most seasons played with the same club without winning a World Series title: 23 (1961 to '83). Yaz did reach the World Series twice with Boston, losing in 1967 and '75 in seven games.
- Bucky Harris is the only manager to win the World Series in his first year with two different teams (1924 with the Senators; 1947 with the Yankees).
- The winning team with the lowest batting average in a seven-game series was the 1918 Boston Red Sox. They hit just .186 to win the World Series in six games over the Cubs. Babe Ruth had one hit in five at-bats for the Red Sox but won two games as a pitcher in the series.
- The 1929 Philadelphia A's had the biggest comeback in World Series history. Down 8-0 in Game 4, they scored 10 runs in the seventh inning to win 10-8.

total access
jeremy schaap

On October 2, 1978, when I was nine years old and a devoted Yankees fan, my father, Dick Schaap, took me to Fenway to watch the Yankees and the Red Sox in a one-game playoff for the AL's Eastern Division title. I still remember watching Bucky Dent's home run float over the Green Monster. I remember the silence as he rounded the bases. But those glaring Boston fans didn't even know the best part: Dad and I were sitting in Bucky's seats."

Q5

Ken Griffey Jr. had another big season in 1998, finishing with 56 home runs.

level 1   *How many 50-home-run seasons has he had in his career?*

level 2   *How many other M's have hit 50 home runs in a season?*

level 3   *When was his first season in the majors, and how many home runs did he hit that year?*

question 5 answers

level 1   Two
level 2   None
level 3   1989, 16 home runs in 127 games

Q6

In '98, the Mariners dealt star left-hander Randy Johnson to the Astros for three players, including promising infielder Carlos Guillen.

level 1   *Which team originally drafted Randy Johnson?*

level 2   *Which team traded Johnson to the Mariners in 1989? Name the key pitcher Seattle dealt in that transaction.*

level 3   *Johnson attended USC on scholarship for two sports. Name the sports.*

question 6 answers

level 1   The Braves in 1982
level 2   Montreal Expos. Mark Langston
level 3   Baseball and basketball

dubious distinctions

- The most batters hit by one pitcher in a game is six, by St. Louis's John Grimes in 1897.
- Dodger Willie Davis holds the record for errors in one inning in the World Series. He had three miscues in the fifth inning of Game 2 in 1966.
- The only team to have a perfect game and a no-hitter thrown against them in the same year is the 1965 Cubs, who were no-hit by Cincinnati's Jim Maloney and then were the victims of Sandy Koufax's perfect game.
- The 1920 Red Sox played the most innings (45) in two consecutive extra-inning contests.
- In 1886, Washington committed 867 errors in 122 games.
- Boston and St. Louis combined for 40 errors in a game on June 14, 1876.
- In 20 postseason games, Ken Griffey Sr. never hit a home run. He went a combined 18-75 (.240) with five doubles and eleven RBIs.
- The most wins ever for a team that didn't make the World Series is 104, shared by the 1909 Cubs, 1942 Dodgers and the 1993 Braves.
- Oakland's Brian Kingman was the last major league pitcher to lose 20 games in a season (8-20 in 1980).
- In 1964, the Cubs acquired Ernie Broglio, Bobby Shantz and Doug Clemens.
  The player of note acquired by the Cardinals in the deal was future Hall of Famer Lou Brock.
- The franchise that has gone the longest without a 100-win season is the Pirates, who last posted three-digit wins in 1909, going 110-42.
- The longest span between postseason wins is 62 years by the Phillies (1915-77).
- The record for most consecutive losses by a major league baseball team to start a season is 21, set by the Orioles in 1988.
- The 1961 Tigers won 101 games and still finished eight games behind the Yankees.
- The record for the most at-bats in a hitless season is 70 by pitcher Bob Buhl of the 1962 Braves. Over the course of his career, Buhl was an .089 hitter, who struck out 389 times in 857 at-bats.
- Bobo Newsom won 20 games for the St. Louis Browns in 1938 despite posting a 5.08 ERA.
- The player with the most regular-season games without playing in the postseason is Ernie Banks (2,528 games).
- On June 3, 1956, White Sox Nellie Fox became the first player to be hit by two pitches in a row.
- In 1946, Giants player-manager Mel Ott became the first manager or player to be thrown out of both ends of a doubleheader.
- The record for most career postseason at-bats without a home run is 197, set by Frankie Frisch, who played in eight World Series for the Giants and Cardinals during his Hall of Fame career.
- The franchise that has gone the longest since having a champion in a Triple Crown batting category is the Dodgers, dating back to 1963, when Tommy Davis led in average.
  (The last Dodger to win an RBI title was Davis in 1962. The last Dodger to win a HR title was Duke Snider in 1956.)
- The highest lifetime ERA in major league history (minimum 500 innings) is 6.24, held by Todd Van Poppel. He pitched 509 ⅓, with a career record of 22-37.
- On August 8, 1976, the White Sox became the first team to wear shorts as part of their uniform, defeating the Royals 5-2.

Q7

Sammy Sosa enjoyed his competition with Mark McGwire in the home run chase.

level 1   *Before 1998, what was Sosa's greatest home run total in one season?*

level 2   *Which team dealt Sosa to the Cubs? Name the player he was traded for.*

level 3   *Which major league team did he debut with in 1989?*

Q8

Kerry Wood made big news in 1998 when he struck out 20 in one game.

level 1   *Name the team that was fanned 20 times by Wood.*

level 2   *He also set the record for most strikeouts in consecutive games. How many were there?*

level 3   *He was the fourth overall pick in the 1995 draft. Name the current major leaguer who went first in that draft.*

cooperstown

⁑ Of the 17 players who have won two or more MVP awards and are eligible for the Hall of Fame, only Roger Maris has not been elected. Two-time winners Dale Murphy and Robin Yount become eligible this summer, while Frank Thomas, Barry Bonds and Cal Ripken Jr. are still active.

⁑ The Yankees have the most career players in Cooperstown: Earle Combs, Bill Dickey, Joe DiMaggio, Lou Gehrig, Whitey Ford, Mickey Mantle and Phil Rizzuto. Lefty Gomez was a Senator for one game, while Yogi Berra was a Met for four.

⁑ The only Hall of Famer to hit a home run in his first major league at-bat was Giants pitcher Hoyt Wilhelm in 1952. It was also his only HR in 21 major-league seasons.

⁑ Rollie Fingers has the fewest wins of any Hall of Fame pitcher (114).

⁑ The Hall of Famer who was elected with the lowest percentage of votes cast was Ferguson Jenkins in 1991 (74.7 percent of votes cast). There has never been a unanimous vote on any player, with Ty Cobb coming the closest at 98.2 percent.

inside the numbers

Cy Young winners from losing teams:

year	pitcher	record, era	team record
1997	Pedro Martinez MTL	17-8, 1.90	78-84
	Roger Clemens TOR	21-7, 2.05	76-86
1996	Pat Hentgen TOR	20-10, 3.22	74-88
1992	Greg Maddux CUBS	20-11, 2.18	78-84
1987	Roger Clemens RSOX	20-9, 2.97	78-84
	Steve Bedrosian PHI	40 saves	80-82
1979	Bruce Sutter CUBS	37 saves	80-82
1976	Randy Jones SD	22-14, 2.74	73-89
1972	Gaylord Perry CLEV	24-16, 1.92	72-84
	Steve Carlton PHI	27-10, 1.97	59-97
1970	Bob Gibson STL	23-7, 3.12	76-86

total access
dave campbell   baseball tonight

"I hit only 20 home runs in my major league career, but five came against Hall of Fame pitchers: Tom Seaver, Bob Gibson, Phil Niekro and Don Sutton (twice). That's one reason I'm thrilled that Don got in the Hall of Fame this year."

Q 9

At the end of the 1998 regular season, Don Baylor was fired as Rockies manager after a six-year stint.

level 1   *How many winning seasons did he post in Colorado?*

level 2   *What was his overall record?*

level 3   *Only two managers had longer tenures with expansion teams. Name them, the teams and length of stay.*

question 9 answers
level 1   Three
level 2   440 wins, 469 losses
level 3   *a*   Bill Rigney was in his ninth season with the Angels when he left.
           b   Gene Mauch spent seven full seasons with the Expos (1969-75).

Q 10

The Cubs had a solid 1998 season, with the excitement including a playoff game against the Giants for the NL wild card berth.

level 1   *The franchise holds the record for getting to 100 wins faster than anyone.*
How many games did it take?

level 2   *Before 1998, who held the Cubs' record for most home runs in a season?*

level 3   *Two pitchers in the team's storied history won 20 or more games six different times. Name the two hurlers.*

question 10 answers
level 1   132 games
level 2   Hack Wilson with 56 in 1930
level 3   Ferguson Jenkins and Mordecai Brown

franchise history

- The Braves are the only franchise to win the World Series in three different cities: Boston, Milwaukee and Atlanta.
- The last team to lead the major leagues in runs scored and fewest runs allowed in a season was the 1944 Cardinals. Only five teams have led the major leagues in runs scored and fewest runs allowed in a season. Three went on to win the World Series (1944 Cardinals, '39 Yankees, '27 Yankees), one lost the World Series (1906 Cubs), and one, the 1902 Pirates, accomplished their double before the World Series existed.
- The franchise that has gone the longest since last having a player hit for the cycle is the Dodgers (Wes Parker on May 7, 1970).
- The A's and Indians are the only teams in the modern era to have a perfect game, a 300-strikeout pitcher and a 50-home run hitter at any time in their histories. For the A's, Rube Waddell had 300-Ks (1903 to '04), Catfish Hunter had the perfect game and Jimmie Foxx and Mark McGwire had 50-homer seasons. For the Tribe, Bob Feller and Sam McDowell were 300-K men, Addie Joss and Len Barker threw perfect games and Albert Belle hit 50 home runs.
- The Dodgers have had a record 16 Rookie of the Year winners since the origin of the award, starting with Jackie Robinson in 1947.
- The Yankees have won the most individual league home run titles in major league history with 26. The first was Wally Pipp with 12 in 1916. The last was Reggie Jackson, tied with Ben Ogilvie with 41 in 1980.
- The 1983 White Sox are the only team to claim Manager of the Year (Tony La Russa), Rookie of the Year (Ron Kittle) and Cy Young (LaMarr Hoyt) in the same season.

inside the numbers

There have only been three occasions on which a perfect game and a cycle occurred on either either consecutive days or on the same day:

date	player	team	feat
May 16, 1998	Mike Blowers	A's	Cycle
May 17, 1998	David Wells	Yankees	Perfect Game
April 29, 1922	Royce Youngs	NY Giants	Cycle
April 30, 1922	Charlie Robertson	White Sox	Perfect Game
October 10, 1908	Addie Joss	Indians	Perfect Game
October 10, 1908	Otis Clymer	Senators	Cycle

did you know?

Rob Dibble was co-MVP (with teammate Randy Myers) in the 1990 NL Championship Series. Dibble, Myers and Norm Charlton combined to form the bullpen trio nicknamed the Nasty Boys.

Q

Roger Clemens has been rocketing for a long time now.

level 1   *How many times has he pitched in the World Series?*

level 2   *How many 20-win seasons did he have with the Red Sox?*

level 3   *Which team originally drafted him?*

question 11 answers

level 1   Once, in 1986

level 2   Three 20-win seasons with Boston

level 3   The Mets in 1981, though he did not sign with them

Q

In the 1972 All-Star Game, a pair of future Hall of Famers were the starting pitchers.

level 1   *Name the dynamic duo.*

level 2   *Did either pitcher get the decision in that All-Star Game?*

level 3   *Did either pitcher win a World Series game that year?*

question 12 answers

level 1   Bob Gibson (NL) vs. Jim Palmer (AL)

level 2   No

level 3   No

all-stars

- The only defending World Series champions to have just one member on the following year's All-Star team are the '98 Marlins (Edgar Renteria), the '65 Cardinals (Bob Gibson) and '46 Tigers (Hal Newhouser).
- The player with the most career All-Star Game at-bats without a home run is Rod Carew with 41. Carew made 15 career All-Star appearances, batting .244 (a far cry from his regular-season career batting average of .328).
- The shortest All-Star Game took place in 1940 (one hour, 53 minutes) and was won 4-0 by the NL, who held the AL to just three hits.
- Six sets of brothers have played in the same All-Star Game: Roberto and Sandy Alomar (1991-92, '96-97), Felipe and Matty Alou (1968), Mort and Walker Cooper (1942-43), Joe and Dom DiMaggio (1941, '49-50), Gaylord and Jim Perry (1970) and Dixie and Harry Walker (1943, '47).

best supporting athletes

- Carl Yastrzemski was the Red Sox left fielder on the day Roger Maris hit his 61st home run in 1961.
- Bill Buckner was the Dodger's left fielder when Henry Aaron hit his record-breaking 715th home run in 1974.
- When Reggie Jackson hit three home runs in Game 6 of the 1977 World Series, they came off three different pitchers: Burt Hooton, Elias Sosa and Charlie Hough.
- When the Yankees and Tigers went 23 innings in 1962, the winning home run was by Mickey Mantle's caddy, Jack Reed. It was also Reed's only major-league homer.

inside the numbers

In 1998, the Atlanta Braves had five pitchers with 15 or more wins. The last team to accomplish that feat was the 1930 Washington Senators:

1998 Braves	1930 Senators
Greg Maddux 18-9	Lloyd Brown 16-12
Tom Glavine 20-6	Sad Sam Jones 15-7
John Smoltz 17-3	Firpo Marberry 15-5
Denny Neagle 16-11	Bump Hadley 15-11
Kevin Millwood 17-8	Alvin "General" Crowder 15-9

Q 13

The 1998 Florida Marlins were the first team to go from World Series champion to posting the worst record in baseball.

level 1　　*What was the Marlins' regular-season record in '98?*

level 2　　*What was the Marlins' regular-season record in '97?*

level 3　　*Prior to '98, what was the Marlins' franchise record for most losses in a season?*

question 13 answers

level 1　54 wins, 108 losses
level 2　92 wins, 70 losses
level 3　Florida lost 98 games in 1993, their first season.

Q 14

The 1969 Miracle Mets were an incredible story. Of course, it helped to have Hall of Famer Tom Seaver and future Cooperstown member Nolan Ryan on the same team.

level 1　　*What team did the Mets beat in the World Series that year?*

level 2　　*Who was the Mets' manager?*

level 3　　*Who was the World Series MVP?*

question 14 answers

level 1　Orioles
level 2　Gil Hodges
level 3　Donn Clendenon

managers and coaches

◌⁘ Only five men have managed both the AL and NL teams in the World Series: Joe McCarthy, Yogi Berra, Alvin Dark, Sparky Anderson and Dick Williams.

◌⁘ The only person to manage both the Cubs and White Sox was Johnny Evers (Cubs in 1913 and '21 and White Sox in 1924).

◌⁘ The Orioles fired manager Cal Ripken Sr. just six games into the 1988 season.

◌⁘ Connie Mack's real name is Cornelius Alexander McGillicuddy.

◌⁘ Hall of Fame pitcher Christy Mathewson was the manager of the Reds from 1916 to 1918. His record was 165-177.

◌⁘ Astros manager Larry Dierker was the team's TV color analyst.

◌⁘ Cardinals manager Tony La Russa has a degree in industrial management from the University of South Florida and a law degree from Florida State University.

◌⁘ Phillies manager Terry Francona was also the minor league manager of Michael Jordan when he played at AA Birmingham.

◌⁘ Mariners manager Lou Piniella was the Opening Day center fielder for the Royals when they debuted in 1969. He was also the Yankees' leading hitter in the 1981 World Series.

◌⁘ Yankees bench coach Don Zimmer was the Opening Day third baseman for the Mets in 1962.

◌⁘ In 1923, Casey Stengel hit the first World Series home run at Yankee Stadium.

◌⁘ In 1965 the Detroit Tigers made future Pirates manager Gene Lamont their No. 1 draft pick, picking him ahead of Johnny Bench.

◌⁘ On April 12, 1966, future Yankees manager Joe Torre hit the first-ever home run at Atlanta Fulton County Stadium.

◌⁘ Only one manager has ever won Manager of the Year honors in both leagues: Bobby Cox with Toronto in 1985 and Atlanta in 1991.

◌⁘ Connie Mack is the only person to manage the same team in the postseason in four different decades. Tommy Lasorda, Casey Stengel, Walter Alston and John McGraw led the same team to the postseason in three decades.

did you know?

Kevin Kennedy began his managerial career in 1984 with the Pioneer League in Great Falls. He was the PCL Manager of the Year at Albuquerque in 1990. In 1991, his Dukes team featured Pedro Martinez and Eric Karros.

Q 15

One of the more intriguing World Series was in 1968 between the Cardinals and the Tigers.

level 1   *Bob Gibson and Denny McLain each posted incredible seasons, yet another pitcher won three games in that World Series. Name him.*

level 2   *What was Gibson's ERA during the regular season?*

level 3   *How many games did McLain win during the regular season?*

question 15 answers

level 1   Mickey Lolich
level 2   An incredible 1.12
level 3   McLain won 31 games, the last pitcher to reach 30.

Q 16

It's known as "The Shot Heard Round the World." On October 3, 1951, Bobby Thomson hit the home run that gave the Giants the NL pennant.

level 1   *Off whom did he hit the home run?*

level 2   *Who was the Dodgers' starting pitcher that game?*

level 3   *A future Hall of Famer was on deck for the Giants when Thomson hit the home run. Name him.*

question 16 answers

level 1   Ralph Branca
level 2   Don Newcombe
level 3   Willie Mays

family secrets

- Mets manager Bobby Valentine is the son-in-law of Ralph Branca, who gave up the home run to Bobby Thomson in the famed Dodgers-Giants playoff game.
- Astro Ken Forsch (1979) and Cardinal Bob Forsch (1978) are the only brothers to pitch no-hitters.
- The first son of a big leaguer to play in the majors was Jack Doscher – son of Herm – who debuted with the Cubs in 1903.
- The only great grandfather/great grandson combination in the history of baseball is Jim Bluejacket (1914-16) and Bill Wilkinson (1985, '87-88).
- Diamondbacks third baseman Matt Williams's grandfather, Bart Griffith, was a first baseman-outfielder for the Brooklyn Dodgers and Washington Senators from 1922 to 1924.
- Reds teammates Bret and Aaron Boone are brothers. Their dad, Bob, was a catcher (Phillies, Angels and Royals) and managed the Royals. Their grandfather, Ray, played for the Indians, Tigers, White Sox, Athletics, Braves and Red Sox.
- Tigers pitcher Herman Pillette led the AL in losses in 1923 (19). Twenty-eight years later, his son, Duane, led the league in losses as a member of the St. Louis Browns with 14.
- Former major league pitcher Luis Tiant's father, Luis Sr., played in the Negro Leagues from 1930 to 1947.
- The A's drafted TCU junior Matt Howe, son of Oakland manager Art Howe, in the 29th round of the 1998 draft.
- Only two sets of brothers have teamed up for 55 or more home runs in one season: Joe and Vince DiMaggio (59 in 1937) and Lee and Carlos May (56 in 1969).

total access
stuart scott

"Five-year-olds at their first big league game are excited, impressionable and naive. There I was at Comiskey Park checking out a double-header between the A's and White Sox, with Vida Blue starting Game 1. The only thing that would've been better for this Chicago fan was for Blue, a black pitcher, to be wearing a White Sox uniform. Between games, my father and uncle started saying that Blue had been traded that very moment and would be starting in Game 2. I didn't know they were joking and there I was, excited, impressionable and naive, waiting for Vida Blue to pitch for my team."

Q 17

Reggie Jackson's three-home-run performance in Game 6 of the 1977 World Series is one of the greatest of all time.

level 1   *Name the three pitchers he hit the home runs against.*

level 2   *What other Yankee player also homered in that game?*

level 3   *Who was the winning pitcher for the Yankees?*

question 17 answers

level 1   Burt Hooton, Elias Sosa and Charlie Hough

level 2   Chris Chambliss

level 3   Mike Torrez

Q 18

On July 17, 1941, Joe DiMaggio's 56-game hit streak came to an end.

level 1   *Which team did the Yankees play that day?*

level 2   *How many hits did DiMaggio have during his 56-game streak?*

level 3   *What did DiMaggio go on the day the streak ended?*

question 18 answers

level 1   The Cleveland Indians

level 2   91

level 3   0 for 3

the draft

::: The first player to go to the major leagues without playing in the minors since the free agent draft began in 1965 was Mike Adamson (Orioles in 1967).

::: Dave Winfield was picked by the Atlanta Hawks in the fifth round of the 1973 NBA draft.

::: Eleven players were chosen in the 1994 draft before Nomar Garciaparra.

::: In the 1995 draft, the Padres picked catcher Ben Davis with the second overall pick. Among players picked after Davis and in the top 10 were Jose Cruz Jr. (third, Mariners), Kerry Wood (fourth, Cubs) and Todd Helton (eighth, Rockies).

::: Roberto Clemente was selected by the Pirates in the minor league draft after being left unprotected by the Brooklyn Dodgers following the 1954 season.

::: Michael Cuddyer (Twins) and John Curtice (Red Sox) of Great Bridge High School in Chesapeake, Virginia, were selected in the first round of the 1997 baseball draft. They form only the second tandem of first-round picks selected from the same high school in the same year (1972: Jerry Manuel and Mike Ondina, Rancho Cordova High School, California).

::: Tony Gwynn was selected in the 10th round of the 1981 NBA draft by the San Diego Clippers on the same day the Padres chose him in the third round of the baseball draft.

::: Jose Canseco was a 15th-round pick by the A's in 1982.

::: Mike Piazza was a 62nd-round pick by the Dodgers in 1988.

::: Ryne Sandberg was a 20th-round pick by the Phillies in 1978.

::: Twenty-one players were chosen before All-Star Craig Biggio was nabbed by the Astros in 1987.

inside the numbers

The 1988 draft class was one of the more memorable in recent years:

draft position	team	player
No. 1	Padres	Andy Benes
No. 2	Indians	Mark Lewis
No. 3	Braves	Steve Avery
No. 4	Orioles	Gregg Olson
No. 8	Angels	Jim Abbott
No. 10	White sox	Robin Ventura
No. 14	Mariners	Tino Martinez
No. 15	Giants	Royce Clayton
No. 17	Indians	Charles Nagy

total access
chris berman

"There have been a lot of memorable home runs over the years. One of my favorites was hit by Reds catcher Ernie Lombardi. He hit in out of Crosley Field and into the back of a truck, which traveled another 30 miles before the driver pulled over. When he finally emptied his truck, sand wasn't the only thing in there – that home run ball came out, too."

Q19

In the 1934 All-Star Game, one of the greatest pitching performances took place: five stars struck out in a row.

level 1   *Name the pitcher who recorded the five strikeouts.*

level 2   *Name the five batters.*

level 3   *Where was the game played?*

question 19 answers

level 1   Carl Hubbell

level 2   Babe Ruth, Lou Gehrig, Jimmie Foxx, Al Simmons and Joe Cronin

level 3   The Polo Grounds

Q20

Don Larsen pitched the only perfect game in World Series history on October 8, 1956.

level 1   *What team did the Yankees beat?*

level 2   *What was the final score of the game?*

level 3   *What position did Jackie Robinson play in that game?*

question 20 answers

level 1   The Brooklyn Dodgers

level 2   The final score was 2-0.

level 3   Robinson played third base.

- The two Yankees who have pitched perfect games, Don Larsen and David Wells, attended the same San Diego high school.
- Angels shortstop Gary DiSarcina and Braves pitcher Tom Glavine were teammates at Billerica High School in Massachusetts.
- Barry Bonds and Lynn Swann are both products of Serra High School in San Mateo, California.
- The first game Harry Caray broadcast was on April 17, 1945, when he was the voice of the St. Louis Cardinals on WTMV Radio. That day the Cardinals lost 3-2 to the Cubs.
- Kirk Gibson holds the Michigan State University record for most touchdown passes caught in a career (24). Gibson is also second in receiving yards (2,347), trailing Andre Rison (2,992).
- Cardinals outfielder Brian Jordan played defensive back for the Atlanta Falcons from 1989 to 1991. He had a career-high three interceptions in 1990.
- Astros outfielder Carl Everett was a member of a Florida track team that won the 4 x 100 at the 1989 Junior Olympics.
- Derek Bell is the only major leaguer to play in two Little League World Series (1980 and '81). He and Gary Sheffield were teammates on the 1980 Belmont Heights team from Florida.
- Twins second baseman Todd Walker was the College World Series MVP for LSU in 1993.
- White Sox first baseman Frank Thomas also played football at Auburn. As a tight end, he had three catches for 45 yards in 1986.
- On September 5, 1989, Deion Sanders hit a home run for the Yankees. Five days later, he returned a punt 68 yards for a touchdown in his debut with the Atlanta Falcons.
- Gene Conley was a member of two pro sports champions in 1957, pitching for the Milwaukee Braves and playing as a reserve center (behind Bill Russell) on the Boston Celtics.
- Cubs pitcher Marc Pisciotta was a member of the 1983 Little League World Series champions from East Marietta, Georgia.
- After graduation from high school, Randy Johnson was originally selected by the Braves in the third round of the June 1982 draft. He opted instead to go to USC on a baseball / basketball scholarship. The Expos drafted the Big Unit in the second round in 1984.
- Wade Boggs and Bob Ojeda played in the longest baseball game ever. A minor league match on April 19, 1981, between Pawtucket and Rochester went 33 innings before Pawtucket finally won 3-2.
- A's pitcher Vida Blue was married on the mound at Candlestick Park before a game on September 24, 1989.

total access

lesley visser

"Five years ago, I was jogging in Central Park, when, in one step, my life forever changed. I tripped over a piece of sidewalk and jammed my knee into the pavement with such force that it shattered my hip like a dropped teacup. While in a hospital bed for 10 weeks, I heard from family and friends, including Mark McGwire, who sent me a carton full of No Fear T-shirts. Like everyone else, I have followed his summer of '98 with great joy and emotion. Mark is so genuine and full of good will that, in the middle of his historic run, he sent me a note, remembering the fifth anniversary of my accident. When it comes to heroes, I think we've found one."

Q21

Dennis Eckersley set a major league record for career pitching appearances during the 1998 season.

level 1   *What is the new record set by Eckersley?*

level 2   *Name the pitcher he passed.*

level 3   *When did Eckersley debut in the majors and with which team?*

question 21 answers

level 1   1,071 games

level 2   Hoyt Wilhelm, who has 1,070 appearances

level 3   Eckersley debuted with the Indians in 1975.

Q22

Mark McGwire not only set the major league home run record in 1998, he also set the NL mark for walks in one season.

level 1   *How many walks did he get in '98?*

level 2   *Whose NL record did he break and what was the previous NL high?*

level 3   *Who holds the major league record for walks in one season?*

question 22 answers

level 1   162 walks

level 2   Barry Bonds, who had 151 walks in 1996

level 3   Babe Ruth, who had 170 walks in 1923

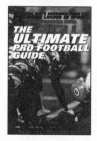